P9-CTP-060

GAMBLING
CRIME OR RECREATION?

Abbey Begun

INFORMATION PLUS REFERENCE SERIES
Formerly published by Information Plus, Wylie, Texas

GALE GROUP

Detroit
New York
San Francisco
London
Boston
Woodbridge, CT

GAMBLING: CRIME OR RECREATION?

was produced for the Gale Group by Information Plus, Wylie, Texas

Information Plus Staff:

Abbey Begun, Author

Jacquelyn Quiram, Designer

Editorial: Cornelia Blair, Barbara Klier, Nancy R. Jacobs, Virginia Peterson, Mei Ling Rein, Mark A. Siegel

The Gale Group Staff:

Editorial: Rita Runchock, Managing Editor; John F. McCoy, Editor

Graphic Services: Randy Bassett, Image Database Supervisor; Robert Duncan, Senior Imaging Specialist

Product Design: Michelle DiMercurio, Senior Art Director; Michael Logusz, Graphic Artist

Production: NeKita McKee, Buyer; Dorothy Maki, Manufacturing Manager

GAMBLING — CRIME OR RECREATION?

CHAPTER I

GAMBLING — AN AMERICAN TRADITION

NATIVE AMERICAN GAMES OF CHANCE

Gambling was a popular pastime in North America long before there was ever a United States. Native Americans played games of chance with dice, sticks, stones, shells, and fruit pits. The dice that Native Americans used were not the six-sided cubes used today, but were nearly always two-sided. Players often tossed the dice in a shallow basket or wooden cup or bowl. The dice would be tossed in the air and caught in the basket, or tossed by hand or shaken and thrown to the ground. *Pugasaing* was a game played with painted sticks and dice, with some colors having a higher value than others. Some Southwestern tribes played a game with a round counting board made of stones. The object of the game was to see which player could move a twig around the complete circle first. The players often staked their possessions — arrows, blankets, pipes, and even horses — on a toss of the dice or a spin of a stone.

COLONIAL PASTIME

Playing cards and dice were brought over by both the British and the Dutch. By the end of the seventeenth century, just about every county seat in colonial America had a lottery wheel. Cockfighting flourished throughout the colonies, especially in the South. Bear-baiting (an old diversion in which dogs were made to torment a chained bear) was also a popular sport, but the Puritans banned it "not because it gave pain to the bear, but because it gave pleasure to the spectators." While strict New Englanders considered gambling a "dis-

order to God" and levied fines and whippings against gamblers, gambling was much less of a moral issue in other parts of the country.

European visitors to America, from English soldiers during the Revolutionary War period to the writer Frances Trollope in the nineteenth century, commented on the American's affinity for gambling. George Washington was an avid, though mediocre, card player and wisely limited his betting. Benjamin Franklin printed and sold playing cards. The controversial Stamp Act levied a one-shilling tax on every pack of cards, raising perhaps as much ire as the tax on tea, since every well-furnished colonial home possessed a card table. In the South, the planter-aristocrat, with his thoroughbred horses, had the opportunity and the wealth to enjoy leisure time pursuits — horse racing being a favorite.

LOTTERIES HELP FINANCE THE GROWTH OF A NATION

During the colonial period, lotteries were a popular means of raising funds. English lotteries provided most of the funding to establish the colony of Virginia, and the original Jamestown settlement was financed by a lottery conducted by the Virginia Company in London, England. In 1748, young Ben Franklin organized a lottery to pay for military supplies to defend Philadelphia from attack by Indian tribes and French soldiers. In 1777, the Continental Congress held a $5 million lottery to help finance the Revolutionary War. Unfortunately, all winnings over $50 were to be paid in promissory notes (to be collected at some future date). The lottery was mismanaged, and several scoundrels abused the trust of their fellow revolutionaries. The lottery was a disaster, and most people holding winning tickets never received their winnings.

Lotteries were also held to raise money for county treasuries, to build bridges, assist churches and schools, and establish relief funds. Lottery proceeds contributed to the establishment of such prestigious Ivy League schools as Harvard, Yale, Columbia, Princeton, and Dartmouth.

ENTERTAINMENT DURING THE JACKSONIAN ERA

President Andrew Jackson believed that a person's destiny should be controlled by the individual, rather than by elected officials. During his administration (1829-1837), popularly known as the era of "the common man," gambling was a form of entertainment enjoyed by large numbers of people, as well as public officials. President Jackson was an avid gambler (he once reportedly bet all of his clothes during a game of chance). During his presidential campaign, Jackson's eventual successor, Martin Van Buren (1837-1841), wagered a new suit and $40,000 on his victory in the elections.

During this period, Americans were well known for their eager and continued interest in all forms of gambling. A northern traveler in the South commented on the heavy betting at cockfights, which were attended by people from all levels of society. A flatboat merchant who plied the Ohio River observed that Kentuckians were completely absorbed in horse racing and gambling. One could hardly talk to a Kentuckian, he wrote, without hearing the phrase, "I'll bet you."

Along the Mississippi and Ohio Rivers, notorious gamblers earned their keep on the riverboats that sailed down the rivers to New Orleans, a gambler's paradise. The first formal casino in New Orleans opened in 1827, and it soon became a model for other "carpet joints," as the lavishly decorated casinos were called. Riverboat gambling continued after the Civil War but never regained its antebellum (pre-Civil War) dash and glamour.

Urban areas were also centers of gambling activity during the Jacksonian Era. While the countryside and riverfront facilities relied on visitors from outlying areas to attend their cockfights, horse races, or casinos, urban areas had a ready-made customer base. New York City was an early gambling center. By 1850, it had approximately 6,000 flourishing gambling houses, an astounding ratio of one gambling house for every 85 New Yorkers.

THE REFORM MOVEMENT

During the 1840s, a reforming spirit swept across America. Societies formed to combat tobacco use, profanity, and the transit of mail on Sunday. The first women's rights movement was organized, and temperance crusaders preached against alcohol use. The abolitionist movement against slavery gained significant momentum during these years.

Many reformers attacked gambling. They were most successful in their fight against the flourishing lottery business. During the 1830s, some newspapers began publishing accounts of corrupt lotteries and their harmful effect on individuals who really could not afford to buy tickets, but did so anyway. As a result of this negative publicity, the number of lottery permits decreased, and lotteries were abolished altogether in most northern states by 1840. The increasing rate of profiteering by lottery middlemen eventually incited public indignation in the South and West as well. By 1860, every state in the nation except Delaware, Kentucky, and Missouri had enacted constitutional or statutory prohibitions against lotteries.

Although illegal in most states by this time, gambling occurred openly in such cities as New York, Chicago, and New Orleans. In reaction to reform efforts, operators of gambling establishments fought to save their lucrative businesses by paying members of local police forces for protection. Policemen staged prearranged raids for appearance's sake, but they were careful not to damage furniture, and they usually returned the gamblers to their places of business after booking them. The very fact that gambling was illegal seemed to add to its popular appeal as an exciting form of entertainment. Any attempts to legalize gambling probably would have been opposed by gamblers, operators, and corrupt police and public officials alike.

During the mid- and late 1860s, the financial demands of the Civil War and Reconstruction once again led to an interest in lotteries in the southern and western states. However, because of their reputation for breeding corruption and a lack of uniform state regulation, federal legislation against lotteries was introduced. Lottery operators mounted efforts to get around anti-lottery laws by forming "gift companies" that operated in essentially the same manner as lotteries.

THE WILD WEST — HONKY-TONKS AND THE GOLD RUSH

The opening of the Far West after the Civil War gave gambling in America a second life. Far from both government controls and the moral interference of reform groups in the East, gambling became so popular and widespread that monte (a card game) tables were often set up in the street in the middle of town. Professional gamblers, rumored to earn as much as $20,000 per month, were glad to relieve hard-working miners of their gold nuggets. Losses were usually taken philosophically. For the unlucky miners, a quick return to their gold mines in the hills would usually replenish whatever they lost at the gaming tables. Gambling houses could easily be found in Kansas City, Dallas, Denver, and San Francisco, as well as nearly every small town located near mining camps, railroad towns, and major cattle trails.

THE LOUISIANA LOTTERY

As noted above, dishonesty and fraud were common in lottery operations during the 1800s.

The Louisiana Lottery, however, took these characteristics to such extremes that, by the turn of the century, gambling and political corruption would be forever linked in the minds of many people.

In 1864, 1868, 1872, and 1876, Congress passed laws to stop the expansion of lotteries by taxing them and limiting the activities they could conduct by federal mail. In 1865, a New York-based gambling syndicate (a group of individuals or corporations formed to undertake an activity, usually one that requires substantial financial backing) applied for approval to operate a lottery in Louisiana. In return for granting a sales monopoly to the syndicate, the Louisiana state treasury would receive $40,000 annually for 25 years to finance the Charity Hospital in New Orleans. The use of profits from gambling for charitable causes became an established tactic to promote the acceptance of gambling within the community.

The approval of the Louisiana Lottery was assured by rigged elections that kept out candidates opposed to the lottery and by bribing legislators to grant licenses. From its inception, the Louisiana Lottery controlled legislatures, newspapers, banks, and governors. It continued operating despite prohibitions by federal laws because enforcement officials would not prosecute lottery managers. Players around the country participated in the Louisiana Lottery by mail, bringing the lottery's profits to an average $13 million per year, a huge sum of money at the time.

Mounting Criticism

National criticism grew as the Louisiana Lottery extended into every state, with the syndicate receiving more than 90 percent of its income from outside Louisiana. Reformers, labor and farm organizations, newspapers, and churches all demanded federal action against the Louisiana Lottery. As a result, the state legislature canceled the lottery, but using the considerable number of dollars at its disposal, the syndicate forced an extension through a Louisiana constitutional convention.

Finally, in 1890, the U.S. Congress passed legislation banning postal delivery of all items dealing with lotteries and prohibiting operation through an agent or representative, such as the New Orleans National Bank. For the first time, violations of this law became punishable by imprisonment. A new provision was also enacted making the offense triable by a court in any jurisdiction through which lottery material had been transported, thereby making it harder for the lottery operators to avoid conviction by bribing local jurors.

The Louisiana Lottery Company moved to Honduras in Central America to avoid postal regulations. In 1895, Congress authorized the Postmaster General to withhold delivery of lottery-related mail and to deny any person representing a lottery company the use of the postal service. Interstate transportation of lottery materials and the use of express mail became illegal in 1895. The anti-lottery laws deprived the Louisiana Lottery Company of the methods by which it had evaded state and federal laws for years, and it had to close. The combined effect of several federal statutes enacted between 1890 and 1895 eliminated lotteries for the next 70 years.

THE PROGRESSIVE ERA —
A SECOND PERIOD OF REFORM

Between 1900 and 1917, a reform-minded group of people called the "Progressives" dedicated themselves to exposing corruption in big business and municipal governments, correcting social evils, and improving living conditions for women, children, and the poor. Progressive reformers had two main goals: to use state power to curb unscrupulous business trusts and to stem the threat of socialism.

Reformers attacked red-light (prostitution) districts, saloons, and alcoholism. Francis E. Willard founded the Anti-Saloon League to crusade against these establishments, considered to be dominated by crooked city officials and political bosses who supported "booze interests," counted poker chips by night, and miscounted ballots by day. Progressive reformers were also instrumental in closing gambling houses and race tracks, as well as policy (see Chapter X) and bookmaking operations. By 1915, only seven states permitted horse racing.

ORGANIZED CRIME

In 1920, Congress instituted Prohibition, which outlawed the manufacture, transportation, and sale of alcoholic liquors in the United States. However, while Congress could make alcohol illegal, it could not curb Americans' appetite for alcohol. With its potential for huge profits, the manufacture and sale of alcoholic beverages became the domain of the underground world of gangsters. Subsequently, organized crime moved on to other profitable and illicit activities, such as gambling.

During the Prohibition Era (1920-1933), illegal gambling was organized into an authoritarian regional and national system. Responsibility for the syndication of gambling is usually attributed to Arnold Rothstein (1881-1928), who invented the inner-city layoff (in which gambling organizations in one city helped those in other cities cover heavy, potentially risky bets). Rothstein is also known for masterminding the "Black Sox" scandal, in which the Chicago White Sox threw the 1919 World (Baseball) Series to the Cincinnati Reds to assure gambling profits.

The Union Pacific Railroad arrived in Las Vegas in 1905, making it a city. At that time, bars and gambling houses began to sprout up, attracting railroad workers and miners. In 1931, during the Great Depression, many workers flocked to Las Vegas to help construct the Hoover Dam. That same year, the state legislators legalized gambling in Las Vegas, and immediately casinos and hotels began to be built, transforming the city overnight into a gambling mecca. Some of those hotels and casinos were owned and run by mobsters, who built fancy hotels like the Flamingo to attract tourists, but also to front for illegal gambling games, slot machines, and bookie operations.

Organized crime no longer possesses the glamorous reputation it enjoyed in movies about the 1920s and 1930s. Findings by the Special Senate Committee to Investigate Organized Crime in Interstate Commerce, headed by Senator Estes Kefauver in 1950, and the McClellan hearings in 1963-64 revealed the brutal activities of the underworld and instigated more vigorous attempts at reform and containment. Most illegal slot machines and walk-in bookie joints disappeared from sight. They still existed, of course, as did floating card and "crap" games — they were just less conspicuous.

LEGAL GAMBLING AGAIN BECOMES ACCEPTABLE

Since the 1970s, the United States has turned full circle in its attitude toward gambling. Three hundred years ago, the "sport," especially in the form of lotteries, was seen as a perfectly acceptable way to raise money for public purposes. During the late 1980s and early 1990s, slow economic growth, cuts in federal funding to states, and growing public needs forced many desperate state and even local governments to seek additional sources of revenue. Most states turned to lotteries, horse and dog racing, and most recently, a growing number of states have resorted to casino gambling as a way to "painlessly" raise money for the public coffers.

Moral issues and concerns about criminal involvement usually play a part in state and local election campaigns to institute legalized gambling. They are, however, almost always overcome by the prospect of even less attractive alternatives: decreased social programs and/or increased taxes. Increased fiscal need and fear of increased taxes often outweigh any moral argument.

Once big business understood the unrealized potential of legal gambling in the United States, it was not long before gambling swept across the nation. While most Americans following business over the last decade have focused on the explosion in high technology, the transformation of the gambling industry has been just as dynamic. Las Vegas, one of the nation's fastest growing metropolitan areas, has more hotels and casinos than anywhere on Earth. While it is the nation's gambling capital, the city now markets itself as a family vacation spot.

After some shaky years, Atlantic City seems to be returning to financial solvency. Well-appointed riverboats, many of them unable to sail, attract millions of Americans along the nation's waterways. Indian reservations, many of them formerly mired in poverty, now host some of the most attractive casinos in the country. Old mining towns in Colorado and South Dakota offer visitors a chance to bet their money. (See Chapter VII.)

CHAPTER II

GAMBLING AND THE GOVERNMENT
LAWS, COURT CASES, LOBBYING, AND POLITICS

PUBLIC POLICY ON GAMBLING

Current gambling policies at the state and federal levels reflect the mixed feelings Americans have toward gambling. Over the years, Americans have generally held one of two or three beliefs about gambling.

- It is morally and socially destructive and it must be eliminated.

- Its enormous popularity makes it a suitable activity for government licensing and taxation.

- It is morally destructive, but if you want to do it, that is your problem.

With the nation's apparently increasing tolerance for once-prohibited activities, coupled with a growing need for state and local revenues, the lure of gambling revenues has prompted most states to reconsider and usually change their gambling policies.

TRYING TO CONTROL CRIME
CROSSING STATE LINES AND BORDERS

The first modern anti-gambling legislation was passed to outlaw the use of "floating casinos." During the 1940s, gambling took place on ships off the California coast, just outside the country's three-mile limit, in order to avoid prohibitions against gambling. The federal government did not approve, and in 1948, Congress passed 18 USC 1081-1083,* which effectively halted the operation of gambling ships off the coast of the United States by prohibiting transportation to and from the ships. (Gambling ships have since become legal.)

The Kefauver Committee investigations (see Chapter I) produced a number of statutes directed at "nation-wide crime syndicates." The Johnson Act (15 USC 1171-1177), a group of statutes produced by the Kefauver Committee, prohibited the interstate transportation of illegal gambling devices. This law supported state policies prohibiting slot machines and successfully eliminated interstate traffic in coin-operated gambling machines.

Throughout the 1950s, most federal efforts to control gambling were undertaken by the Internal Revenue Service (IRS). The IRS attacked illegal gambling operations under the Wagering Excise Tax (26 USC 4401) and Wagering Occupational Stamp Tax statute (26 USC 4411). (See below.)

The (John F.) Kennedy Administration (1961-1963) was committed to controlling illegal gambling. During the 1960s, Congress passed statutes that attacked large gambling syndicates operating across state lines (18 USC 1081-1804 and 18 USC 1952). With the passage of these statutes, the federal government attempted to suppress large-scale interstate gambling operations by allowing local and state governments to extend their investigations across state boundaries.

---

* This and the following citations refer to the United States Code. The number preceding USC is the volume. The number after USC is the section.

The interstate transportation of wagering para-phernalia is defined under Public Law (PL) 91-452 (18 USC 1952-53) and contains the broadest anti-gambling provisions. It prohibits interstate travel or the use of interstate facilities to promote illegal gambling enterprises. Statutes 18 USC 1084 and 18 USC 1952 have been most effective against interstate bookmaking operations and were essential in closing down the lavish, large-scale illegal casinos that flourished in major cities during the 1940s and 1950s. Before these statutes were passed, a large interstate layoff bookmaking operation (in which a bookie turns to other bookies to help handle larger bets) existed throughout the country (see Arnold Rothstein, Chapter I) and supported bookmaking establishments in a number of states.

Federal law enforcement agencies were more effective in combating interstate gambling syndicates than were state or local governments because federal authorities could operate more easily across state lines, and they were somewhat less susceptible to payoffs. The federal effort substantially reduced interstate bookmaking operations controlled by organized crime and eliminated all but the two most prevalent forms of illegal gambling — the numbers game and bookmaking.

TARGETING ORGANIZED CRIME

Despite all the government's previous efforts to control syndicated gambling, Congressional hearings and research revealed that gambling was still the largest single source of income for organized crime. The passage of the Organized Crime Control Act of 1970 (PL 91-452) significantly expanded federal jurisdiction over gambling.

Provision 18 USC 1955, originating from the Organized Crime Control Act changed the federal government's basis for attacking organized gambling. First, it defined an illegal, organized gambling operation as one that involved five or more people in the conduct, financing, directing, managing, or ownership of a gambling business grossing $2,000 per day or operating continually over a 30-day period, in violation of the law in a particular state. It also broadened the federal government's control over interstate commerce by requiring only general, rather than specific, knowledge of illegal activities as cause to apprehend lawbreakers.

Corrupt public officials often play a major role in organized crime operations. Statute 18 USC 1511, originating from the Organized Crime Control Act, prohibits an elected or appointed public official from using his or her position to hinder an investigation of illegal gambling activity.

GAMBLING AND RACKETEERING

Statutes 18 USC 1961-68 provide civil remedies for illegal gambling activities. These provisions, enacted as part of the Organized Crime Control Act of 1970, are collectively known as the RICO (Racketeer-Influenced and Corrupt Organizations) statutes. The RICO statutes permit the federal government to act in a civil or criminal case against anyone engaged in two separate acts of "racketeering activity" (obtaining money illegally). The transmission of gambling information, interstate transportation of wagering paraphernalia, and illegal gambling businesses became offenses punishable by imprisonment.

The civil remedy provision, 18 USC 1964, does not normally involve imprisonment. However, this provision permits a court to order individuals to divest themselves of interests that are in violation of RICO statutes, to impose reasonable restrictions on future activities and investments of such persons, and to order the dissolution or reorganization of such enterprises involved in racketeering activities. These long-term preventive actions, while not putting the violator in jail, can sometimes provide more practical protection from racketeering activity than criminal punishment.

An extremely important part of statute 18 USC 1964 is that a defendant who violates a court order must show cause why he or she should not be held in contempt of court, while the government must only show that the order has been violated. This lowers the government's burden of proof and thereby allows a rapid response to any violations of the court's order. Finally, in a civil case, the government need only prove by "a preponderance of the evidence" (or the bulk of the evidence) that the defendant is likely in the future to engage in conduct that violates the law. This means that a violator can be put in prison, not because he or she has been guilty "beyond a reasonable doubt," as in all criminal proceedings, but because the "preponderance of the evidence" shows that a court order has been violated.

The RICO statutes have had great success in stemming illegal gambling in the United States, but many civil libertarians question the use of this law, which has been used as an easy way to prosecute alleged lawbreakers, ranging from those charged with pornography to those arrested for picketing abortion clinics.

TAXABLE EARNINGS

Since the Prohibition Era (1920-1933), tax laws have been used as one method to control organized crime. In fact, Al Capone was indicted for income-tax evasion even before the investigation of his illegal bootlegging activities was completed, and he went to jail for failing to pay his taxes, not for his many other criminal activities.

On the other hand, some tax laws have contributed to the success of illegal gambling operations and thereby promoted organized crime. Section 61 of the Internal Revenue Service code describes as taxable income "any accretion to wealth ... unless specifically exempt," which means gambling winnings are taxable. Since most persons wager or bet for entertainment, few small winners coming home from a moderately successful trip to Las Vegas or Atlantic City are likely to declare their winnings. Few gamblers are net winners during a given year or, for that matter, during their gambling careers, but most gamblers think that at some time they will become big winners.

Winners who properly declare their gambling income are not permitted to carry back or carry forward losses from previous or later years as a deduction against their current winnings (an economic disadvantage), as they would in the case of normal investment earnings. Consequently, the tax laws tend to encourage patronage of illegal games. Furthermore, a big winner knows that a legal gambling establishment will report his or her winnings to the IRS, while the winner in an illegal game can safely assume that the operator will not file a report of his business activities.

Certainly one of the most controversial recommendations made by the Commission on the Review of the National Policy Toward Gambling in 1976 was to repeal taxes on gambling winnings in order to take away a major edge held by illegal gambling. Some experts believe that if taxes on gambling were repealed, it could have a significant impact in eliminating illegal gambling operations. A change in the tax policy, however, is most unlikely.

In 1951, in an attempt to raise money, Congress passed the Wagering Excise Tax (26 USC 4401) and the Wagering Occupational Stamp Tax (26 USC 441). Originally, for those engaged in gambling activities, the excise tax was 10 percent of earnings plus a $50 charge for the occupational stamp required for each person involved in gambling operations. On December 1, 1974, Congress changed these requirements to 2 percent and $500, respectively, in an effort to enable legal bookmakers, who pay the taxes, to compete more effectively with their illegal competitors. This wagering tax applies only to sports, horse bookmaking, and numbers games; it does not apply to pari-mutuel betting, coin-operated machines, state lotteries that base winnings on horse race results, or casino games.

Although the laws discussed here were intended to limit illegal gambling activity, not much money or manpower has been devoted to their enforcement. In fact, these laws have hurt legal state-sanctioned gambling operations because legal operators are far more likely to pay taxes than illegal operators; hence, they are unable to offer the same return on a wager as the illegal operations. Therefore, the Commission on the Review of the National Policy Toward Gambling recommended that the excise and occupational taxes be eliminated, as well as the $250 Occupational Tax on Coin-Operated Devices (26 USC 4411), passed in 1941. None of the tax recommendations made by the Commission was ever instituted.

State Gambling Taxes — Some Examples

States have a variety of ways to collect gambling taxes. Nevada and New Jersey have taxed gambling for many years, since they have been gambling meccas longer than any other states. Colorado, Illinois, Indiana, Iowa, Louisiana, Mississippi, and South Dakota are more recent gambling-tax collectors.

Nevada levies a tax on each admission fee to a Nevada riverboat or casino. The state also imposes extensive gambling license fees. There are 10 categories of annual state licenses, depending on the number of games that are being played in an establishment. Nevada collects different quarterly license fees for small operators (fewer than 10 games) and large operators (more than 10 games). In addition, Nevada imposes monthly county license fees based on the number of games and devices being operated in a gambling house. A $250 annual tax is imposed on each slot machine over and above any other license fee and gaming tax.

New Jersey charges an annual 8 percent tax on gross revenues from its casinos. In addition, an initial fee of at least $200,000 is required for a casino license. The annual renewal for this license is a minimum of $100,000.

Arkansas taxes all admission charges for bingo games and on gross receipts (all money gambled) from any apparatus used in playing the game. (No admission tax is levied on charitable or non-profit organizations.) Arkansas also imposes a "dog rac-

ing privilege tax" of 3 percent of all money gambled.

Florida takes in 7.6 percent of the gross proceeds from betting pools. Florida also taxes horse racing with a harness horse tax of 1 percent per race. A 3 percent thoroughbred horse tax is levied from January 10 through March 1, which coincides with Florida's heaviest tourist season. The dying sport of jai alai is taxed at a rate of 5.5 percent of receipts per performance.

New York has a complex horse racing tax structure, which includes 17 categories of taxes on both regular and multiple bets. The state taxes pari-mutuel winnings at between 2.5 percent and 7.5 percent of the total pool. New York also taxes admissions to racetracks. Licensed simulcasts (programs being broadcast as they occur on television or radio or both) of races are taxed on earned money equal to 1.5 percent. Any city in New York with a population of 1 million or more people may collect gambling taxes up to 5 percent of bets at off-track facilities located in that city.

ADVERTISING FOR LOTTERIES

Title 18 USC Para. 1302 prohibits the mailing of any "publication of any kind containing any advertisement of any lottery, gift enterprise, or scheme of any kind offering prizes dependent in whole or in part upon lot or chance, or containing any list of the prizes drawn or awarded by means of any such lottery, gift, enterprise, or scheme." This law dated back to the 1940s, when lotteries were illegal. By the 1980s, most states had a lottery, and many wanted to advertise the lottery through promotions sent out directly through the mail and/or in newspapers, which are often sent through the mail.

The Minnesota Newspaper Association challenged the law. A federal district court, in *Minnesota Newspaper Assn., Inc. v. Postmaster General* (677 F. Supp. 1400, 1987), ruled the law valid as it applied to advertisements but unconstitutional as applied to prize lists, since the law could prevent the publication of prize lists in news reports, and that would be a violation of the freedom of the press.

The case was appealed all the way to the U.S. Supreme Court. However, before the Supreme Court could hear the case, the U.S. Congress reached a legislative remedy to this problem. Congress passed and President Ronald Reagan signed into law the "Charity Games Advertising Clarification Act of 1988" (PL 100-625). This law indicates that the existing federal law should not apply to advertisements or radio broadcasts concerning lotteries prepared by either state or non-profit organizations that are published or broadcast in a state that conducts a lottery. The law also applies to private companies that use a lottery as a promotional activity ("but only a promotional activity and only occasional[ly]").

Based on this new law, the Postmaster General agreed that the law no longer applied to the noncommercial publishing of prize lists. The Supreme Court, in *Frank, Postmaster General of the United States v. Minnesota Newspaper Association, Inc.* (490 US 225, 1989), finding there was no longer a controversy, declared the case moot and referred it back to the lower court to be dismissed.

BROADCAST ADVERTISING FOR CASINO GAMBLING

In June 1999, the Supreme Court unanimously struck down a ban on television and radio advertising of casino gambling in states where such gambling is legal. In *Greater New Orleans Broadcasting Association v. United States* (119 S.Ct. 1923), Justice John Paul Stevens wrote for the court that the ban "may not be applied to advertisements of private casino gambling that are broadcast by radio or television stations located in Louisiana, where such gambling is legal."

The ruling is a major victory for the casino industry and for broadcasters who began to challenge the ban after 1988, when Congress permitted gam-

bling advertising by casinos owned by Native American tribes.

SPORTS GAMBLING

During the late 1980s and early 1990s, several states tried to introduce sports betting, either as part of the lottery (similar to a sports pool) or as sports bookmaking. Legal attempts to introduce sports bookmaking in California to counter the sports bookmaking operations across the Mexican-American border in northern Baja California, Mexico, have failed, as have attempts in New York, Illinois, and New Jersey. Oregon has tied sports betting with its lotteries.

Fear of Gambling in the Sports Industry

Nonetheless, the leaders of the nation's sports industry, including the National Basketball Association (NBA), the National Football League (NFL), and Major League Baseball, were concerned that the states, in their desperation to raise monies, might begin to tie sports betting with their lotteries. They began to put strong pressure on state legislatures not to introduce sports betting. The sports industry also started lobbying Congress, and as a result, several bills were introduced in the U.S. Congress to limit the growth of sports wagering, either as part of a lottery or as sports bookmaking. The most notable were two similar bills, one (S 474) proposed by then-Senator Dennis DeConcini (D-AZ) and the other (HR 74) by former Representative John Bryant (D-TX).

Gambling Is Bad for Sports

At hearings on HR 74, representatives from the NBA and the NFL strongly supported the bill. They believed that legal gambling on sports would threaten the integrity of their games. Any missed basketball shot or field goal that hooked away from the goal posts would be suspect. Had the player missed the shot or the kick because some gambler had paid him money? What about a terrible call by the referee? Was the game fixed? These are questions the sports leagues believe could threaten their businesses. (See Chapter XI for a discussion of public attitudes as to whether various sporting events are fixed.)

NFL Commissioner Paul Tagliabue declared that

We do not want our games used as bait to sell gambling. Sports gambling should not be used as a cure for the sagging fortunes of Atlantic City casinos or to boost public interest in state lotteries. We should not gamble with our children's heroes.

NBA Commissioner David Stern added that

Sports betting alters the interest of spectators from that of fans, who are principally interested in the ultimate outcome of the game, to that of gamblers, who are principally interested in beating the point spread and winning their bets.

Finally, some legislators believe that sports gambling could be a bad influence on young people. Former Senator DeConcini indicated that

The spread of legalized sports gambling threatens to lure our youth into all types of gambling. It threatens the very foundation of professional and amateur sporting events, which is to provide wholesome entertainment for all ages.

Sports Is Just Another Opportunity for Gambling

Opponents of the bills, mainly representatives from the various states considering such gambling possibilities in order to raise money, plus the North American Association of State and Provincial Lotteries (NASPL), believed the sports leagues were being hypocritical. They wondered why the sports businesses were willing to accept sports betting in Nevada but would not accept it in other states that need the money just as badly. Furthermore, they argued, the sports leagues were aware that billions of dollars are bet illegally on sporting events, so that the opportunity for gamblers' influence on players and referees already existed.

NASPL President James Hosker observed,

More than $1.5 billion is wagered annually on sports in Nevada and an estimated $15 billion to $20 billion nationwide. The leagues have long been aware of this activity and have taken virtually no action to prevent it. If this has not undermined the integrity of professional sports, state-sponsored sports lotteries will not do so.

Similarly, Oregon Lottery Director James Davey observed,

The leagues have long known of extensive wagering in Nevada and the publication of point spread in virtually every major newspaper and have done nothing.... The leagues' attempts to ban carefully regulated, state-run sports pool lotteries cannot be justified.

Proponents further pointed out that the various pre-game sports shows (usually for football games) featured the point spreads (see Chapter VIII) that the sports leagues knew were used for betting on the games. Apparently stung by such criticism, the National Football League (NFL) has tried to pressure the networks carrying their games not to discuss the odds or point spread on these pre-game shows, although without success. Moreover, virtually every sports page in every newspaper carries the point spread and other odds attached to the game. The National Basketball Association (NBA) sued the Oregon Lottery Commission to forbid them from using the scores of basketball games as the basis of their lottery's sports lottery game. The NBA and the Commission settled out of court, with the Commission agreeing not to offer betting on professional basketball games for the next five years.

The Professional and Amateur Sports Protection Act of 1992

On October 28, 1992, former Senator DeConcini's and then-Representative Bryant's bills became law as the Professional and Amateur Sports Protection Act of 1992 (PL 102-559). The law forbids betting on professional and collegiate sports but exempts all existing sports betting in Delaware, Nevada, Oregon, and Montana. New Jersey had until January 1, 1994, to introduce sports betting should it choose, which it did not. Horse racing, dog racing, and jai alai were in no way affected by this law.

GAMBLING ON CRUISE SHIPS

When ships are three miles off the coast of the United States, there generally has been no regulation over the gambling that may or may not take place on board. In 1992, Congress approved a general maritime law (PL 102-251) that included a section permitting gambling on cruise ships. The law allowed U.S. flag ships within the 3-mile limit to operate gambling facilities on board as long as gambling was not the sole purpose of the cruise. Gambling was permitted only on international and interstate (between states) voyages. This law actually applied to very few cruise ships since, of the 100-plus cruise ships that dock at American ports, barely 2 percent are registered in the United States.

Any gambling that took place in ports located within a single state would be regulated by that state. "Cruises to nowhere," gambling trips in which the ship sails out into international waters and then cruises around while the passengers gamble, would be controlled by the state from which the ship left port. Currently, only Florida, Georgia, and Texas allow "cruises to nowhere."

Some cruises leaving Los Angeles stopped at other California ports (Catalina and San Diego). Up until the passage of the new legislation, foreign ships had been operating casino games as they traveled between California ports. Dan Lungren, attorney general of California, decided to reconsider the situation in light of the new legislation, which allowed the individual states to regulate such intrastate cruises operated by foreign owners.

As a result, in 1992, California passed a law (AB3769) banning gambling on both American and foreign registered ships traveling between ports in the state. The law also reemphasized the state's ban on "cruises to nowhere." Faced with a loss of gambling revenue, several cruise lines cancelled stops in Catalina and San Diego, whose tourist industry lost many millions of dollars in revenue as a result.

The cruise ship industry was dealt another severe blow in Alaska. Cruises up the coast to Alaska have become very popular, offering travelers the opportunity to see whales, polar bears, and some of the most beautiful scenery in the world. Up until recently the ships have been sailing the inland passages and waterways of Alaska with the casinos open and producing revenues. Then, in 1993, the Federal Bureau of Investigation (FBI) ruled that these cruise ships had been violating the law because they were sailing in Alaska waters, and Alaska did not permit casino gambling. The FBI ordered the casinos closed when they were in Alaskan waters.

As a result, the Alaska state legislature quickly passed a bill to allow the casinos to operate in Alaskan waters. Tourism is the state's number-one industry, and cruise ships are an important part of that business. Much to the surprise of many, former Governor Walter Hickel vetoed the bill, declaring he was "fundamentally opposed to gambling, because it adds nothing to civilization." This was an economic blow to the cruise industry since the casinos will now likely be open perhaps one day each way as they travel through international waters to and from Alaska.

GAMBLING ON AIRCRAFT

Gambling has become so widespread that some legislators were concerned wagering would be introduced in the nation's commercial airliners. In the early 1990s, many airlines were suffering financially, and lengthy international flights in jumbo jets that can be reconfigured to include small gambling areas were considered an opportunity to earn additional revenue. The Federal Aviation Administration Authorization Act of 1994 (PL 103-305) forbade the use of "any gambling device on board an aircraft in foreign air transportation."

GAMBLING ON NATIVE AMERICAN RESERVATIONS

Gambling on Indian reservations can be found in well over half the states in the country, the product of a three-decade long effort by Native Americans to develop an industry many of them believe will benefit their people and their reservations. (Thirty-three states have tribal casinos.)

Because of historical tribal treaties, Native American reservations have been under exclusive federal jurisdiction and thereby exempt from the laws of the state in which they are located. However, under PL 83-280, passed in 1968, Congress granted civil and criminal jurisdiction over reservations to the states, as long as the move was approved by tribal consent. This statute was passed with the understanding that federal supervision would gradually be eliminated and state jurisdiction would prevail. The most controversial issue arising from PL 83-280 concerns taxation — it prohibited the states from collecting a tax on Indian activities. Nevertheless, many state governments, searching for additional sources of revenue, have shown an interest in collecting such taxes, but their efforts, so far, have failed.

Turning to Bingo

Like the states, Native American tribes saw their federal funding cut back during the 1980s, and they began looking for another source of income. Many tribes decided to take advantage of their unique sovereign status and set up gambling (mainly bingo) operations on their reservations. By the end of the 1980s, Native American tribes were sponsoring over 100 gambling operations, most of them high-stakes bingo games, which were producing more than $100 million in revenues annually for the tribes. Some bingo games became so big that prizes reached $100,000.

Wanting a Part of the Take — Trying to Tax the Income

Not surprisingly, many states in which these reservations were located wanted to regulate and, perhaps, tax the income from gambling. Florida wanted to regulate bingo games played on Seminole land, but, in 1981, the Fifth Circuit Court of Appeals, in *Seminole Tribe of Florida v. Butterworth* (658 F.2d 310), ruled that the state could not regulate bingo on the reservation if the game were legal in the state. The Supreme Court denied *certiorari* (would not hear) (455 US 1020, 1982), letting the lower court decision stand. *Barona Groups of Captain Grande Band of Mission Indians v. State of Wisconsin* (694 F.2d 1185, 1982) and *Oneida Tribe of Indians v. State of Wisconsin* (518 F. Supp. 712, 1981) produced similar rulings.

In 1987, the U.S. Supreme Court, in *California v. Cabazon of Mission Indians* (480 US 202), ruled that states generally may not regulate gaming on Native American reservations, but that the federal government does have the authority to regulate or forbid Native American gaming enterprises and to delegate authority to the states.

In 1986, the Bureau of Indian Affairs (BIA) reversed a long-standing policy by notifying Indian tribes that the BIA must approve bingo management contracts with outside companies. This ruling was an attempt by the federal government to become involved in what had previously been a state-regulated gambling industry. The federal government was concerned about the possibility of organized crime controlling gambling on Native American reservations and the possibility that large gambling winnings might go unreported, since tribal revenues are unaudited and cannot be taxed.

The Indian Gaming Regulatory Act

Meanwhile, Congress had already begun to try to resolve the problem. Like many controversial issues, it took a long time (six years) to reach a compromise that would satisfy the competing factions. The federal government claimed to be concerned that organized crime would take over the Native American games, the states were offended by any gambling activities within their borders that they did not regulate, and the Native Americans resented any intrusion on their lands or tribal rights.

In 1988, Congress passed, and President Ronald Reagan signed into law, the Indian Gaming Regulatory Act (IGRA, PL 100-497), which permits

> Indian tribes [to] have the exclusive right to regulate gaming activity on Indian lands if the gaming activity is not specifically prohibited by Federal law and is conducted within a State which does not, as a matter of criminal law and public policy, prohibit such gaming activity.

The law creates three different categories of gambling. "Class I gaming" refers to "social games solely for prizes of minimal value or traditional forms of Indian gaming" which would be regulated only by the tribe. "Class II gaming," which includes bingo, lotto, and other games similar to bingo (and specifically does not include baccarat, chemin de fer, or blackjack), would be under the regulation of a National Indian Gaming Commission set up by the law. "Class III gaming" refers to all other forms of gambling, including casinos, slot machines, and horse and dog racing. These gambling activities would not take place on Native American lands unless they were permitted in the state and unless the tribe reached an agreement with the state.

A "grandfather clause" permitted certain card games, most notably blackjack, to continue to be played in the states of Michigan, North Dakota, South Dakota, and Washington, since they were already in operation.

The National Indian Gaming Commission consists of three full-time members, the chairman appointed by the president of the United States with the advice and consent of the Senate, and the other two appointed by the Secretary of the Interior. No more than two members can come from the same political party, and at least two members have to be enrolled in a Native American tribe. The commission has the power to regulate Class II and Class III gambling on Native American lands, although Class III gambling is also controlled by agreements between the tribe and the state within which the reservation is located. Finally, the states could not tax the Native American earnings from gambling, and, in fact, the law specifically states that a court "shall consider any demand by the State for direct taxation of the Indian tribe or of any Indian lands as evidence that the State has not negotiated in good faith."

State-Tribal Compacts

As a result of the law, states and tribes have entered legal agreements called compacts to permit gambling facilities to be developed on Native American lands. By July 30, 1999, 160 tribes in 24 states had reached 179 compacts with the governments in the states within which their lands were located. Many of these compacts have already led to very successful casino operations, and more will likely develop in the near future. (See Chapter VII.)

Not Always Easy

Nonetheless, the procedure of making state compacts has not always been easy. Some states, including California and New Mexico, have been reluctant to negotiate with Native Americans. On the other hand, many Native American leaders resent having to deal with state officials. In the past, they have only had to deal with federal officials. In addition, many Native American leaders believe that having to reach a compact agreement with states compromises their authority as sovereign nations.

Several states have gone to court in order to avoid reaching a compact with a Native American tribe. The states claimed the Tenth Amendment reserves to the states all powers not delegated to the federal government by the Constitution. They also argued that the Eleventh Amendment declares that a state may not be sued by individuals based on federal legislation (unless clearly so stated by Congress).* In many states, including Washington, North Carolina, Arizona, New Mexico, and Massachusetts, state and tribal authorities have clashed. In Alaska, the state passed a law banning Monte Carlo nights so that they would not have to agree to permit casino gambling on land belonging to the Klawock Band of Tlingit Native Alaskans.

THE STATES AND NATIVE AMERICANS GO TO COURT OVER IGRA

Several federal courts of appeals reached mixed findings on these questions.

Cheyenne River Sioux Tribe v. South Dakota

In *Cheyenne River Sioux Tribe v. South Dakota* (3 F.3d 273, 1993), the Eighth Circuit Court of Appeals held that the Indian Gaming Regulatory Act (IGRA) did not violate either the Tenth or the Eleventh Amendments of the United States Constitution. The Cheyenne River Sioux had gone to court claiming that South Dakota had refused to negotiate in good faith with them. The tribe had wanted to offer keno because the Cheyenne River Sioux claimed that the state permitted video keno. The state claimed the games were quite different, and the circuit court agreed, indicating that South Dakota did not have to permit keno because it did not allow keno in the state. Furthermore, the state could impose a $5 betting limit on Indian gam-

bling because "bet limits are established by state law" and covered all other betting in the state.

However, the court ruled that IGRA did not violate the Tenth Amendment because (quoting from an earlier case) "Congress, when acting pursuant to the Indian Commerce Clause, has the power to abrogate (invalidate) the States' immunity."

Concerning the Tenth Amendment, the circuit court ruled that IGRA did not force states to negotiate since the states can refuse to respond. There are a number of options, and if the state refuses to negotiate, a mediator can choose to accept the tribe's proposed compact. Obviously, negotiating is in the best interest of the state, but it does not have to do it. "Therefore," declared the court, "we hold the IGRA does not force the state to compact with Indian tribes regarding the Indian gaming and does not violate the Tenth Amendment."

Rumsey Indian Rancheria of Wintun Indians v. Wilson, Governor; State of California

In *Rumsey Indian Rancheria of Wintun Indians v. Wilson, Governor; State of California* (41 F 3d 421, 1994), the Ninth Circuit Court of Appeals agreed with the Eighth Circuit. (See above.) The Rumsey Indian tribe had asked permission to have casino games such as slot machines and blackjack. The tribe noted that the state already permitted video lottery terminals, pari-mutuel horse racing, and poker, which were "functionally similar" to the games the tribe wanted.

The Ninth Circuit Court did not agree. The games that the Rumsey tribe wanted were different from the ones already permitted in the state. Simply because a state permitted some gambling did not mean it had to permit all types of gambling. "We agree with the approach taken by the Eighth Circuit," said the court.

---

* "The Judicial power of the United States shall not be construed to extend to any suit in law or equity, commenced or prosecuted against one of the United States by Citizens of another State, or by Citizens or subjects of any Foreign State."

IGRA does not require a state to negotiate over one form of a gaming activity simply because it has legalized another, albeit similar, form of gaming. Instead, the statute says only that, if a state allows a gaming activity "for any purpose by any person, organization, or entity," then it also must allow Indian tribes to engage in that same activity. In other words, a state need only allow Indian tribes to operate games that others can operate, but need not give tribes what others cannot have.

Spokane Tribe of Indians v. Washington State

The Spokane Tribe of Indians and the state of Washington met a number of times from 1989 through 1991 in an unsuccessful attempt to reach a mutually acceptable compact. Unsatisfied, the tribe filed a complaint against the state of Washington, claiming the state had failed to negotiate in good faith and asking for an injunction ordering the parties to conclude a compact within 60 days. The State of Washington claimed that the suit had no validity because the state had immunity based on the Eleventh Amendment of the U.S. Constitution. The Ninth Circuit Court of Appeals, in *Spokane Tribe of Indians v. Washington State* (28 F.3d 991, 1994), did not agree.

Concerning whether Congress intended to abrogate the state's immunity, the court observed

> Our discussion of congressional intent need not be lengthy. Every federal court that has considered the issue has concluded that the IGRA's language reveals a clear intent to abrogate the states' Eleventh Amendment immunity.

Concerning the Indian Commerce Clause and the Interstate Commerce Clause, the court observed that it

> Cannot agree ... that the differences between the Indian and the Interstate Commerce Clauses support state immunity from tribal suit where, as here, Congress has authorized such suits. Congress' power

over both Indian and interstate commerce is set forth in Article I, & 8:

> The Congress shall have power ... [t]o regulate commerce with foreign nations, and among the several states, and with the Indian tribes.
>
> ... Congressional power pursuant to the Indian Commerce Clause, then, cannot be less than its authority under the Interstate Commerce Clause.

The Ninth Circuit Court concluded that

> Congress tried to fashion a plan (IGRA) that would enable the states to have a choice in how tribal gaming should operate and to enforce to some degree the states' own laws. The states' immunity from suits under the Eleventh Amendment should not frustrate that goal. Indeed, principles of state sovereignty are singularly out of place in such a scheme, where the federal government is tailoring a limited grant of power to the states. In this case, sovereign immunity would undermine rather than remove the assertion of state interests.

The court strongly disagreed with the Eleventh Circuit Court's conclusion in *Seminole Tribe of Florida v. Florida* (see below) that the case could always be referred to the Secretary of the Interior. The Secretary of the Interior, said the Ninth Circuit Court, should be only "a matter of last resort." The compact should be reached through negotiations between the state and the tribe so that resolution benefiting both sides can be reached. Using the Secretary of Interior as the expected, eventual arbitrator of the issue "would turn the Secretary of the Interior into a federal czar, contrary to the congressional aim of state participation."

Seminole Tribe of Florida v. Florida

When the State of Florida refused to negotiate with the Seminole Tribe of Florida, the tribe took the state to court to compel them to negotiate under the terms of the Indian Gaming Regulatory Act (IGRA). The State of Florida countered that they were under no obligation to negotiate because the Eleventh Amendment of the U.S. Constitution granted the state sovereign immunity from being sued. The Eleventh Circuit Court of Appeals, in *Seminole Tribe of Florida v. Florida* (11 F.3d 1016, 1994), agreed with the State of Florida and said that the Seminole tribe did not have the right to sue the State of Florida.

The court agreed with the earlier cases that the Congress had, indeed, clearly intended to void the states' Eleventh Amendment immunity. On the other hand, unless the state had consented to be sued, which they had not, "Congress, when it enacted IGRA pursuant to the Indian Commerce Clause, lacked the power to abrogate (void) the states' sovereign immunity" and, therefore, the state could not be sued. The court recognized the right of the states, under certain circumstances, to be sued under the Interstate Commerce Act, but the Indian Commerce Act was not the Interstate Commerce Act and did not apply. Consequently, the court concluded, "The principles of federalism and sovereign immunity exemplified in the Eleventh Amendment prevent Congress from abrogating the states' immunity."

The court closed, noting that

Nevertheless, we are left with the question as to what procedure is left for an Indian tribe faced with a state that not only will not negotiate in good faith, but also will not consent to sit. The answer, gleaned from the statute, is simple. One hundred and eighty days after the tribe first requests negotiations with the state, the tribe may file suit in district court. If the state pleads an Eleventh Amendment defense, the suit is dismissed, and the tribe ... then may notify the Secretary of the Interior of the tribe's failure to negotiate a compact with the state. The secretary then may prescribe regulations governing class III gaming on

the tribe's lands. This solution conforms with IGRA and serves to achieve Congress' goals....

This case was appealed to the U.S. Supreme Court, and in *Seminole Tribe of Florida v. Florida* (517 US 44, 1996), the High Court upheld the findings of the Eleventh Circuit Court of Appeals. The Court noted that

Notwithstanding Congress' clear intent to abrogate the States' sovereign immunity, the Indian Commerce Clause does not grant Congress that power, and therefore ... cannot grant jurisdiction over a State that does not consent to be sued.

The High Court concluded, "The Eleventh Amendment prohibits Congress from making the State of Florida capable of being sued in federal court." The Seminoles' claim against the state of Florida was dismissed.

However, while it might have appeared that Indian tribes had suffered a defeat, some Indian observers thought the decision might work to their benefit. The Supreme Court had not resolved the issue of whether the Indian tribes could go directly to the Department of Interior as recommended in the Court of Appeals ruling (see above). Tom Wapato, National Indian Gaming Association Executive Director, observed that "the result ... is that the case returns the tribes to pre-IGRA time where the Interior Secretary is responsible for completing gaming agreements with tribes."

Apparently, the states, instead of having at least some power to control the development of Indian gambling casinos within their state borders, may now be left out of the process. Decisions in which they had had at least some input would now be decided by federal authorities in Washington. Many Indian leaders believe that they will get better treatment from the Department of the Interior than they had received from some reluctant states. The states, on the other hand, might have achieved a Pyrrhic victory (a too costly victory). While they might have won their case, they may not be better off. (See Chapter VII for political problems that have developed.)

NATIONAL INDIAN GAMING COMMISSION

Finally, after several years, the National Indian Gaming Commission (NIGC) reached full membership and began to prepare long overdue guidelines to provide some oversight for the Native American gambling industry. Beginning in 1993, the National Indian Gaming Commission began daily oversight of Class II gaming (mainly bingo) and, with approval of management, contracts, and tribal rules on Class III gaming (casinos, slot machines, etc.). Most regulation on Class III gaming, however, will be established in the state-tribe compacts.

Many tribal leaders resent NIGC having any control over them. They feel they have had two hundred years of oversight by federal agencies, most notably the Bureau of Indian Affairs, and it has done them little good. They further think they are fully capable of running their reservations and the business done on those reservations, and they do not need NIGC looking over their shoulders. The tribal leaders know that certainly some of them will fail, and others may be cheated by unscrupulous business people, but these circumstances happen in all sorts of business endeavors, and there is no reason they should be singled out for oversight.

On the other hand, Tony Hope, former Chairman of the National Indian Gaming Commission, believed that regulation would actually promote the profitability for gambling on Indian reservations. When customers know that the Indian casinos are regulated, they will have more faith in the integrity of the games and will, therefore, be more likely to go to the reservations to gamble. Hope believed that regulation is not an issue of tribal sovereignty, but a matter of sound business. His successor, Harold Monteau, also indicated his desire to take "a leadership role in encouraging the development of strong tribal regulatory structures."

According to the Bureau of Indian Affairs, there are 554 federally recognized tribes in the United States, and it will not be easy for the NIGC to find agreement among this large group. Like any group of hundreds of different sovereign entities, they have hundreds of different positions and needs. Just as there is no single generic nation in the world, there is no single generic Native American tribe. The NIGC faces a considerable challenge and will have to recognize this diversity and learn to work with this wide variety of opinions and situations.

Attempts in Congress to Limit Native American Gambling

The rapid growth of casino gambling on Native American reservations has led to the introduction of several proposed pieces of legislation designed to change the Indian Gaming Regulatory Act (IGRA). In 1993, Representative Robert Torricelli (D-NJ) and Senator Harry Reid (D-NV) introduced, on the same day, similar bills calling for the limiting of Class III Native American gambling. Representative Torricelli's bill, the Gaming Integrity and State Enforcement Act of 1993, and Senator Reid's proposal, the Indian Gaming Regulatory Act Amendments, both prohibited Native American gambling compacts unless the state permitted the gaming as part of a commercial, for-profit enterprise within the state. In addition, just because a state permitted one type of Class III gaming, most notably a lottery, did not mean that it had to permit other forms of Class III gaming, such as a casino.

Both bills also proposed to make the state a more equal power in the preparation of the compact and less subject to the threat that they were not bargaining in good faith. Both congressmen claimed that Native American gaming had gotten out of control. Meanwhile, Senator Daniel Inouye (D-HI), Chairman of the Senate Indian Affairs Committee, had spent a great deal of time meeting with Native American leaders and government officials in an effort to reach a compromise that would essentially leave IGRA intact. Neither bill ever became law.

In the following 104th Congress (1995), Senate advocates of stricter control of Native American gambling introduced a bill (S 487) that would require Native American tribes to license games, conduct strict background checks on important casino workers, and provide the federal government with periodic accounting of gambling revenues and profits. Initially, the bill had included provisions that allowed tribes to bypass states that refused to negotiate compacts. Tribes in many states had been blocked in their efforts to draw up compacts and introduce gambling on their reservations.

Despite all of the other proposals that the tribal authorities had considered offensive, this provision was considered so important that it led many Indian leaders to support S 487. Native American leaders found that their support was considered unnecessary since this provision was removed from the bill before it won approval from the Senate Committee on Indian Affairs.

In the House of Representatives, legislators proposed a bill calling for the federal government to tax Indian gaming. Thinking they would be more successful in the Senate, Native American representatives lobbied Senate leaders to oppose the House bill when it reached the Senate for consideration. Their efforts focused upon then-Senate Majority Leader Robert Dole (R-KS). They reminded him that tribal governments had never been taxed before, that much of the money earned was being used for social needs, that this was the only successful economic activity on Indian reservations, and finally, that the Republicans had promised no new taxes, and this pledge should include Native Americans. Senator Dole, through a spokeswoman, indicated that he opposed the tax and would fight to keep it out of the Senate budget. The proposal, however, never made it out of House committee.

Using Tribal Winnings
to Replace Tribal Allocations

Native American tribes receive Tribal Priority Allocations (TPA) from the Department of Interior to provide educational and social services on their reservations. These fundings are essential for the operation of the reservations. In 1995, the Senate Interior Appropriations Committee proposed that the Secretary of the Interior, the administrator responsible for providing funding to Indian reservations, use a "means test" to determine how much funding each tribe should get. Initially, the draft bill indicated, "Notwithstanding any other provision of law, the Secretary of the Interior may reduce the funds provided in this act for tribes receiving gaming revenues in order to minimize the need for funding reductions for other tribes." This meant that those tribes earning monies from gambling would receive less money, an amount likely equal to their earnings from gambling.

Although the provision was eventually removed from the funding bill, this attitude still likely prevails. Congress is looking everywhere to cut spending, and Native Americans have relatively little political clout in Congress. In addition, the success of gambling on many Indian reservations has led many people to think that Native Americans are rolling in money. While many Indian casino ventures have proved quite successful, most have not earned enough to lift their reservations out of the economic hardship that characterizes most reservations.

DEALING WITH STATE GOVERNMENTS

In the recent past, when the nation's major concern was to control illegal gambling, the federal government was the main enforcement level of government. Gambling was illegal almost everywhere in the country. Gambling laws were designed to control gambling and catch bookies, operators of illegal card games, and the members of criminal syndicates who dominated illegal gambling. Gambling was a criminal matter, and federal laws were designed to put those who ran the illegal operations behind bars. Even in the few places where it was legal, most notably Las Vegas, it was thought, quite correctly, that criminal elements played a major role in gambling operations.

During the past several years, the political landscape has been turned upside down. Few people are arrested for illegal gambling (see Chapter III), and many Americans tolerate gambling as readily as they accept other forms of entertainment, such as movies and sporting events. While the federal laws are still on the books, they seem to have little applicability to the modern gambling industry.

Gambling has become a major part of the entertainment industry. Companies offering gambling are like any other businesses in the entertainment industry. Like so many businesses, expansion has been the order of the day. Unlike the growth in many industries, most political issues have not passed through Washington, DC, but rather through state capitals such as Jackson, Mississippi; Jefferson City, Missouri; Baton Rouge, Louisiana; Des Moines, Iowa; and Denver, Colorado.

Making Gambling Interests Heard

State legislatures decide if gambling will become legal in the individual states. Currently, some form of gambling is legal in all states except Hawaii and Utah. While success is never assured, revenue-hungry state governments are virtually always willing to give gambling interests a hearing.

Like any industry, gambling companies want their interests to be heard in the state capitals. They hire lobbyists and donate to political campaigns. While major donations do not necessarily buy votes, they usually earn the right to be heard. In 1996, gambling interests saturated the state of Arkansas with one of the industry's largest campaigns for casino gambling. Arkansas rejected the proposal. Six other states — Ohio, Washington, Colorado, Iowa, Nebraska, and Louisiana — also rejected wagering proposals on election day. Only Michigan voters passed a proposal to permit casinos in economically depressed Detroit. (Louisiana rejected one gambling proposal, but passed two others.)

Political contributions by gambling corporations have led to scandals in Louisiana, Missouri, Arizona, Kentucky, South Carolina, and West Virginia. For example, it is suspected that video poker operators in Louisiana had bribed state legislators to kill proposed anti-gambling legislation. (As a result of that scandal, in 1996, Louisiana voters voted to end video poker in 33 of the state's 34 parishes.) The attorney general of Pennsylvania pleaded guilty to hiding contributions from operators of illegal video poker games. Legislators in Arizona, Kentucky, South Carolina, and West Virginia have been convicted of taking bribes from gambling interests. When so much money is involved, there is always the chance for corruption.

Modern gambling is generally a well-regulated business. Virtually every state that permits casino gambling or pari-mutuel betting has a state racing or gambling commission to monitor gambling activities. While today's gambling industry is big business run by huge corporations, virtually every state regulatory commission feels it must show it is making sure that no underworld or syndicate figures play a role in its state gambling activities. The commissions also control other activities, such as how late casinos may stay open and whether there will be limits on betting. Since these regulations are usually determined by state legislatures, it is only natural that gambling companies try to influence their decisions through lobbyists and political donations.

At the same time, however, although the gambling business is now controlled by major entertainment corporations, they still must bear the stigma of their history. Gambling money was once mob money. Twenty years ago, if a legislator was found to have accepted money to handle a gambling matter, it was assumed that it was syndicate money, and the legislator's career was likely in jeopardy. Today, although gambling has become just another matter handled by state legislatures, gambling money still appears as tainted money to some.

Some Money Still Goes to Washington

Although state capitals have become more important than the federal capital in regulating

21

gambling, it does not mean that the gambling industry has forgotten the federal government. For example, The Center for Public Integrity, a Washington-based research organization, reported that gambling interests had contributed more than $200,000 to Bob Dole's presidential campaign and $60,000 to President Clinton's campaign in 1996. The amount of these contributions were eight times more than the industry had ever donated previously to a presidential election. The Center for Responsive Politics, a nonpartisan watchdog organization, reported that the gambling industry donated more than $130,000 to Republican congressional candidates and $53,000 to Democratic congressional candidates in 1995. Between 1991 and 1998, gambling interests contributed more than $13 million to the Democratic and Republican National Committees, other party committees, and the campaign treasuries of candidates running for federal offices.

OPPOSITION TO GAMBLING

The rapid expansion of gambling across the United States has not been well received by all Americans. The failure of many gambling initiatives over the past few years indicates an opposition powerful enough to either influence state legislators to drop proposed legislation allowing various forms of gambling or to garner enough votes to defeat initiatives that would do the same thing.

Varied Reasons for Opposition

Opposition to gambling can include a wide variety of interests. Some business people might fear that a casino could draw spending away from their restaurants or hotels. Many point out that gambling casinos rarely bring in as much income to the area or tax revenues to the government as gambling promoters claim. Others fear that crime will increase as more people are drawn to gambling. One gambling interest might oppose another gambling interest. For example, horse and track owners often oppose the introduction of casino gambling, as do owners of "cruise ships to nowhere," which leave Florida ports and sail into international waters so that passengers can gamble on the casinos onboard.

A Moral Issue

Many who oppose gambling consider it morally or theologically wrong. The domestic violence and crime that might result from compulsive gambling could lead to the breakdown of the family and divorce. Gambling, especially the lotteries, contribute to the attitude that a person can get something for nothing, a belief many people consider particularly harmful to the nation's morality. They believe that the states, by administering the lotteries, have become party to this. By sanctioning gambling, government authorities have contributed to making gambling publicly acceptable. Many opponents believe that government and community leaders have had a choice between money and morality and, in all too many cases, have chosen money. Not only have they degraded their own integrity, but they have also debased the values of their communities.

Some people consider gambling a social and economic, as well as a moral, issue. In many instances, poorer people will spend a higher proportion of their income on gambling. A gambler might gamble away his or her paycheck or even the family savings. The family might end up on welfare, costing the government money. A gambler might steal from his or her job in order to pay off gambling debts and get fired for stealing, or might become indebted to a loan shark who will charge extremely high interest and harm him if he does not pay. Under pressure from his debts, he might beat his wife and/or children. The gambler, deep in debt, his whole world crumbling around him, might commit suicide.

Major gambling cities, such as Las Vegas and Reno, Nevada, and Atlantic City, New Jersey, have been found to have suicide rates that are four times higher than in cities of similar size where gambling is not legal. Visitors to the city commit many of these suicides. During one 8-day period in August 1999, three men killed themselves in Atlantic City, New Jersey, after losing money. A young lawyer from Florida lost $87,000 in two days and jumped off the roof of one of the casino/hotels. A casino dealer suffering financial and personal problems leaped off the top of a casino/hotel parking garage, and a German tourist fell to his death from the tenth floor of a parking garage.

Increased Addiction

An estimated 0.7 percent of Americans are addicted to gambling. The spread of lotteries and casino gambling has increased the opportunities for those already addicted to gamble more, and for those who have the potential to become addicted, but who have never been exposed to gambling, to become hooked. Some observers estimate that, with the increased opportunities to gamble, the proportion of compulsive gamblers has increased to 2 to 5 percent of those who gamble.

According to *Gambling Impact and Behavior Study*, a 1999 report to the National Gambling Impact Study Commission (National Opinion Research Center, University of Chicago, Chicago, Illinois), pathological and problem gamblers comprise 2.5 percent of adults and account for about 15 percent of casino, lottery, and pari-mutuel receipts from the gamblers who are represented in surveys. They consider this a significant percentage, certainly high enough to make anyone think twice about introducing gambling into his area. In the long run, opponents claim, the treatment of compulsive gamblers and their families, the effects of increased crime, and the loss of business in other areas will cost far more than any revenues produced by the casinos or lotteries.

THE NATIONAL COALITION AGAINST LEGALIZED GAMBLING

The National Coalition Against Legalized Gambling (Birmingham, Alabama) believes that "this surge toward legalized gambling must stop before it destroys our communities." The National Coalition supports the passage of legislation to study the social and economic effects of gambling on the United States. (The National Gambling Impact Study Commission Act; PL 104-169, signed into law by President Bill Clinton in 1997. See below.)

The National Coalition also hopes to stop the development of interactive gambling on the Internet or cable television. "The Case Against Legalized Gambling," a Coalition release, summarizes the arguments against gambling (Table 2.1). In 1996, the National Coalition opened an office in Washington, DC, to lobby Congress more effectively.

The Reverend Tom Grey, Executive Director of the National Coalition Against Legalized Gambling, in testimony before the House Judiciary Committee (September 29, 1995), summed up the Coalition's position when he observed that

> to many Americans, government's promotion of gambling is a cop-out and a double-cross. We see public officials sacrificing our communities to a predatory enterprise — for money. Citizens see government living off gambling profits, taken from the poorest and weakest of our citizens, instead of facing up to rational choices regarding budgets and taxes.

The National Coalition (its president and executive director are both ministers) received considerable support from conservative Christian groups, such as Focus on the Family and the Christian Coalition, as well as many mainline churches. This backing gave the organization considerable grassroots support and the ability to mobilize letters to Congressmen or votes in ballot initiatives. The National Coalition claims to have played a major role in the defeat of dozens of proposed gambling casinos.

THE AMERICAN GAMING ASSOCIATION

To present the best image of the industry to state and federal governments and to the public, the gambling industry has established the American Gaming Association as an industry trade group. Frank J. Fahrenkopf, Jr., former national chairman of the Republican Party and former lawyer in Reno,

TABLE 2.1

THE CASE AGAINST LEGALIZED GAMBLING

Gambling costs far more than it benefits. Studies show that for every dollar gambling produces for a regional economy, three dollars are lost because of the economic and social costs of gambling. When government legalizes more gambling, taxpayers lose -- whether they gamble or not.

Gambling cannibalizes local businesses. A hundred dollars spent in a slot machine is a hundred dollars that is not spent in a local restaurant, theater or retail store. As Donald Trump told the Miami Herald, "People will spend a tremendous amount of money in casinos, money that they would normally spend on buying a refrigerator or a new car. Local businesses will suffer because they'll lose customer dollars to the casinos."

Gambling triggers addiction. The more legalized gambling available, the more addictive behavior is triggered. In 1989, only 1.7% of Iowa's adults were gambling addicts, but after riverboat casinos were legalized, the rate of addiction more than tripled to 5.4%. The Florida Office of Planning and Budgeting conducted a study which concluded that the costs to government of gambling addiction far outweighed all revenues that might be generated by casino gambling.

Gambling addiction has become an epidemic among youth. Researchers now call gambling the fastest-growing teenage addiction, with the rate of pathological gambling among high school and college-age youth about twice that of adults. According to Dr. Howard Shaffer, Director of the Harvard Medical School Center for Addiction Studies, "Today, there are more children experiencing adverse symptoms from gambling than from drugs...and the problem is growing."

Gambling attracts crime. A comprehensive report by the Attorney General of Maryland concludes, "Casinos would bring a substantial increase in crime to our State. There would be more violent crime, more crimes against property, more insurance fraud, more white collar crime, more juvenile crime, more drug and alcohol-related crime, more domestic violence and child abuse, and more organized crime."

Gambling victimizes the poor. The poorest citizens spend the largest percentage of their incomes on gambling. Those who can afford it the least gamble the most. Both public and private gambling businesses target advertising directly at the weakest individuals in society because they are gambling's best customers.

Gambling presents a bad example to our children. Gambling promotes the idea that luck, not education and hard work, is the key to success. Gambling produces no wealth for society, and suggests that productivity is not important. Gambling sets up artificial risks and glorifies individuals who take the biggest, most foolish risks.

Gambling corrupts government. So much money is at stake, and gambling companies are so dependent on governmental decisions for a piece of those profits, that corruption is inevitable. Wherever gambling has gone, bribery, extortion and payoffs have followed.

National Coalition Against Legalized Gambling
110 Maryland Avenue, N.E.
Washington, D.C. 20002

Source: Used by permission of the National Coalition Against Legalized Gambling, Washington, DC, no date

Nevada, was chosen as the group's first president. One of his main responsibilities is to see that the federal government is aware of the gambling industry's position on whatever gambling issues the federal government might consider. In addition to lobbying the federal government concerning the needs and position of the nation's gambling industry, the AGA also educates the public about the industry and acts as a clearinghouse for information about the industry.

The industry believes that American consumers want to enjoy gambling as a form of entertainment. Certainly the huge increases in gambling revenues show both that the American marketplace wants gambling and that need has not yet been filled. Gambling brings employment, as has been shown by the many tens of thousands of workers employed at gambling casinos and riverboats.

The industry considers syndicate control of gambling very much a thing of the past. Gambling is now a major entertainment industry owned by public companies that are monitored by the Securities and Exchange Commission. Today, the mob probably could not raise the many hundreds of millions of dollars needed to develop a new resort complex.

The industry does not accept the argument that gambling does not produce anything. They note that, in the same sense, Disneyland or Disney World do not produce anything either. People go to Las Vegas and Disneyland to be entertained and have fun. It is not appropriate to compare a Las Vegas casino or Disney World with a manufacturing plant such as General Motors or Gateway Computers. One is a service or entertainment industry; the other is a manufacturing industry. People go to a casino or to Disneyland to have fun. If they have a good time, then they have gotten their money's worth.

Supporters of gambling claim that increased crime does not accompany gambling. State gaming commissions work very hard to make sure that casino ownership and management do not have any links to organized crime. Local crime increases proportionately no more than the growth in the population caused by the gambling casino. The crime rate in Orlando, Florida (where Disney World is located), is significantly higher than that in Las Vegas, Nevada, yet no one would claim that Mickey Mouse and Donald Duck contribute to crime.

The industry recognizes that, for a small percentage of gamblers, addiction is a real problem. The industry has been supporting many states in the creation of agencies to help those people needing assistance. The industry also works hard to make sure that those under 18 years old do not gamble at casinos.

Finally, while some people may feel that gambling is morally unacceptable, they do not have the right to force their moral or religious views on others. If they do not want to gamble, they do not have to gamble. However, if their neighbor wants to gamble, that should be his or her choice.

See Chapters XII and XIII for a more complete debate on the issue of gambling.

GAMBLING COMMISSION FORMED

President Bill Clinton signed a bill creating a commission to study the impact of legalized gambling into law on August 3, 1997 (HR 497 — PL 104-169). The commission was formed in response to the rapid nationwide growth in legalized gambling from 1976, when only two states permitted legal gambling, to 1996, when 48 states had some form of legalized wagering.

The legislation, sponsored by Frank R. Wolf (R-VA) in the House and Paul Simon (D-IL) in the Senate, created a nine-member federal commission to investigate all facets of gambling in America, including casinos, lotteries, sports betting, and Indian gambling. The purpose of the law was to give policy makers advice on how to bring gambling into a state or community, or whether to bring it in at all.

The commission, with power to subpoena documents, was given two years to submit a report to Congress showing the economic impact of gambling on an area's families and businesses. The report was also to include the commission's findings on American Indian gambling, gambling on the Internet, and any relationship between gambling and crime.

In June 1999, the National Gambling Impact Study Commission (NGISC) released the results of the study. The NGISC recommended a pause in the spread of casinos, lotteries, and slot machines nationwide. The purpose in stopping the growth of legalized gambling was to urge state and local governments to form their own gambling study commissions to consider gambling's explosive growth before building more casinos or introducing more lottery games. Furthermore, the NGISC addressed problem gambling. Many of the recommendations in the report dealt with research on and treatment for problem gamblers, who, according to the commission, account for 15 percent of the industry's gross revenues.

Other recommendations included

- Permitting only those ages 21 and older to gamble.

- Banning Internet gambling, betting on college and amateur sports, and all political contributions to state and local campaigns by gambling companies.

- Reducing lottery advertising and decreasing the number of outlets selling lottery products.

- More federal oversight of casinos operated by Native American tribes.

For more information on the NGISC report, see individual chapters.

GAMBLING — HERE TO STAY?

People in the United States are still torn between the perceived evils of gambling and its potential for raising money for social needs, such as education and care for the elderly. Politicians see it as a way to avoid raising taxes. Many Americans consider it just plain fun. Despite moral misgivings of some, the United States has become far more tolerant of gambling in recent years. Most states now operate lotteries, and an ever-growing number of states and communities have turned to some form of casino gambling to generate income.

CHAPTER III

AN OVERVIEW OF GAMBLING*

SOME DEFINITIONS

As with any industry or occupation, gambling has its own vocabulary. Following are a few terms that have a specific meaning in the gambling industry.

- Gaming — same as gambling.

- Wager — same as "bet," that is, the amount of money a person spends on a gambling activity.

- Handle — the total amount of money wagered by all bettors on a specific gambling event or activity.

- Take-out — the percentage of the handle that is taken out by the operator of the gambling activity (the race track operator, for example) and by the state (in the form of taxes and license fees, etc.).

- Pay-off — the amount of money left over after the take-out; the amount that is distributed among the winning bettors.

TYPES OF LEGAL GAMBLING

Gambling is inevitable. No matter what is said or done by advocates or opponents in all its various forms, it is an activity that is practiced, or tacitly endorsed, by a substantial majority of Americans. — Final Report, Commission on the Review of the National Policy Toward Gambling, Washington, DC, 1976

There are five principal forms of legal gambling in the United States: bingo, lotteries, parimutuel betting, off-track betting, and casinos. According to the Organized Crime Control Act of 1970 (PL 91-452), the term gambling includes, but is not limited to, pool-selling; bookmaking; maintaining slot machines, roulette wheels, or dice tables; conducting lotteries, policy, bolita, or numbers games; and selling chances to these games. Either a state or a private enterprise can conduct legal gambling operations. Gambling operations must follow federal statutes but are generally regulated by state governments.

In 1999, some form of legal gambling was either operating or authorized to operate in 48 states plus Washington, DC, and the jurisdictions of Puerto Rico and the U.S. Virgin Islands. The only states that have no form of legal gambling either authorized or operating are Hawaii and Utah (which permits quarterhorse racing but no pari-mutuel gambling). North Carolina permits only charitable bingo.

---

* Most of this chapter has been based on *International Gaming and Wagering Business*, 1998 and 1999. Note that the industry uses the word "gaming" instead of gambling. Since its inception in 1979, this Information Plus publication has used the word gambling. To change the use of the term might indicate a lack of balance in the presentation, and therefore, this publication will continue to use the word gambling.

TABLE 3.1

United States Gaming at a Glance

	Charitable bingo	Charitable games	Card rooms	Casinos & gaming	Non-casino devices	Indian casinos	Indian bingo	Sports betting	Lottery operated games: Video lottery	Keno-style games	Instant/pulltabs	Lotto games	Numbers games	Parimutuel wagering: Greyhound	Jai-alai	Harness	Quarter horse	Thoroughbred	Inter-track wagering	Off-track wagering	Telephone wagering
Alabama	●						●							●		◆	■	■	●		
Alaska	●	●					●														
Arizona	●	●				●	●				●	●	★	●			◆	●	●	●	
Arkansas														●			◆	●	●	●	
California	●	●	●			●	●			●	●	●	●			●	●	●	●	●	
Colorado	●	●	●	●		●	●			■	●	●	●	●		◆	◆	◆	●	●	
Connecticut	●	●				●	●				●	●	●	●	●	◆	◆	◆	●	●	●
Delaware	●	●							●		●	●	●			●		●	●	●	
D.C.	●	●									●	●	●								
Florida	●	●				●	●				●	●	●	●	●	●	■	●	●	●	
Georgia	●										●	●	●								
Hawaii																					
Idaho	●	●				☆	●				●	●					●	●	●		
Illinois	●	●		●							●	●	●	●		●	◆	●	●	●	
Indiana	●	●	●	●							●	●	●			●	◆	●	●	●	
Iowa	●	●		●		●	●				●	●	●	●		●	●	●	●		
Kansas	●	●				●	●			●	●	●	●	●		■	●	○	●		
Kentucky	●	●									●	●	●			■	●	●	●	●	●
Louisiana	●	●		●	●	●	●				●	●	●			■	●	●	●	●	
Maine	●	●									●	●	●			●	●	●	●	●	
Maryland	●	●			●					●	●	●	●			●	●	●	●	●	◆
Mass.	●	●								●	●	●	●			●	●	●	●		
Michigan	●	●		★		●	●				●	●	●			●	●	●	●	●	
Minnesota	●	●	◆			●	●				●	●	●			●	●	●	●		
Miss.	●	●		●			●				●	●									
Missouri	●	●		●							●	●	●			■	◆	■	◆	◆	
Montana	●	●	●	▼	●	●	●	●		●	●	●	●			●	◆	●	●	●	
Nebraska	●	●				▲				●	●	●	●	●		■	●	●	●		
Nevada	●		●	●	●	●	●	●						■	■	●	●			●	●
N.H.	●										●	●	●	●		●	●	●	●		
New Jersey	●	●		●	●						●	●	●			●		●	●	●	
New Mexico	●	●				★	●				●	●	●				●	●	●	●	
New York	●	●				●	●			●	●	●	●			●	●	●	●	●	●
N. Carolina	●			▼		●	●														
N. Dakota	●	●	●			●	●	●								■	●	●	●	●	
Ohio	●	●									●	●	●			●	●	●	●	●	●
Oklahoma	●	●				☆	●									◆	●	●	●	●	★
Oregon	●	●				●	●	●	●	■	●	●	●	●		●	●	●	●	●	●
Penn.	●	●									●	●	●			■	●	●	●	●	●
R. Island	●	●							●	●	●	●	●	●		■					
S. Carolina	●				●																
S. Dakota	●	●	●	●	●	●	●		●		●	●	●			■	●	●	■	●	
Tennessee																◆	◆	◆	◆	◆	
Texas	●	●					●				●	●	●				●	●	●		
Utah																	○				
Vermont	●	●									●	●	●			■	●	◆	●		
Virginia	●	●									●	●	●				●	●	●	●	
Wash.	●	●	●	▲		▲	●			●	●	●	●			■	●	●	●		
W. Virginia	●	●							●	●	●	●	●	●		◆	■	●	●		
Wisconsin	●	●				●	●				●	●	●	●			◆	●	●		
Wyoming	●	●															◆	●	●	●	
Puerto Rico	●			●								●	●						●	●	
Virgin Islands				◆					●										●	●	

● Legal and operative
★ Implemented since June 1998
▲ Table games only (no slots)
◆ Authorized but not yet implemented
▼ Commercial bingo, keno, or pulltabs only

■ Permitted by law and previously operative
○ Operative but no parimutuel wagering
◻ Previously operative but now not permitted
☆ Compacts signed for non-casino gaming, such as parimutuel wagering and lotteries; however, casino games may be operating

Source: Patricia A. McQueen, "North American Gaming at a Glance," *International Gaming and Wagering Business*, vol. 20, no. 9, September 1999. Copyright © 1999, *International Gaming and Wagering Business* magazine. Reproduced with permission.

TABLE 3.2

Canadian Gaming at a Glance

	Charitable bingo	Charitable games	Card rooms	Casinos & gaming	First Nation casinos	First Nation bingo	Lottery operated games							Parimutuel wagering					
							Sports betting	Video or slots	Keno games	Instant/pulltabs	Lotto games	Numbers games	Passive games	Harness	Quarter horse	Thoroughbred	Inter-track wagering	Off-track wagering	Telephone wagering
Alberta	●	●		▼		●	●	●		●	●	●	●	●	●	●	●	●	●
British Columbia	●	●		★	◆	●	●	●	●	●	●	●	●	●	●	●	●	●	●
Manitoba	●	●		●		●	●		●	●	●	●	●	●	●	●	●	●	●
New Brunswick	●	●				●	●		●	●	●	●	●	●	●	◆	●		◆
Newfoundland	●	●					●	●	●	●	●	●	●	●	■	●			◆
Northwest Territories	●	●	●			●	●		●	●	●	●	●	◆	●	◆	●	◆	◆
Nova Scotia	●	●		●		●	●	●	●	●	●	●	●	●	■	■	●	●	◆
Ontario	●	●		●	●	●	●	★	●	●	●	●	■	●	●	●	●	●	●
Prince Edward Island	●	●				●	●	●	●	●	●	●	●	●	●	◆	●	●	◆
Quebec	●	●		●		●	●	●	●	●	●	●	●	●	●	■	●	●	◆
Saskatchewan	●	●		●	●	●	●		●	●	●	●	●	●	●	●	●	●	◆
Yukon Territory	●			●			●		●	●	●	●	●	◆	◆	◆	◆	◆	◆

● Legal and operative
★ Implemented since June 1998
◆ Authorized but not yet implemented
▼ Charity casinos only
■ Permitted by law and previously operative

Source: Patricia A. McQueen, "North American Gaming at a Glance," *International Gaming and Wagering Business*, vol. 20, no. 9, September 1999. Copyright © 1999, *International Gaming and Wagering Business* magazine. Reproduced with permission.

Bingo is the most common form of legalized gambling (46 states, Washington, DC, and Puerto Rico). Forty-three states (although not necessarily operating), Puerto Rico, and the Virgin Islands permit thoroughbred horseracing. Lotteries are allowed in 37 states, Washington, DC, Puerto Rico, and the Virgin Islands. Twenty-four states and Puerto Rico permit casino gambling.

Table 3.1 shows the types of gambling activities available throughout the United States and its jurisdictions and their operating status. Table 3.2 shows the same information for provinces and territories in Canada.

A BIG BUSINESS

Gambling is a big business in which dramatic changes have occurred over the past few years. Casino gambling was once limited to two states, and only bingo parlors could be found on Native American reservations. Today, almost 100 casinos are operating in 24 states. States without lotteries are now the exception and even many southern states, such as Texas and Georgia, which were once reluctant to have lotteries, now aggressively market them.

As a result, horse and dog racing has generally suffered during this period of rapid change as gamblers bet their money elsewhere. Many states have permitted off-track betting and simulcasting (see Chapter IV) to maintain betting on these races, and many racetrack operations have introduced other forms of gambling to their tracks. Jai alai, a game in which the players hurl a small ball against the walls of the court using a curved basket attached to one arm, has virtually disappeared.

In 1997, a record $50.9 billion was earned by legal gambling companies (earnings came from the gamblers' losses), a 6.2 percent increase from just the year before. Most of the earnings came from casinos (40 percent) and lotteries (32.5 percent). (See Table 3.3.) This was about four times the amount earned by gambling only a dozen years before. To understand how extensive gambling has become, the revenues from gambling ($50.9 bil-

TABLE 3.3

1997 Gross Gambling Revenues by Industry and Change From 1996

(dollars in millions)

	% Retained	1996 Gross Revenues (Expenditures)	1997 Gross Revenues (Expenditures)	Increase/Decrease in Gross Revenues (Expenditures) Dollars	Increase/Decrease in Gross Revenues (Expenditures) Percent
Parimutuel					
Horse Total	21.2%	$3,181.4	$3,251.4$	$69.99	2.2%
Greyhound Total	22.3%	538.8	509.4	(29.39)	(5.5%)
Jai Alai Total	22.8%	61.4	50.1	(11.30)	(18.4%)
TOTAL PARIMUTUEL	**21.3%**	**$3,781.6**	**$3,811.0**	**$29.31**	**0.8%**
Lotteries					
Video Lotteries	9.3%	892.3	1,101.9	209.57	23.5%
Traditional Games	44.9%	15,309.5	15,464.9	155.43	1.0%
TOTAL LOTTERIES	**35.8%**	**$16,201.8**	**$16,566.8**	**$365.00**	**2.3%**
Casinos					
Nevada/NJ Slot Machines	5.7%	7,292.1	7,611.0	318.91	4.4%
Nevada/NJ Table Games	2.1%	3,775.9	3,913.4	137.55	3.6%
Deepwater Cruise Ships	7.1%	234.0	244.1	10.06	4.3%
Cruises-to-nowhere	7.1%	200.0	219.6	19.60	9.8%
Riverboats	5.3%	5,543.3	6,170.5	627.16	11.3%
Other Land-Based Casinos	6.0%	458.2	474.5	16.26	3.5%
Other Commercial Gambling	34.9%	158.4	157.5	(0.91)	(0.6%)
Non-Casino Devices	10.7%	1,482.5	1,737.0	254.54	17.2%
TOTAL CASINOS	**4.4%**	**$19,144.5**	**$20,527.6**	**$1,383.16**	**7.2%**
Legal Bookmaking					
Sports Books	3.7%	76.4	89.7	13.30	17.4%
HORSE BOOKS	**4.6%**	**10.1**	**6.6**	**(3.56)**	**(35.2%)**
TOTAL BOOKMAKING	**3.7%**	**$86.5**	**$96.3**	**$9.74**	**11.3%**
Card Rooms	6.7%	684.3	700.2	15.86	2.3%
Charitable Bingo	24.5%	959.1	956.9	(2.19)	(0.2%)
Charitable Games	25.9%	1,471.0	1,562.2	91.22	6.2%
Indian Reservations					
Class II		873.8	899.2	25.34	2.9%
Class III	7.5%	4,731.3	5,779.3	1,048.01	22.2%
TOTAL INDIAN RESERVATIONS	**8.3%**	**$5,605.1**	**$6,678.5**	**$1,073.35**	**19.1%**
GRAND TOTAL	**8.0%**	**$47,933.9**	**$50,899.3**	**$2,965.4**	**6.2%**

Note: Columns may not add to totals due to rounding.

Christiansen/Cummings Associates, Inc.

Source: Eugene Martin Christiansen et al., "A New Entitlement," *The United States Gross Annual Wager — 1997*. Copyright © 1998, *International Gaming and Wagering Business* magazine. Reproduced with permission.

lion) dwarf the revenues from such mainstays of American life as movies ($6.2 billion); spectator sports such as football, baseball, and basketball ($6.3 billion); theme parks ($7.6 billion); video games ($7.5 billion); and recorded music ($12.2 billion). Revenues from all publications sold were $51.9 billion.

If the total $50.9 billion in revenue earned by gambling were represented as the sales revenue for one single company, that company would have been the eleventh largest company in the 1997 Forbes Sales 500 for the year, up from number 19 just five years before in 1992.

GROSS WAGERS (THE HANDLE)

In 1998, Americans bet $677.4 billion on legal gambling in the United States, more than five times as much as the $125.7 billion bet in 1982. Nearly 3 out of 4 dollars (72 percent) were wagered at casinos, mostly in Las Vegas, Nevada, or Atlantic City, New Jersey. Most of the remainder was bet at games on Indian reservations (14.7 percent) or on the lotteries (7 percent). (See Table 3.4.)

TABLE 3.4
Trends in Gross Wagering (Handle), 1982-1998 (Dollars in millions)

	1982 Gross Wagering (Handle)	1997 Gross Wagering (Handle)(Revised)	1998 Gross Wagering (Handle)	1982-1998 Increase/(Decrease) in Gross Wagering (Handle)		Average Annual Rate 1982-1998
				Dollars	Percent	
Pari-Mutuels						
Horses						
On-Track	$9,990.60	$3,603.20	$3,481.40	($6,509.20)	-65.15%	-(6.38%)
ITW		6,115.00	6,320.40	6,320.37	N/A	N/A
OTB	1,707.30	5,620.40	5,870.40	4,163.14	243.85%	8.02%
Total	11,697.90	15,338.60	15,672.20	3,974.31	33.97%	1.84%
Greyhounds						
On-Track	2,208.60	1,306.50	1,236.90	(971.68)	-44.00%	-(3.56%)
ITW		797.3	820.8	820.78	N/A	N/A
OTB		147.4	146.5	146.49	N/A	0.54-(1)
Total	2,208.60	2,251.10	2,204.10	(4.4)	-0.20%	-0.01%
Jai Alai	622.8	212.6	198.4	(424.35)	-68.14%	-6.90%
Total Pari-Mutuels	14,529.20	17,802.40	18,074.80	3,545.55	24.40%	1.37%
Lotteries						
Video Lotteries		11,862.20	14,181.60	14,181.59	N/A	N/A
Other Games	4,088.30	34,241.70	34,350.20	30,261.91	740.21%	4.23%
Total Lotteries	4,088.30	46,103.90	48,531.80	44,443.50	1087.09%	16.72%
Casinos						
Nevada/NJ Slot Machines	14,400.00	133,895.20	137,519.10	123,119.06	854.99%	15.15%
Nevada/NJ Table Games	87,000.00	189,250.40	181,757.20	94,757.23	108.92%	4.71%
Deepwater Cruise Ships		3,437.70	3,692.10	3,692.09	N/A	N/A
Cruises-to-nowhere		3,093.00	3,884.50	3,884.51	N/A	N/A
Riverboats		115,817.80	135,505.70	135,505.73	N/A	N/A
Other Land-Based Casinos		7,932.90	7,982.60	7,982.57	N/A	N/A
Other Commercial Gambling		451.8	466.8	466.78	N/A	N/A
Non-Casino Devices		16,188.70	17,089.90	17,089.94	N/A	N/A
Total Casinos	101,400.00	470,067.40	487,897.90	386,497.90	381.16%	10.32%
Legal Bookmaking						
Sports Books	415.2	2,431.40	2,269.10	1,853.90	446.55%	11.20%
Horse Books	122.8	141.5	137	14.19	11.56%	0.69%
Total Bookmaking	538	2,572.90	2,406.10	1,868.09	347.25%	9.81%
Card Rooms	1,000.00	10,423.60	11,007.30	10,007.35	1000.73%	16.17%
Charitable Bingo	3,000.00	3,910.40	3,972.90	972.92	32.43%	1.77%
Charitable Games	1,200.00	6,034.10	6,172.90	4,972.86	414.40%	10.78%
Indian Reservations						
Class II		2,997.20	3,180.80	3,180.77	N/A	N/A
Class III		78,934.30	96,174.90	96,174.90	N/A	N/A
Total Indian Reservations		81,931.50	99,355.70	99,355.67	N/A	N/A
Internet Gambling		N/A	N/A	N/A	N/A	N/A
Grand Total	$125,755.50	$638,846.10	$677,419.30	$551,663.80	438.68%	11.10%

Note: Lottery handles for 1982 are for the twelve months ending June 30th
Columns may not add to totals due to rounding.
(1) Average annual rate from 1984 to 1995

In the 16 years between 1982 and 1998, the amount bet in non-Nevada/New Jersey card rooms (places where gamblers get together and play card games for money) rose elevenfold, while the amount wagered on lotteries increased twelvefold. (The handle from card rooms in Las Vegas and Atlantic City are included in their table games.) The amount bet on legal bookmaking (where the gambler bets on sporting events or horseraces) rose more than fourfold over the same period, virtually all of the increase attributable to sports books. Gambling at the slot machines in Nevada and New Jersey rose more than ninefold over this period, while the wagering at the tables at these two gambling centers doubled. Gambling on Native American reservations, which hardly existed in 1982, and was estimated at $1.3 billion in 1990, soared to an estimated $99.4 billion in 1998. (See Table 3.4.)

TABLE 3.5

Trends in Gross Revenues (Consumer Spending)

	1982 Gross Revenues (Spending)	1997 Gross Revenues (Spending)(Revised)	1998 Gross Revenues (Spending)
Pari-Mutuels			
Horse Total	$2,250.00	$3,245.00	$3,306.80
Greyhound Total	430	506	493.7
Jai Alai Total	112	48.4	45.2
Total Pari-Mutuels	2,792.00	3,799.30	3,845.70
Lotteries			
Video Lotteries		1,102.70	1,281.60
Other Games	2,170.00	15,394.90	15,398.60
Total Lotteries	2,170.00	16,497.60	16,680.20
Casinos			
Nevada/NJ Slot Machines	2,000.00	7,611.00	8,091.80
Nevada/NJ Table Games	2,200.00	3,913.80	3,834.60
Deepwater Cruise Ships		244.1	262.1
Cruises-to-nowhere		219.6	275.8
Riverboats		6,170.50	7,293.90
Other Land-Based Casinos		474.5	526
Other Commercial Gambling		157.5	162.7
Non-Casino Devices		1,737.00	1,830.00
Total Casinos	4,200.00	20,527.90	22,277.00
Legal Bookmaking			
Sports Books	7.7	89.7	77.4
Horse Books	18	6.6	(5.8)
Total Bookmaking	25.8	96.3	71.6
Card Rooms	50	700.2	739.4
Charitable Bingo	780	956.9	972.2
Charitable Games	396	1,562.20	1,598.10
Indian Reservations			
Class II		913.1	954.2
Class III		5,920.10	7,213.10
Total Indian Reservations		6,833.20	8,167.30
Internet Gambling[1]		300	651.2
Grand Total	$10,413.80	$50,973.60	$54,351.60

Note: Lottery handles for 1982 are for the twelve months ending June 30th
Columns may not add to totals due to rounding.
(1) Since Internet gaming is international, its revenues are not included in U.S. totals

Source: Eugene Martin Christiansen, "Steady Growth for Gaming," *International Gaming and Wagering Business*, vol. 20, no. 8, August 1999. Copyright © 1999, *International Gaming and Wagering Business* magazine. Reproduced with permission.

On the other hand, the amount of pari-mutuel wagering (betting on horses, greyhounds, and jai alai) rose only 24.4 percent. Without off-track betting (OTB) and inter-track wagering (ITW), it would have actually dropped. In 1982, pari-mutuel betting had accounted for about 12 percent of all money wagered; by 1998, it accounted for only 2.7 percent. Betting on the horses at the racetrack fell 65.2 percent from 1982, and wagering on jai alai tumbled 68.1 percent. On-track betting for greyhound racing posted a 44 percent loss over this period.

Most experts agree that pari-mutuel wagering has been the most affected by the expansion of lotteries and casino gambling. Wagering on charitable games was up fivefold, while charitable bingo has leveled off with an increase of only 32.4 percent from 1982 to 1998. (See Table 3.4.)

How Much Does the House Keep?

Of the $638.8 billion wagered in 1997, the United States gambling industry kept $50.9 billion in gross revenues, or about 8 percent of the amount bet. Nevada/New Jersey table games and slot machines, Native American casinos, cruise ships, riverboats, and card rooms throughout the country kept less than 8 percent of the amount bet, while traditional lotteries retained almost half (44.9 percent) of all the money bet. Operators of charitable bingo, and other charitable games kept about one-fourth of the amount bet. Pari-mutuel games kept about one-fifth. (See Table 3.3.)

GROSS REVENUES (THE TAKE)

Not surprisingly, the gross revenues (the amount the house has after giving out the winnings) rose (or fell) right along with the increase (or decrease) of the total wagering. As shown in Table 3.4, total gross wagering for most forms of gambling increased from 1982 through 1998, so it should not be surprising that gross revenues also rose. Gross revenues quintupled over this period, increasing from $10.4 billion in 1982 to $54.4 billion in 1998. (See Table 3.5.)

SHARE OF THE GAMBLING MARKET

Casinos had, by far, the largest market share (40 percent) of gambling revenues in 1997, most of which came from the slot machines and casino tables of Las Vegas and Atlantic City (22.6 percent). Just a few years ago almost all casino revenues came from Las Vegas and Atlantic City. In 1997, riverboats (12 percent of all gambling revenues) accounted for a significant proportion of the revenues earned from casino gambling. (See Table 3.6.)

Lotteries (32.6 percent) were the second largest proportion of the market in 1997. Total pari-mutuel betting on horses, greyhounds, and jai alai brought in 7.5 percent, while charitable games (3.1 percent) and charitable bingo (1.9 percent) accounted for most of the rest. Gambling on Native American reservations brought in about 13.1 percent, most of which came from newly built casinos. (See Table 3.6 and Figure 3.1.)

The makeup of the gambling market has changed dramatically over the past dozen years. In 1982, the pari-mutuels, betting on horses and dogs, accounted for 1 of every 4 dollars earned; in 1997, barely 1 in 14 dollars. Less than 20 years ago, gambling on Native American reservations played no role in the market; in 1997, it earned 1 in 8 gambling dollars. In 1982, lotteries earned about one-fifth of total revenues; in 1997, they made about one-third. Casinos earned about 2 in 5 gambling dollars in 1982 and in 1997. Lotteries, casinos, and Native American gambling have all helped drive the huge increase in gambling in the United States. Pari-mutuel gambling has not.

ILLEGAL GAMBLING

International Gaming and Wagering Business, the monthly magazine that covers the gambling industry and the data source for much of this chapter, no longer includes illegal gambling when it counts gambling revenues. Eugene M. Christiansen, who prepares the *International Gaming and Wagering Business* annual review of gaming, has noted that there is not enough reliable data to make an estimate. (See Chapter X for a further discussion of estimates of illegal gambling.)

**GAMBLING ON
NATIVE AMERICAN RESERVATIONS**

As discussed in Chapter II, the Indian Gaming Regulatory Act (IGRA; PL 100-497) permits Native American tribes to introduce gambling on their reservations. Many tribes had already been holding bingo games on their reservations, but the new law opened up the possibility that other forms of gambling could be played on Native American lands. It also meant that the Native American tribes would play a major role in the large expansion of gambling that was occurring throughout the country.

While returns from bingo, the major form of gambling that was being played on reservations, were beginning to level off, many Native American tribes recognized that casino games were being offered in a growing number of places throughout the United States. (See Chapter VII.) They saw this as an opportunity to bring some prosperity to their reservations.

IGRA permitted the tribes to conduct, on their reservations, any type of gambling that was permitted in the state where the reservation was located. The law also called for the tribe and the state to negotiate agreements or "compacts" that would allow this gambling. The state was required to bargain with the tribes in good faith. If not, or if the tribe was not satisfied with the process, the law permitted the tribe to take the issue to court. (See Chapter II for a complete discussion.) By July 1999, according to the Bureau of Indian Affairs, almost 160 tribes in 24 states had negotiated compacts that permit casino gambling, a trend likely to continue.

The amount of money bet on Native American reservations rose from nothing in 1982 to an estimated $99.4 billion in 1998. The reservation retains about 8 percent of the handle, giving the tribes an estimated $8.2 billion in 1998. (See Tables 3.4 and 3.5.) Of this amount, about $7.2 billion came from casino gambling and about $954.2 million

came from bingo. Gambling revenue from reservations has been increasing rapidly, with income quadrupling from 1992 alone. In all likelihood, these numbers will continue to increase, although not at such a dramatic rate. (See Chapter VII for a more complete discussion of gambling on Native American reservations.)

SPORTS GAMBLING

Sports gambling is legal and operating in Montana, Nevada, North Dakota, and Oregon, and is legal, but not operative, in Delaware. Bookmaking on sports is legal statewide only in Nevada, while it takes place in limited localities in Montana and North Dakota and is used in Oregon as part of its lottery program. Sports betting is also legal in a number of locations in Baja California,

TABLE 3.6

Market Share 1996 vs. 1997

	1996 Revenue Market Share	1997 Revenue Market Share	Increase
Class III	9.21%	11.35%	2.14%
Riverboats	10.27%	12.12%	1.86%
Video Lotteries	1.37%	2.16%	0.80%
Non-Casino Devices	3.10%	3.41%	0.31%
Card Rooms	1.48%	1.38%	0.05%
Cruises-to-nowhere	0.40%	0.43%	0.03%
Sports Books	0.18%	0.18%	0.00%
Deepwater Cruise Ships	0.50%	0.48%	-0.03%
Horse Books	0.05%	0.01%	-0.04%
Other Land-Based Casinos	0.97%	0.93%	-0.04%
Other Commercial Gambling	0.35%	0.31%	-0.04%
Jai Alai Total	0.15%	0.10%	-0.05%
Class II	1.84%	1.77%	-0.07%
Charitable Games	3.22%	3.07%	-0.15%
Charitable Bingo	2.16%	1.88%	-0.21%
Greyhound Total	1.31%	1.00%	-0.31%
Horse Total	6.80%	6.39%	-0.41%
Nevada/NJ Slot Machines	15.65%	14.95%	-0.70%
Nevada/NJ Table Games	8.51%	7.69%	-0.82%
Traditional Lottery Games	32.49%	30.38%	-2.11%
TOTAL INDIAN RESERVATIONS	11.05%	13.12%	2.07%
TOTAL CASINOS	39.75%	40.33%	0.58%
TOTAL BOOKMAKING	0.22%	0.19%	-0.04%
TOTAL PARIMUTUEL	8.25%	7.49%	-0.76%
TOTAL LOTTERIES	33.86%	32.55%	-1.31%

Source: Eugene Martin Christiansen et al., "A New Entitlement," *The United States Gross Annual Wager — 1997.* Copyright © 1998, *International Gaming and Wagering Business* magazine. Reproduced with permission.

Mexico, which borders California. The overwhelming majority of bettors visiting these border locations are Americans, mainly Californians. (For illegal sports betting, see Chapter X.)

Almost all the money wagered legally on sports books is bet in Nevada. In 1997, $2.4 billion was wagered on sports in Nevada, with about $89.7 million retained by the house. This is a retained percentage of 3.7 percent, much less than the 5.7 percent take in 1994. The 1994 revenues were inordinately high, and sports bettors will have to be very unlucky to allow the house to earn that high rate of return in the future.

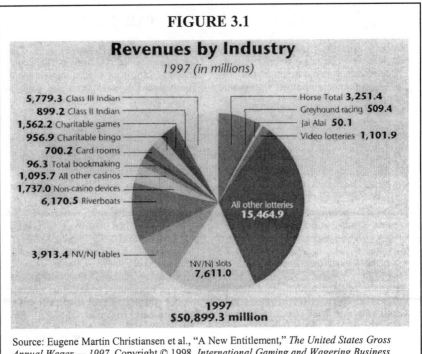

FIGURE 3.1

Revenues by Industry

1997 (in millions)

- 5,779.3 Class III Indian
- 899.2 Class II Indian
- 1,562.2 Charitable games
- 956.9 Charitable bingo
- 700.2 Card rooms
- 96.3 Total bookmaking
- 1,095.7 All other casinos
- 1,737.0 Non-casino devices
- 6,170.5 Riverboats
- 3,913.4 NV/NJ tables
- Horse Total 3,251.4
- Greyhound racing 509.4
- Jai Alai 50.1
- Video lotteries 1,101.9
- All other lotteries 15,464.9
- NV/NJ slots 7,611.0

1997
$50,899.3 million

Source: Eugene Martin Christiansen et al., "A New Entitlement," *The United States Gross Annual Wager — 1997*. Copyright © 1998, *International Gaming and Wagering Business* magazine. Reproduced with permission.

GAMBLING IN THE HIGH-TECHNOLOGY WORLD

According to the National Gambling Impact Study Commission, on-line betting will totally change the way Americans gamble because it allows people to gamble 24 hours per day from home. (For more information on the National Gambling Impact Study, see individual chapters.)

As more people use the Internet and likely become more comfortable with on-line financial transactions, larger numbers of people will be attracted to Internet gambling. It is difficult to measure the actual numbers of people who gamble online, but many observers agree that the growth has been considerable and swift. Christiansen/ Cummings Associates, Inc., an independent consulting and financial services firm that serves the communications, entertainment, gambling, and sports industries and the government agencies that regulate such activities, estimates that the number of people who used the Internet to gamble rose from 6.9 million in 1997 to 14.5 million in 1998.

Estimated revenues more than doubled during that same one-year period from $300 million to $651 million. Christiansen/Cummings estimates that Internet gambling revenues will reach $2.3 billion by 2001. (See Table 3.7.) These are huge increases over a short period of time, and there is little reason to believe that the Internet will not affect gambling as dramatically as it has affected other forms of business.

Internet Gambling Sites

It is difficult to accurately report the number of gambling sites on the Internet. The industry is in its infancy; companies enter and leave the market constantly, and there is no central registry. However, industry experts estimate that, at the end of 1998, between 800 and 1,000 gambling-related sites existed. (This may be somewhat misleading as many of those sites are parts of a single operation and many on-line gambling operations are subsidiaries of other companies.) Every expert expects the number of sites to grow.

Gambling sites offer a great variety of games to play, including interactive games, broadcast

TABLE 3.7

Estimated Worldwide Internet Gambling Revenues ($ in millions)					
	1997	1998	1999	2000	2001
Adult home users (in millions)	46	81	121	145	159
% users conducting on-line transactions	15%	18%	21%	24%	27%
Potential Internet gamblers (in millions)	6.9	14.5	25.4	34.8	43
Per-capita expenditure	$146	$154	$155	$16	$16
Potential Internet gambling revenues	$1,009	$2,182	$3,933	$5,555	$7,080
Estimated actual Internet gambling revenues	$300	$651	$811	$1,520	$2,330

Source: Sebastian Sinclair, "Legitimacy Fuels Internet Gaming Growth," *International Gaming and Wagering Business*, vol. 20, no. 1, January 1999. Copyright © 1999, *International Gaming and Wagering Business* magazine. Reproduced with permission.

races in real-time video, sports gambling, lotteries, and bingo. Casino-style gambling, such as blackjack, poker, slot machines, and roulette is also offered. Before a customer may gamble, most sites require the person to fill out registration forms and to either buy "chips" or set up accounts with a preset minimum amount. The gambler pays with credit or debit cards, money transfers, or some other form of electronic payment.

Underage Gamblers, Pathological (Compulsive) Gamblers, and Criminals

The Internet can be used anonymously, and access to on-line gambling can be dangerous to certain groups of people. Usually, a gambler need only fill out a registration form in order to play, and most sites trust the user to fill out the form accurately. Rarely do Internet companies try to verify any information, including the user's age.

Youngsters who have access to their parents' credit cards or have cards of their own may register and open accounts on Internet gambling sites. According to *American Demographics* magazine, 69 percent of 18- to 24-year-olds use computers for hobbies and entertainment, and it is possible that some may turn to on-line gambling as a form of entertainment. The National Collegiate Athletic Association (NCAA) has noted that sports betting, tournaments, and sweepstakes are very attractive to underage gamblers and is concerned about increased gambling among college students, who have easy access to the Internet.

Pathological gamblers find Internet gambling easily accessible 24 hours a day, instantly gratifying, and private, all of which may make their problems worse. Experts who deal with addiction to gambling fear that abuse of this technology will magnify the problems that already exist.

As online gambling companies are neither regulated nor accountable to any trade group, there is considerable potential for a number of criminal activities. Most Internet service providers (ISPs) that host Internet gambling operations are not physically located in the United States but are based off shore. These operators can change, move, or remove sites within minutes, making it easy for them to "take the money and run" by emptying funds from deposited accounts or taking credit card numbers and closing down. In addition, computer hackers or gambling operators may alter gambling software to control the games.

Furthermore, gambling on-line offers a fairly easy way to launder money earned from criminal activities, as it offers anonymity, remote access, and the ability to send coded messages. If a gambler wishes to launder money, he simply deposits money into an offshore account, uses the funds to gamble, making sure to lose some of the original funds, and cashes out the balance.

The Law Addressing Internet Gambling

Currently, the most widely applied federal statute addressing Internet gambling is 18 USC 1084 from the Wire Communications Act of 1961 (PL

87-216), which makes it illegal to use wire communications to place bets or wagers. However, due to the ambiguity of some of the act's language, it is not clear if "wire communications" include the Internet or if "contests" include all types of Internet gambling.

Of course, when the law was written in 1961, there was no Internet technology. Consequently, some observers claim that the intent of the law applies only to telephone communications. However, since Congress did not specify "telephone communications" in the statute, others insist that it was intended to include any and all wire communication devices. (In the future, information on the Internet may not use hard wire connections at all, but cellular technology and direct satellite feeds to computers.) The statute specifies that "sports wagering" is not legal, but it does not include a clear definition of "contests." Whether or not "contests" include bingo, lotteries, or casino-style games is unclear.

Senator Jon Kyl (R-AZ) has sponsored a bill (S692) to extend the current federal telephone and wire gambling prohibition by amending the Wire Communications Act to cover new technologies such as microwave transmission and fiberoptic cable. According to Senator Kyl,

> We need to update the law to help it keep up with technology and close the loopholes that have allowed this activity to flourish. By passing this law, Congress will ensure the ability to prosecute the same gambling crimes tomorrow that are illegal today.

Kyl's bill would permit fining and/or imprisoning people who conduct business or participate in illegal gambling, as well as taking measures against Internet service providers (ISPs) that provide communications service to Internet gambling Web sites. Opponents of the legislation, notably the racing industry and ISPs, have claimed that it is not enforceable because most of the sites are not located in the United States.

Individual states have made efforts to regulate or prohibit Internet gambling. Illinois, Louisiana, Nevada, and Texas have introduced and/or passed legislation prohibiting Internet gambling, and Florida, together with Western Union, has taken steps to stop the money transfer service of 40 offshore sports books.

But the Internet Is International

In 1999, governments in 25 countries had licensed or passed legislation allowing Internet gambling, further confusing the issue. They include five territories within Australia, Antigua and Barbuda, Austria, Belgium, Cook Islands, Costa Rica, Curaçao, Dominica, Dominican Republic, Finland, Germany, Grand Turk, Grenada, Honduras, the territory of Kalmykia in Russia, Liechtenstein, Mauritius, St. Kitts and Nevis, St. Vincent, South Africa, Trinidad, Turks and Caicos Islands, four territories in the United Kingdom, Vanatu (an island nation located in the southwest Pacific), and Venezuela. American law cannot control activities on the Internet that originate from another country.

INTERNATIONAL GAMBLING

This publication examines gambling only in the United States. However, the explosion in gambling is taking place worldwide. Many other countries of the world have always permitted gambling, but now gambling is becoming as common throughout the world as it has become in the United States. Just as in the United States, other industrially developed and financially strained countries are considering the growing gambling market as an opportunity to increase tax revenues. Less developed countries see gambling as a tool to increase tourism and attract more foreign dollars.

Just as in other areas of commerce, much of the development of gambling is being financed and managed by companies in the industrially developed world. Many of the companies that play a major role in the development of America's gambling market are investing in overseas markets to develop gambling in those countries. Should the American gambling market become overcrowded or if political opposition stops its expansion, which is a possibility, these companies will be in position to continue developing in the world market.

Reflecting this change in the gambling marketplace, *International Gaming & Wagering Business* (IGWB), the monthly publication that covers the industry, has reformatted its presentation. Not only has the magazine cover been given a facelift, but the United States, while still the most important country covered, is now one of many countries being considered. For example, the December 1999 issue features a report on Russia's gambling revolution. According to IGWB, the outlook for wagering within Russia is good even though the economy is poor and the political climate is unstable.

Additional articles in the December 1999 issue discuss Internet gambling in the United Kingdom, the success of gambling in Estonia, and the success of the new Halifax casino in Nova Scotia, Canada. Stories covering gambling in the United States lead with the dateline of the country's name, just as stories from the other countries covered.

IGWB recently began publishing an annual special supplement, the *European Casino Report,* featuring a country-by-country study of the casinos in Austria, Belgium, the Czech Republic, Denmark, France, Germany, Great Britain, Greece, Hungary, Italy, the Netherlands, Poland, Portugal, Spain, and Switzerland. The report includes information about the number of casinos, tax rates, total gross gaming revenues, values for slots and table games, summaries of relevant laws and regulations, and legal games.

COMPULSIVE GAMBLERS

As can be concluded from the many surveys taken on gambling, for most people who bet, gambling is a form of recreation and fun. (See Chapter XI.) While they receive enjoyment from the game, they can take or leave it. Even when they lose, they usually look upon it as the cost of entertainment.

For some people, however, gambling is a compulsion, an addiction they cannot easily control.

These people may become addicted to gambling, and like alcoholism, it may take control of their behavior and destroy their lives. The addiction may cause them to gamble away their paychecks or go deeply into debt. It may threaten their marriages and their relationships with their children, relatives, and friends. According to the National Center on Problem Gambling, Inc., a not-for-profit agency dedicated to addressing the issue of problem and pathological gambling, there are nearly 3 million Americans with pathological (compulsive) gambling disorders and another 5 to 8 million who have gambling problems. The National Council on Problem Gambling offers a nationwide hotline for those needing assistance (1-800-522-4700).

The Council on Compulsive Gambling of New Jersey, Inc., an affiliate of the National Council on Compulsive Gambling, Inc., "aims to reduce and prevent this insidious disease by mobilizing public support through public information and education and through interaction with professional groups concerned with the growing impact of pathological gambling." The agency offers a toll-free line, 1-800-GAMBLER, to provide help to compulsive gamblers.

The New Jersey Council considers compulsive gambling "the Hidden Epidemic." In 1997, 23,606 people called the helpline, significantly more than the 14,577 people who phoned in 1993. In 1998, the average gambling debt of callers to the New Jersey Council's toll-free number was $38,000, an amount that can leave families in debt for many years.

Gamblers Anonymous

Gamblers Anonymous offers a 12-step program similar to Alcoholics Anonymous. Currently, people attend Gamblers Anonymous meetings at over 1,100 locations across the nation, up from 800 locations just a few years ago. All members share two goals — to stop themselves from gambling and to help other compulsive gamblers to do the same. Gamblers Anonymous can be reached by calling (213) 386-8789, faxing (213) 386-0030, or writing Gamblers Anonymous, International Service Office, P.O.Box 17173, Los Angeles, California 90017. It will supply the address of the nearest Gamblers Anonymous location. All information is kept confidential.

In addition, most states that permit gambling have developed some sort of state-supported system to assist compulsive gamblers. Those needing help from these state agencies should be able to find out their phone number from the state gaming commission or the lottery commission. Some gambling companies have recognized the seriousness of the problem and are contributing to some of these programs.

In 1999, in an unusual move, the casino industry joined forces with therapists and researchers in an attempt to address the dangers of gambling addiction. A conference, sponsored by the National Center for Responsible Gaming, brought together 150 experts to discuss the biological causes and possible treatments for compulsive gambling. While gambling opponents claim that the alliance undermines impartial study, organizers believe that the conference focused new medical attention on gambling addiction.

NATIONAL GAMBLING IMPACT STUDY COMMISSION RECOMMENDATIONS

The nine-member National Gambling Impact Study Commission (NGISC), set up in 1997 to investigate gambling in America, concluded that more research on problem and pathological gambling must be a clear priority. It recommended that the gambling industry, government, foundations, and other sources of funding provide long-term continued support for those who need treatment. NGISC anticipates that more people will develop gambling problems as opportunities for gambling increase, and the Commission suggests that future research should not only include treatment for the disorder but should also include efforts in prevention and intervention that may help to stop problem and pathological gambling before it begins.

The Commission recommended that all relevant governmental gambling regulatory agencies require that every applicant for legalized gambling establishments (including lotteries) adopt a mission statement as to policy on problem and pathological gambling and name a high-ranking official to oversee the preparation of the mission statement. Other recommendations included contracting with a professional to train staff to recognize potential problems, refusing service to any customer whose behavior exhibits indications of a problem, providing said customer with a state-approved list of treatment programs and self-help groups, and providing medical insurance for employees of wagering facilities who have gambling addictions.

The Commission also recommended that

- Each state and tribal government enact a Gambling Privilege Tax from which sufficient amounts of money can be used to create a fund for development and support of problem gambling-specific research, prevention, education, and treatment programs.

- States mandate that private and public insurers and managed care providers identify successful treatment programs, educate participants about problem and treatment options, and offer coverage under their plans.

- Each gambling facility implement procedures to permit gamblers to ban themselves from a gambling establishment for a specific period of time.

- Encouragement be given to private groups and associations, nationwide, to solve problem gambling.

- Each state-run or approved gambling operation be required to post and distribute telephone numbers of at least two state-approved providers of problem-gambling information, treatment, and referral support services.

For more information on the National Gambling Impact Study Commission recommendations, see individual chapters.

CHAPTER IV

PARI-MUTUEL BETTING — HORSES, DOGS, AND JAI ALAI

HOW PARI-MUTUEL BETTING WORKS

The term "pari-mutuel" describes a method of betting in which the persons who pick the winners in a given event divide the total amount of money bet in proportion to their wagers. Winnings, or payoffs, are paid on the win (first place), place (second place), and show (third place) categories of a given event, or on certain combinations of these categories.

The amount of the payoff depends on the total amount bet on a given race or game. If the winners are heavily favored, the payoff per individual is much smaller than if the winners have little money wagered or "riding" on them. For example, if a horse is a 5-to-1 favorite, it means that for every dollar bet on that horse, $5 has been bet on the other entries. If the horse has negative odds, or is an "odds-on" favorite, let us say 1 to 2, it means that for every two dollars bet on that horse, one dollar was bet on all the other horses in the race. Bettors are constantly informed of the changing odds in an event (as people place their bets) by computerized totalizator machines, which flash new betting totals and odds on the "tote board" every 60 to 90 seconds.

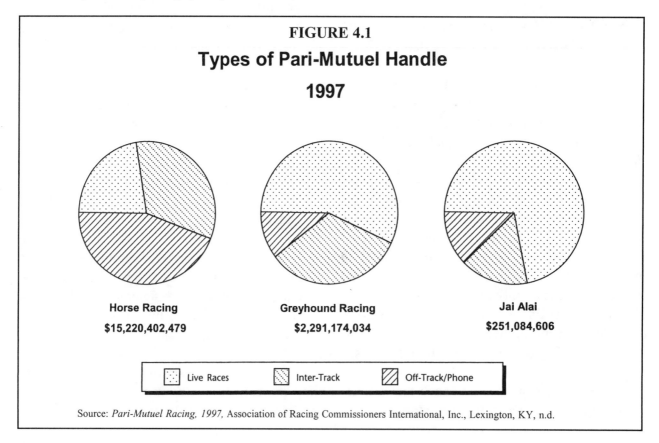

FIGURE 4.1

Types of Pari-Mutuel Handle

1997

Horse Racing	Greyhound Racing	Jai Alai
$15,220,402,479	$2,291,174,034	$251,084,606

Live Races   Inter-Track   Off-Track/Phone

Source: *Pari-Mutuel Racing, 1997,* Association of Racing Commissioners International, Inc., Lexington, KY, n.d.

The minimum amount for a pari-mutuel wager is $2, but the bettor may wager any additional amount in denominations of $5, $10, $50, or $100. Before the winning bettors collect their money, a percentage of the total amount of money bet is taken by the agency conducting the betting operation, for example, the racetrack operator, and by the state, in the form of taxes. Of the total amount wagered on a particular race, approximately 78 to 80 percent is returned to winning bettors in the form of payoffs.

TABLE 4.1

PARI-MUTUEL WAGERING IN THE UNITED STATES

TOTAL PARI-MUTUEL REVENUE TO GOVERNMENT 1959 - 1997

Year	Revenue	Year	Revenue
1997	545,588,566	1977	819,201,638
1996	594,897,481	1976	821,311,348
1995	625,521,148	1975	871,345,367
1994	656,123,006	1974	729,533,116
1993	693,214,593	1973	657,647,137
1992	725,585,548	1972	595,253,462
1991	792,767,083	1971	572,277,744
1990	897,426,844	1970	539,742,764
1989	862,718,105	1969	508,545,672
1988	870,233,100	1968	468,077,649
1987	880,558,761	1967	432,076,514
1986	852,535,313	1966	424,252,115
1985	876,005,323	1965	402,705,421
1984	875,243,184	1964	379,914,405
1983	856,888,828	1963	343,228,047
1982	858,251,794	1962	313,438,030
1981	876,384,974	1961	287,920,639
1980	899,996,920	1960	280,090,399
1979	861,706,557	1959	262,810,999
1978	835,846,080		

(Note: Does not include jai-alai prior to 1978.)

Source: *Pari-Mutuel Racing, 1997,* Association of Racing Commissioners International, Inc., Lexington, KY, n.d.

In most states where pari-mutuel gambling is legal, a person must be at least 18 years old to wager at a racetrack, although in Illinois a 17-year-old may bet. In Birmingham and Macon County, Alabama, Nebraska, and Wyoming, the age is 19 years, while in New York, Nevada, and Texas, the legal age for wagering is 21 years. Most states do not have an age restriction on simply attending an event, although several do require that an adult accompany a minor.

HISTORY OF THE PARI-MUTUEL SYSTEM

Pari-mutuel betting, the standard form of wagering on horses, was invented in France in 1865. This new method of wagering made its first American appearance in 1871 at New York's Jerome Park and became an established feature of horse racing when it was successfully used at the 1908 Kentucky Derby.

Before pari-mutuel wagering was introduced, the racetrack bookmaker was a dominant figure. The bookmaker was an agent, or professional bettor, against whom the layman (non-professional) bettor wagered his own expertise and hunches. As a competitor to the layman, the bookie held a clear advantage. With the invention of pari-mutuel wagering, the bookie's position was weakened because the pari-mutuel system allowed the bettor to wager against his peers, instead of against professional bookmakers. This system also increased the bettor's return on his investment by allowing him to receive payoffs on second and third place finishes.

PARI-MUTUEL BETTING TODAY

Pari-mutual wagering is the most common form of betting on horse races (thoroughbred, harness, and quarter horse), dog races, and jai alai games. Most pari-mutuel betting is done at the racetrack or game site where the event is actually taking place, but in many states, bettors can also place pari-mutuel bets at off-track and simulcast sites (see below) and via telephone. Pari-mutuel wagering is legal in all but six states (Alaska, Georgia, Hawaii, Mississippi, North Carolina, and South Carolina) and Washington, D.C.

41

TABLE 4.2

Live Racing Days

	Thoroughbred	Quarter Horse	Harness	Mixed	Total
Alabama		No Live Horse Racing Conducted			
Arizona				284	284
Arkansas	60				60
California	473	142	136	105	856
Colorado				38	38
Connecticut		No Live Horse Racing Conducted			
Delaware	149		160 E		309
Florida	383		192		575
Idaho				82	82
Illinois	400		607		1,007
Indiana	57		85		142
Iowa				98	98
Kansas				48	48
Kentucky	287		59		346
Louisiana	246			117	363
Maine			246		246
Maryland	228		183		411
Massachusetts	168		90		258
Michigan	161		523	31	715
Minnesota			5	53	58
Montana				54	54
Nebraska	117				117
Nevada				9	9
New Hampshire	100		12		112
New Jersey	231		418		649
New Mexico				214	214
New York	435		895		1,330
North Dakota				6	6
Ohio	429	4	796		1,229
Oklahoma	107			201	308
Oregon				138	138
Pennsylvania	423		367		790
Rhode Island		No Live Horse Racing Conducted			
South Dakota				13	13
Texas	234	110		45	389
Vermont			14		14
Virginia	30				30
Washington	224			28	252
West Virginia	385				385
Wisconsin		No Live Horse Racing Conducted			
Wyoming				23	23
Totals	5,327	256	4,788	1,587	11,958

Source: *Pari-Mutuel Racing, 1997,* Association of Racing Commissioners International, Inc., Lexington, KY, n.d.

AN OVERVIEW OF THE INDUSTRY

Some Real Problems

The pari-mutuel industry has been hard hit by many of the recent changes in the gambling industry. The nation's bettors have been provided with many other options. The huge growth of lotteries over the past decade has given gamblers another place to spend their money. Even more serious has been the recent explosion of casino gambling on riverboats in selected counties in a number of states, and the ever-growing number of casinos on Na- tive American reservations. Racetracks in Minnesota, Wisconsin, and Connecticut, where Native American casinos have been most successful, have been badly hurt.

Pari-mutuel betting has been barely holding its own over the past dozen years, a period of dramatic change in the gambling industry. As recently as 1982, pari-mutuel gambling played a dominant role in the gambling business, accounting for 27 percent of the wagering. Just 12 years later, in 1994, pari-mutuels brought in only 9 percent, and in 1997, 7 percent. With the nationwide spread of lotteries and casino gambling, pari-mutuel gambling has almost become a minor player in the gambling business.

In 1982, Americans wagered $14.5 billion on pari-mutuel betting; by 1997, wagering had increased to $17.8 billion, not enough to keep up with inflation. (The figures do not account for inflation.) From 1997 to 1998, the pari-mutuel handle (total amount of money wagered by all bettors on a specific gambling event or activity) increased by $272.4 million (up about 1.6 percent). According to *International Gaming and Wagering Business* (IGWB), its small index of pari-mutuel stocks kept pace with the Dow Jones Industrial Average for that year. IGWB sees this as an encouraging sign for the future of horse racing.

On the other hand, from 1982 to 1998, betting at the greyhound track fell 44 percent. It toppled 65.2 percent at the horsetrack, and plunged 68.1 percent at the jai alai frontons. Without the introduction of off-track betting (OTB),* intertrack wagering (ITW),** and simulcasting,*** pari-mutuel gambling may have disappeared. (See Table 3.4 in Chapter III.) Figure 4.1 shows how OTB and ITW have become fundamental to the earnings of pari-mutuel gambling.

Revenues from pari-mutuel gambling rose from $2.8 billion in 1982, when it accounted for 27 percent of the market, to $3.8 billion in 1998, when it accounted for 7 percent of the market. (See Table 3.5 in Chapter III.) The decline in the fortune of pari-mutuels can also be seen in the drop in the amount of money the government collected. In 1990, state and local governments made nearly $900 million from pari-mutuel wagering; by 1997, that figure had dropped to $545.6 million. (See Table 4.1.)

Despite the success of some tracks, such as Remington Park (Oklahoma), Penn National (Pennsylvania), and Churchill Downs (Kentucky),

---

* Off-track betting (OTB) means exactly what it says — a person places a bet on a horse or dog race at some location other than the track where the race actually takes place. Off-track bets are usually placed at a track branch office or a betting shop. Some states permit a bettor to call in his or her bet over the telephone. In 1998, according to the National Gambling Impact Study Commission Report, nearly $550 million was wagered through telephone accounts. Revenues are distributed to state and local governments and the racing industry (which includes the OTB corporations themselves, racetrack operators, etc.). Many observers hope that locating OTBs in attractive places, such as restaurants, special OTB theaters, or gambling casinos, will make these operations more effective. Some people associate OTB with the parlors in New York, many of which have become sleazy and unappealing.

** Intertrack wagering (ITW) is the programming of thoroughbred, harness, quarterhorse, or greyhound racing shown via television at a site away from the actual racetrack where the event is taking place for the purpose of pari-mutuel wagering. This may occur at a special betting parlor or, more likely, another racetrack. The person watching the television simulcasting is watching the race "live" and may bet on it as if he or she were at the actual track where the race was being run. In the case of ITW, the racetrack has opened solely for the purpose of showing these televised races. There is no live racing going on at the track. Both the track where the race is being run and the place where the ITW is occurring share in the revenues from the races.

*** Simulcasting is the programming of thoroughbred, harness, quarterhorse, or greyhound racing shown via television at a site away from the actual racetrack where the event is taking place for the purpose of pari-mutuel wagering in order to augment a live schedule of racing. Technically, simulcasting and ITW are the same thing, but with simulcasting, the transmitted races add to the existing show, while with ITW, the transmitted races are the only show.

TABLE 4.3

Live Meeting Attendance

	Thoroughbred	Quarter Horse	Harness	Mixed	Total
Alabama					
Arizona				549,527	549,527
Arkansas	704,050				704,050
California	8,546,811	755,266	666,818	1,015,016	10,983,911
Colorado				N/A	N/A
Connecticut					
Delaware	N/A		N/A		N/A
Florida	1,563,089		382,897		1,945,986
Idaho				145,482	145,482
Illinois	1,518,073		842,459		2,360,532
Indiana	73,900		95,809		169,709
Iowa				N/A	N/A
Kansas				32,689	32,689
Kentucky	1,694,853		38,253		1,733,106
Louisiana	1,098,395			59,522	1,157,917
Maine			N/A		N/A
Maryland	2,073,407		362,834		2,436,241
Massachusetts	940,494		50,164		990,658
Michigan	644,983		1,422,858	31,454	2,099,295
Minnesota			9,653	311,879	321,532
Montana				N/A	N/A
Nebraska	203,857				203,857
Nevada				N/A	N/A
New Hampshire	260,702		N/A		260,702
New Jersey	1,438,204		1,441,097		2,879,301
New Mexico				451,173	451,173
New York	2,596,616		826,649		3,423,265
North Dakota				N/A	N/A
Ohio	840,740	N/A	1,733,978		2,574,718
Oklahoma	317,830			314,530	632,360
Oregon				N/A	N/A
Pennsylvania	2,276,774		978,910		3,255,684
Rhode Island					
South Dakota				N/A	N/A
Texas	1,158,190	393,607		128,346	1,680,143
Vermont			N/A		N/A
Virginia	108,591				108,591
Washington	714,363			31,385	745,748
West Virginia	N/A				N/A
Wisconsin					
Wyoming				N/A	N/A
Totals	**28,773,922**	**1,148,873**	**8,852,379**	**3,071,003**	**41,846,177**

Source: *Pari-Mutuel Racing, 1997,* Association of Racing Commissioners International, Inc., Lexington, KY, n.d.

overall pari-mutuel gambling is a struggling industry. Industry officials know they must turn to either very innovative marketing or introduce new forms of gambling at the racetracks in order to survive.

HORSE RACING — THE SPORT OF KINGS

Horse racing has changed over the centuries from a sport associated with the aristocracy into, until recently, one of the more popular pastimes in America. The first known form of horse racing was practiced by the Sumerians over 6,000 years ago and was similar to the chariot races occasionally seen in the movies. "Flat Racing," in which a rider is mounted directly on the horse instead of sitting in a rig drawn by an animal, was first popularized about 3,000 years ago. The first recorded horse race took place in Greece about 600 B.C.E. Horse racing became one of the major diversions of the British royalty between the twelfth and seventeenth centuries, and thereafter, horse racing was known as the "Sport of Kings."

Horse racing was popular in colonial America, and, true to its English heritage, was limited to the

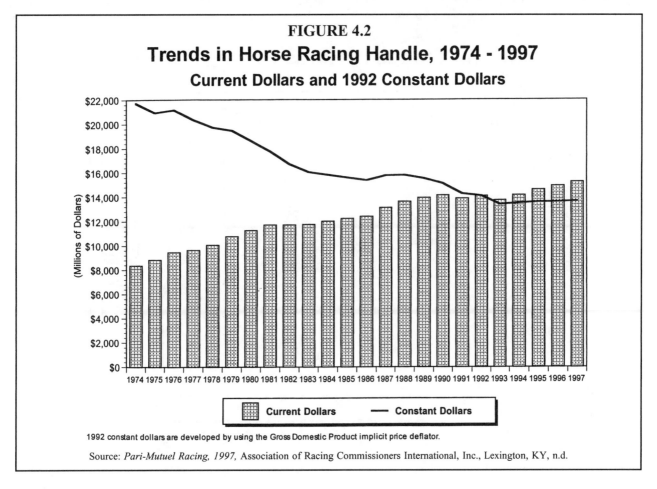

FIGURE 4.2
Trends in Horse Racing Handle, 1974 - 1997
Current Dollars and 1992 Constant Dollars

1992 constant dollars are developed by using the Gross Domestic Product implicit price deflator.

Source: *Pari-Mutuel Racing, 1997,* Association of Racing Commissioners International, Inc., Lexington, KY, n.d.

aristocracy or "gentry." In early colonial days, concern over the lack of quality horses in America prompted colonial governors to sponsor races as a means of identifying the fastest horses for selective breeding. The first racetrack in America was the Newmarket Course, built in 1665 in Hempstead, New York.

By the 1800s, horse racing was conducted at county fairs or at gypsy (traveling) tracks, most notably in Maryland, Virginia, and Kentucky. The first big racetracks opened around the turn of the century, with New York's Belmont Park leading the way in 1905. The first American stakes race, offering a purse for the winner, was the Traveler's Stakes at Saratoga Springs, New York. In 1934, California's Santa Anita track opened. The largest track in the United States, New York's Aqueduct, opened in 1959. Racetracks are usually operated by private investors but are regulated by State Racing Commissions.

Growing Competition

Fifteen years ago, if a person wanted to gamble, he went to the racetrack, placed his bet, and rooted for his favorite horse or dog. The only other option was to call a bookie, who would take bets on those same dog or horse races. Today the situation has changed dramatically. The gambler can go to his local convenience store and buy a lottery ticket, visit a local truck stop and play a video lottery terminal, ride a riverboat and play casino games, cruise on a "trip to nowhere" and play roulette, or visit an old mining town in Colorado or South Dakota and play the slot machines.

All of these gambling opportunities have captured many of the gambling dollars that were once bet on the horses and dogs. As a result, horse racing's popularity has been dropping over the past decade, a decline from which it may never recover.

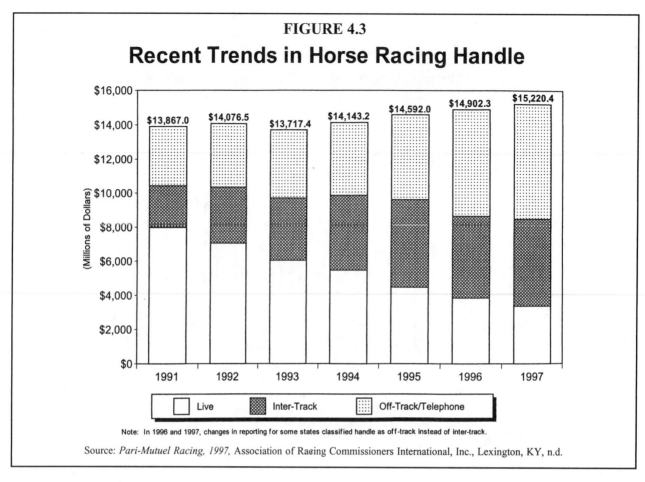

FIGURE 4.3
Recent Trends in Horse Racing Handle

Note: In 1996 and 1997, changes in reporting for some states classified handle as off-track instead of inter-track.

Source: *Pari-Mutuel Racing, 1997,* Association of Racing Commissioners International, Inc., Lexington, KY, n.d.

Average attendance at two of the country's most famous tracks, Aqueduct and Belmont Park in New York, has decreased 40 percent in the past 15 years, and attendance is down at many other tracks. Roosevelt Raceway on Long Island, New York, one of the most famous harness racing tracks, closed in 1988. Florida's Hialeah track, a stalwart of the thoroughbred industry, shut down in 1990.

Canterbury Downs in Minnesota, built at a cost of $80 million (which saddled it with a heavy debt payment) in 1985 to be the ultimate harness track, could not compete with neighboring Indian casinos and went under in 1992. Citing competition from the newly opened riverboat at nearby Elgin, the ownership of Arlington Racetrack near Chicago decided to cancel the 1995 racing season (although they later agreed to do a shortened meet). Finally, no longer able to compete, the track shut down in October 1997. Much was expected from the Sam Houston Race Park in Texas, but it soon went bankrupt as well.

Types of Horse Racing Events

There are three major forms of horse racing: thoroughbred, harness, and quarter horse racing. In the United States, thoroughbred is, by far, the most popular form of horse racing, followed by harness and then quarter horse racing.

Thoroughbred Racing

Anatomically, the thoroughbred horse is distinguished from other breeds of horses by its greater height and longer legs, although in order to be registered as a thoroughbred, other criteria must be met. In 1894, the prestigious Jockey Club was formed in New York for the purpose of organizing and regulating thoroughbred racing. Traditionally, a thoroughbred horse must be registered with the New York Jockey Club, and a horse may be registered only if his sire (father) and dam (mother) are already on the rolls. In other words, the lineage of all thoroughbreds must be genetically traceable

TABLE 4.4
Total Pari-Mutuel Handle ($)

	Thoroughbred	Quarter Horse	Harness	Mixed	Total
Alabama	32,653,338				32,653,338
Arizona				127,666,919	127,666,919
Arkansas	151,816,516				151,816,516
California	1,951,752,966	127,567,307	93,134,740	188,273,797	2,360,728,810
Colorado				55,417,788	55,417,788
Connecticut				199,526,008	199,526,008
Delaware	30,379,849		6,131,351	113,087,968	149,599,168
Florida	637,624,105		96,194,506		733,818,611
Idaho				28,509,502	28,509,502
Illinois	840,350,966		339,682,748		1,180,033,714
Indiana	116,334,351		30,622,378		146,956,729
Iowa				45,785,177	45,785,177
Kansas				37,346,642	37,346,642
Kentucky	598,843,088		10,726,292		609,569,380
Louisiana	346,207,077			13,659,423	359,866,500
Maine			12,523,729	59,825,462	72,349,191
Maryland	465,225,433		82,462,587		547,688,020
Massachusetts	183,883,697		18,607,549	7,238,188	209,729,434
Michigan	241,136,791		233,184,449	287,338	474,608,578
Minnesota	51,629,948	299,255	2,559,632	11,529,848	66,018,683
Montana				10,044,878	10,044,878
Nebraska	88,265,678				88,265,678
Nevada	462,142,000	588,468	39,146,642	295,363	502,172,473
New Hampshire	132,600,549		21,727,836		154,328,385
New Jersey	765,248,376		390,535,985	51,647,218	1,207,431,579
New Mexico				98,784,974	98,784,974
New York	2,228,269,424		439,862,787		2,668,132,211
North Dakota				6,107,461	6,107,461
Ohio	102,291,841	147,549	98,499,980	399,857,446	600,796,816
Oklahoma	62,530,336			167,387,064	229,917,400
Oregon				59,907,087	59,907,087
Pennsylvania	845,855,685		227,271,822		1,073,127,507
Rhode Island				59,857,162	59,857,162
South Dakota				6,956,820	6,956,820
Texas	79,593,935	18,538,969		340,535,135	438,668,039
Vermont			361,612	73,529	435,141
Virginia	75,590,038		19,504,123		95,094,161
Washington	171,044,586			1,209,590	172,254,176
West Virginia	93,496,630				93,496,630
Wisconsin				54,796,437	54,796,437
Wyoming				10,138,756	10,138,756
Totals	**10,754,767,202**	**147,141,548**	**2,162,740,748**	**2,155,752,980**	**15,220,402,479**

Source: *Pari-Mutuel Racing, 1997,* Association of Racing Commissioners International, Inc., Lexington, KY, n.d.

back to three oriental stallions, Godolphin, Byerly, and Darley, the prototypes of the breed.

Harness Racing

In harness racing, the rider sits in a carriage (sulky) and guides the horse around the track. The horses are trained to be either trotters or pacers. On a trotter, the left-front and right-rear legs of the horse move forward almost simultaneously; then the right-front and left-rear legs move. On a pacer,

both left legs move forward in unison, then both right legs move.

Quarter Horse Racing

The quarter horse (the word quarter referring to the quarter-mile sprint it runs) evolved in colonial Virginia where breeders crossed native English horses with those of Spanish ancestry. This cross breeding resulted in a swift horse that could outrun other breeds in short-distance races. Unlike

47

TABLE 4.5
Pari-Mutuel Handle — Live Races ($)

	Thoroughbred	Quarter Horse	Harness	Mixed	Total
Alabama					
Arizona				29,597,942	29,597,942
Arkansas	67,454,297				67,454,297
California	570,582,983	41,208,046	20,434,321	40,911,533	673,136,883
Colorado				2,770,889	2,770,889
Connecticut					
Delaware	30,379,849		6,131,351		36,511,200
Florida	250,714,652		31,772,234		282,486,886
Idaho				5,435,000	5,435,000
Illinois	136,155,793		65,053,036		201,208,829
Indiana	5,264,793		5,647,918		10,912,711
Iowa				8,536,154	8,536,154
Kansas				2,007,228	2,007,228
Kentucky	196,761,930		2,513,558		199,275,488
Louisiana	57,454,246			4,536,528	61,990,774
Maine			9,649,867		9,649,867
Maryland	84,697,147		18,626,244		103,323,391
Massachusetts	39,704,839		3,425,795		43,130,634
Michigan	39,735,043		75,043,071	287,338	115,065,452
Minnesota			253,241	11,090,168	11,343,409
Montana				3,768,877	3,768,877
Nebraska	9,433,185				9,433,185
Nevada				295,363	295,363
New Hampshire	18,662,839		690,421		19,353,260
New Jersey	127,852,913		204,357,008		332,209,921
New Mexico				22,181,004	22,181,004
New York	433,949,732		91,499,299		525,449,031
North Dakota				68,214	68,214
Ohio	102,291,841	147,549	98,499,980		200,939,370
Oklahoma	19,913,222			21,829,770	41,742,992
Oregon				7,938,021	7,938,021
Pennsylvania	109,961,239		31,818,056		141,779,295
Rhode Island					
South Dakota				253,395	253,395
Texas	79,593,935	18,538,969		6,612,030	104,744,934
Vermont			361,612		361,612
Virginia	5,481,303				5,481,303
Washington	61,264,578			1,209,590	62,474,168
West Virginia	37,312,711				37,312,711
Wisconsin					
Wyoming				1,602,044	1,602,044
Totals	**2,484,623,070**	**59,894,564**	**665,777,012**	**170,931,088**	**3,381,225,734**

Source: *Pari-Mutuel Racing, 1997,* Association of Racing Commissioners International, Inc., Lexington, KY, n.d.

the thoroughbred, quarter horses can also be used for farm work and transportation.

Racing Days and Number of Races

Racetracks are not open every day of the year, but rather operate for relatively short periods called "meets." A track might have two meets in a year, often one in the spring and one in the fall. State regulatory agencies usually approve the times for these meets and try to schedule them so that neighboring tracks do not have conflicting meets.

In 1997, there were a total of 11,958 racing days in the United States, down from 13,841 in 1990. New York had the greatest number of racing days (1,330), followed by Ohio (1,229), Illinois (1,007), and California (856). North Dakota (6), Nevada (9), and South Dakota (13) had few racing days, and Alabama, Connecticut, Rhode Island, and Wisconsin had none (Table 4.2).

Attendance

Almost 42 million people visited the track in 1997 (Table 4.3), a huge (34 percent) drop from

TABLE 4.6
Pari-Mutuel Handle — Inter-Track Wagering ($)

	Thoroughbred	Quarter Horse	Harness	Mixed	Total
Alabama	32,653,338				32,653,338
Arizona		Included in Off-Track Wagering			
Arkansas	84,362,219				84,362,219
California		Included in Off-Track Wagering			
Colorado		Included in Off-Track Wagering			
Connecticut		Included in Off-Track Wagering			
Delaware				113,087,968	113,087,968
Florida	386,909,453		64,422,272		451,331,725
Idaho				23,074,502	23,074,502
Illinois	300,772,625		99,852,875		400,625,500
Indiana		Included in Off-Track Wagering			
Iowa				37,249,023	37,249,023
Kansas				35,339,414	35,339,414
Kentucky	367,815,483		8,212,734		376,028,217
Louisiana	121,842,472			2,171,876	124,014,348
Maine			96,941	26,010,611	26,107,552
Maryland	314,274,778		51,799,896		366,074,674
Massachusetts	144,178,858		15,181,754	7,238,188	166,598,800
Michigan	201,401,748		158,141,378		359,543,126
Minnesota	51,629,948	299,255	2,306,391	439,680	54,675,274
Montana					
Nebraska	78,832,493				78,832,493
Nevada					
New Hampshire	113,937,710		21,037,415		134,975,125
New Jersey	532,237,673		157,328,325	47,121,141	736,687,139
New Mexico				76,603,970	76,603,970
New York	228,932,077		78,705,222		307,637,299
North Dakota					
Ohio				399,857,446	399,857,446
Oklahoma	19,197,908			106,781,191	125,979,099
Oregon		Included in Off-Track Wagering			
Pennsylvania		Included in Off-Track Wagering			
Rhode Island				59,857,162	59,857,162
South Dakota					
Texas				333,923,105	333,923,105
Vermont				73,529	73,529
Virginia	2,091,561		272,993		2,364,554
Washington	75,404,226				75,404,226
West Virginia	56,183,919				56,183,919
Wisconsin				54,796,437	54,796,437
Wyoming					
Totals	**3,112,658,489**	**299,255**	**657,358,196**	**1,323,625,243**	**5,093,941,183**

Source: *Pari-Mutuel Racing, 1997,* Association of Racing Commissioners International, Inc., Lexington, KY, n.d.

the more than 63.8 million people who attended horse racing events at the track in 1990. On-track attendance at tracks in California tumbled from 13.7 million in 1990 to 11 million in 1997. New York attendance fell from almost 7 million in 1990 to 3.4 million in 1997. Daily average attendance dropped from 4,610 persons per track in 1990 to 3,499 persons per track in 1997.

Horse Racing Handle

Figure 4.2 indicates the steady slide in constant dollars (which account for inflation) in horse racing handle between 1974 and 1993. Since then, the handle has held steady or increased very slightly. Figure 4.3 shows the growing importance of non-live betting to the industry. Pari-mutuel bettors wagered $15.2 billion on horse races in 1997 (Table 4.4). About $3.4 billion was bet at the track, which generally includes simulcasting (Table 4.5), and $5.1 billion was bet on intertrack races (Table 4.6). Over $6.7 billion, including telephone betting, was wagered at off-track betting establishments (Table 4.7). New York ($2.7 billion), California ($2.4 billion), Illinois and New Jersey ($1.2 billion each) accounted for about half of all the

TABLE 4.7

Pari-Mutuel Handle — Off-Track & Telephone ($)

	Thoroughbred	Quarter Horse	Harness	Mixed	Total
Alabama					
Arizona				98,068,977	98,068,977
Arkansas					
California	1,381,169,983	86,359,261	72,700,419	147,362,264	1,687,591,927
Colorado				52,646,899	52,646,899
Connecticut				199,526,008	199,526,008
Delaware					
Florida					
Idaho					
Illinois	403,422,548		174,776,837		578,199,385
Indiana	111,069,558		24,974,460		136,044,018
Iowa					
Kansas					
Kentucky	34,265,675				34,265,675
Louisiana	166,910,359			6,951,019	173,861,378
Maine			2,776,921	33,814,851	36,591,772
Maryland	66,253,508		12,036,447		78,289,955
Massachusetts					
Michigan					
Minnesota					
Montana				6,276,001	6,276,001
Nebraska					
Nevada	462,142,000	588,468	39,146,642		501,877,110
New Hampshire					
New Jersey	105,157,790		28,850,652	4,526,077	138,534,519
New Mexico					
New York	1,565,387,615		269,658,266		1,835,045,881
North Dakota				6,039,247	6,039,247
Ohio					
Oklahoma	23,419,206			38,776,103	62,195,309
Oregon				51,969,066	51,969,066
Pennsylvania	735,894,446		195,453,766		931,348,212
Rhode Island					
South Dakota				6,703,425	6,703,425
Texas					
Vermont					
Virginia	68,017,174		19,231,130		87,248,304
Washington	34,375,782				34,375,782
West Virginia					
Wisconsin					
Wyoming				8,536,712	8,536,712
Totals	5,157,485,644	86,947,729	839,605,540	661,196,649	6,745,235,562

Source: *Pari-Mutuel Racing, 1997*, Association of Racing Commissioners International, Inc., Lexington, KY, n.d.

money bet on horseracing (Table 4.4). Most money (71 percent) was bet on thoroughbred racing (Table 4.4). The average on-track bettor wagered $115.45.

Return to Bettors and to the Winning Horse Owners

The total pari-mutuel takeout was $3.2 billion or 21 percent of the handle. That means that an average of 79 percent of the money wagered on pari-mutuel horse races in 1997 was returned to the bettors. Owners of winning horses claimed about $882 million in prize money, down from the $951 million in prize money in 1990.

Government Revenues

In 1997, state and local governments received nearly $422 million from horse racing, down from $624 million in 1990. Horse racing revenue to government peaked at $780 million in 1975. With a few small hitches along the way, it has been dropping ever since. (See Table 4.8.) Table 4.9 shows how much each state received from horse racing.

TABLE 4.8

HORSE RACING
IN THE UNITED STATES

HORSE RACING REVENUE TO GOVERNMENT
1934 - 1997

1997 ... 421,768,972	1981 ... 680,199,584	1965 ... 369,892,036	1949 ... 95,327,053
1996 ... 443,882,538	1980 ... 712,727,523	1964 ... 350,095,928	1948 ... 95,803,364
1995 ... 455,764,292	1979 ... 680,919,798	1963 ... 316,570,791	1947 ... 97,926,984
1994 ... 451,546,549	1978 ... 673,063,831	1962 ... 287,930,030	1946 ... 94,035,859
1993 ... 471,735,474	1977 ... 700,239,986	1961 ... 264,853,077	1945 ... 65,265,405
1992 ... 491,259,606	1976 ... 714,629,120	1960 ... 258,039,385	1944 ... 55,971,233
1991 ... 523,249,392	1975 ... 780,081,431	1959 ... 243,388,655	1943 ... 38,194,727
1990 ... 623,839,806	1974 ... 645,980,984	1958 ... 222,049,651	1942 ... 22,005,278
1989 ... 584,888,183	1973 ... 585,201,524	1957 ... 216,747,621	1941 ... 21,128,173
1988 ... 596,202,319	1972 ... 531,404,550	1956 ... 207,456,272	1940 ... 16,145,182
1987 ... 608,351,461	1971 ... 512,838,417	1955 ... 186,989,588	1939 ... 10,369,807
1986 ... 587,357,677	1970 ... 486,403,097	1954 ... 178,015,828	1938 9,576,335
1985 ... 625,159,697	1969 ... 461,498,886	1953 ... 167,426,465	1937 8,434,792
1984 ... 650,262,852	1968 ... 426,856,448	1952 ... 142,489,696	1936 8,611,538
1983 ... 641,387,176	1967 ... 394,381,913	1951 ... 117,250,564	1935 8,386,255
1982 ... 652,888,463	1966 ... 388,452,125	1950 98,366,167	1934 6,024,193

Source: *Pari-Mutuel Racing, 1997,* Association of Racing Commissioners International, Inc., Lexington, KY, n.d.

California ($96 million) and New York ($109.5 million) got nearly half of all the revenues gained by the states. State governments collected $25 million in uncashed pari-mutuel tickets, that is, winnings that were never claimed.

Marketing Horse Racing and Making It Easier to Bet

As an industry facing stiff competition from other forms of gambling, horse racing must do something to make itself more attractive and more accessible if the industry is to survive. While it might be nice to see full stands at the racetrack, the tracks may have to bring the horse races to the customer. In New Haven, an updated Sport Haven that offers both large screens and individual screens to bettors in a modern, comfortable environment has replaced the old Connecticut Teletrack. Other states are also trying to make off-track betting easier by permitting OTB in restaurants and bars where people are already comfortable.

Efforts are also being made to make it easier to bet. Today, telephones are not only available at home or in the office, but in the automobile or wherever a small cellular phone can be carried.

Telephone betting is legal in Connecticut, Kentucky, Maryland, Nebraska, Nevada, New York, Ohio, Oregon, and Pennsylvania. In New York and Pennsylvania, cable television shows broadcast the latest racing information to make it easier for the bettor to phone in his bet.

In 1999, the Racing Network, a partnership of Greenwood Racing (operating Philadelphia Park), Ladbroke Racing Corporation, the Ontario Jockey Club, and International Investment & Underwriting Limited began televising pari-mutuel contests 24 hours per day. The partnership has received commitments from a number of North American racetracks to provide programming. Known as "the industry's network," the Racing Network will begin with five channels, two for thoroughbred racing and one each for harness, greyhound, and Canadian-based racing.

Each channel will provide up to three simultaneous racing programs, allowing the service to offer programming from up to 100 racetracks per day. The satellite system is capable of expanding to 10 or 12 channels. This venture, based on digital mini-dish technology, requires subscribers to purchase a small satellite dish for $320 and pay a $14.99

TABLE 4.9
Total Government Revenue ($)

	Thoroughbred	Quarter Horse	Harness	Mixed	Total
Alabama	983,770				983,770
Arizona				75,719	75,719
Arkansas	4,490,833				4,490,833
California	86,269,532	2,086,344	1,610,180	6,105,358	96,071,415
Colorado				457,715	457,715
Connecticut				7,394,908	7,394,908
Delaware (E)	230,289		14,626	177,548	422,464
Florida	14,509,993		2,221,500		16,731,493
Idaho				735,623	735,623
Illinois	37,427,740		16,615,511	1,325,231	55,368,482
Indiana	3,204,630		843,546	256,949	4,305,125
Iowa				2,466,513	2,466,513
Kansas				918,213	918,213
Kentucky	14,843,453		320,220		15,163,673
Louisiana	5,918,522			295,508	6,214,030
Maine			329,223	1,647,168	1,976,391
Maryland	4,395,441		489,228	2,500	4,887,169
Massachusetts	1,395,772		338,543	27,143	1,761,458
Michigan	8,923,635		8,064,529	88,854	17,077,018
Minnesota	32,701	190	1,621	109,333	143,844
Montana				147,171	147,171
Nebraska	684,092				684,092
Nevada	4,834,018	6,603	421,111	2,954	5,264,686
New Hampshire	2,529,126		364,365		2,893,491
New Jersey (E)	779,149		694,322	30,988	1,504,459
New Mexico				836,502	836,502
New York	63,822,301		11,103,682	34,588,397	109,514,380
North Dakota				111,350	111,350
Ohio	3,075,270	14,254	3,043,948	10,535,986	16,669,458
Oklahoma	1,655,961			5,083,399	6,739,360
Oregon				958,829	958,829
Pennsylvania	15,625,249		3,135,522		18,760,771
Rhode Island				3,048,429	3,048,429
South Dakota		All revenues allocated back to the racing industry			
Texas	1,695,501	394,915		5,834,963	7,925,379
Vermont			16,082	2,465	18,547
Virginia	1,945,137		494,832		2,439,969
Washington	4,028,931			6,328	4,035,259
West Virginia	1,403,600				1,403,600
Wisconsin				925,148	925,148
Wyoming				242,235	242,235
Totals	284,704,648	2,502,306	50,122,590	84,439,428	421,768,972

Source: *Pari-Mutuel Racing, 1997,* Association of Racing Commissioners International, Inc., Lexington, KY, n.d.

per month programming fee. Most early subscribers (about 2,000) are located in the Philadelphia area. The Racing Network hopes to attract serious horseplayers and fans, horse owners, trainers, and breeders. Currently, the Racing Network is not linked to a wagering system, but "odds are" they ultimately will be.

Another network, Television Games Network, also began to televise racing in 1999. Television Games Network does incorporate an interactive wagering system into its television channel. These two new television-based systems join You Bet!, an interactive PC-based betting service already operating, in bringing racing into the home for the first time.

Tying More Tracks Together

The growing use of ITW may benefit racetracks throughout the country. A racetrack in the north cannot have horses racing during the winter. As a result, a huge financial investment stands idle, not earning any money. However, these racetracks can open up and have people come to the enclosed areas of the racetrack and bet on races being run in a warmer climate, such as Florida or California. Today, some northern tracks might have a half

TABLE 4.10

GREYHOUND RACING, 1997

	Number of Live Performances	Number of Live Races	Attendance			
			Live Racing	Average	ITW	OTW
Birmingham, AL	466	6,782	537,895	1,154	Included in Live	
Greene County, AL	No Live Greyhound Racing					
Macon County, AL	505	6,565	427,061	848		
Mobile County, AL	461	5,992	297,754	646		
Alabama Total	1,432	19,339	N/A	N/A		
Arizona	804	11,522	333,262	415		461,001
Arkansas	415	5,683	686,360	1,654		
Colorado	784	N/A	1,094,223	1,396	Included in Live	
Connecticut	416	6,239	241,007	579		
Florida	4,437	61,770	5,193,983	1,171		
Idaho	No Live Greyhound Racing					
Iowa	526	7,635	N/A			
Kansas	708	N/A	573,371	810		
Massachusetts	985	N/A	1,220,599	1,239		
New Hampshire	868	N/A	422,461	487		
Oregon	110	1,422	N/A			
Rhode Island	350	5,250	N/A			
South Dakota	No Live Greyhound Racing					
Texas	905	10,793	1,066,266	1,178		
West Virginia	790	11,850	1,162,933	1,472		
Wisconsin	1,027	N/A	1,048,387	1,021		
Totals	14,557	N/A	N/A	N/A		N/A

Note: Number of races in Macon County, Rhode Island, and West Virginia are estimated.

Source: *Pari-Mutuel Racing, 1997,* Association of Racing Commissioners International, Inc., Lexington, KY, n.d.

dozen different racing programs going on at the same time.

Meanwhile, racetracks in warmer climates, such as Gulfstream in southern Florida and Santa Anita in California, can have people betting on their races and adding to their revenues, even though they might be thousands of miles away. The viewing and betting on the big races all across the country benefit the originating track and all the tracks where these races are shown.

Trying to Get Organized

In 1998, the National Thoroughbred Racing Association (NTRA) introduced a plan intended to unite the racing industry together under one umbrella. NTRA's goal is to streamline the racing industry, cut expenses, and educate fans. Individual racetracks that contribute to the organization will benefit through cooperative advertising, packaged customer retention and fan education programs, and savings from group purchasing of supplies and services. ESPN2's 2Day at the Races (a television show covering major races) has changed to NTRA 2Day at the Races. NTRA-generated advertisements will appear, giving the public information about every racetrack, large or small. NTRA hopes that a more united industry, along with the support of the tracks, owners, breeders, and affiliated companies, will enable thoroughbred racing to become more successful.

Expanding the Gambling Options at the Track

Many track owners are strongly considering an "if you can't beat them, join them" approach. In a number of states, tracks are introducing casino forms of gambling into their facilities. Tracks that offer this combination of racing and casino gambling are called "racinos." For example, Mountaineer Park in West Virginia instituted video lottery terminals (VLTs) at the racetrack. Across the coun-

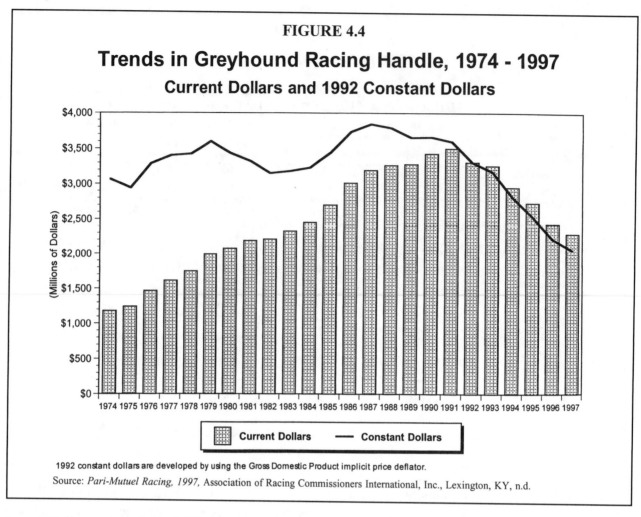

FIGURE 4.4

Trends in Greyhound Racing Handle, 1974 - 1997

Current Dollars and 1992 Constant Dollars

1992 constant dollars are developed by using the Gross Domestic Product implicit price deflator.

Source: *Pari-Mutuel Racing, 1997,* Association of Racing Commissioners International, Inc., Lexington, KY, n.d.

try, at Hollywood Park in California, a casino for card games has been built right next to the track. In Delaware, Dover Downs and Delaware Park introduced slot machines to their tracks. Others have considered actually integrating a complete casino with the racing facility. Currently, only Regina Exhibition Park in Regina, Saskatchewan, offers gamblers an integrated casino-racetrack facility, but this may be the wave of the future if the industry is to survive.

The potential opening of a casino, a riverboat, or Indian gaming nearby, however, constantly imperils these options. To succeed, racetracks will have to make their offerings more attractive, more comfortable, and more alluring than their potential competitors. Finally, some people in the horse racing industry believe the industry has failed to effectively educate the public about how exciting horse racing can be.

Particular Problems of Harness Racing

The problems faced by the harness racing industry were highlighted in a 1993 report of the New York State Advisory Commission on Racing in the 21st Century. The report found that harness racing attendance in New York State had plunged from 9.3 million in 1970 to just 1.6 million in 1993. The on-track handle nosedived from $843.7 million in 1970 to only $231.9 million in 1993.

At the same time, revenue to the state plummeted from $86.7 million in 1970 to only $3.7 million in 1993. (None of these figures account for inflation, so the decline is even worse than it appears. For example, the $86.7 million paid to the state in 1970 would be $323 million in 1993 dollars, which would account for inflation.) The report recommended lower taxes on the handle, more simulcasting, less regulation, more televised races, larger purses to attract better horses, and a greater effort to increase the integrity of the sport. (In 1997, harness racing attendance in New York State fell even further to 827,000 and the on-track handle to $91.5 million. Revenue to the state was $5.3 million.)

Harness racing has had a particularly difficult time appealing to younger people. It has never really caught on in the South and the West. Harness racing occurs at night, and by then, many gamblers have already wagered their money. Many people choose the VCR or cable television for their nighttime entertainment rather than the racetrack. In addition, because of the fear of crime, some people are afraid to go out at night.

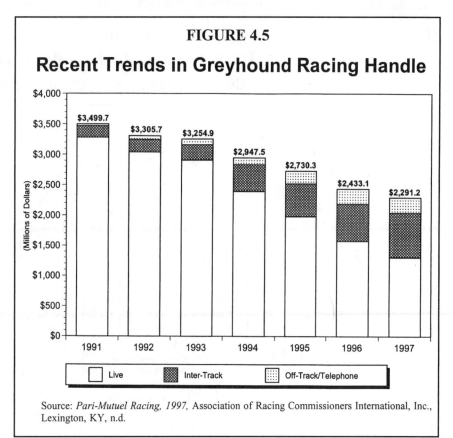

FIGURE 4.5

Recent Trends in Greyhound Racing Handle

Source: *Pari-Mutuel Racing, 1997,* Association of Racing Commissioners International, Inc., Lexington, KY, n.d.

Just as for thoroughbred racing, simulcast and inter-track wagering have helped the harness racing industry to survive. However, since harness racing is not as popular nationwide as thoroughbred racing, its market is more limited.

DOG RACING — THE SPORT OF QUEENS

Dog racing developed from a hunting sport called "coursing" in which a hare was released and then a pair of greyhounds was set in pursuit. The race was judged on the dogs' performance as they ran down the hare. Coursing was very popular during the reign of Queen Elizabeth I of England in the last half of the sixteenth century. For this reason, it became known as the "Sport of Queens." The modern version of dog racing developed from a coursing event in South Dakota in 1904. The sponsor of the contest, Owen Patrick Smith, loved the sport but detested the killing of the hare. Smith spent 15 years

perfecting a mechanical lure, thus eliminating one of the more inhumane aspects of the sport.

Dog racing took off in Florida during the 1920s as a nighttime alternative to daytime horse racing. From there, it spread, eventually becoming legal in 19 states. Interest in dog racing peaked in the mid-1980s with a number of new racetracks being built in order to take advantage of the growing attendance. Unfortunately, the 1990s have not been as kind to the industry. The same factors that hurt horse racing and jai alai also hit dog racing. Lotteries and casino gambling have lured bettors away. While some tracks have stayed even, many are struggling to survive, and a number have closed.

Total Performances, Number of Races, and Attendance

During 1997, 14,557 performances took place, down from 16,110 in 1995. Thirty percent of all races were held in Florida. Total attendance tumbled in just six years from 30.5 million in 1991 to just 14.3 million in 1997. (See Table 4.10.)

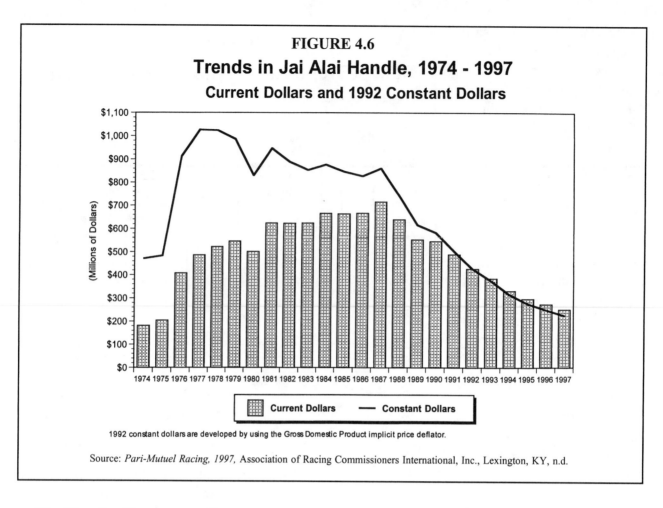

FIGURE 4.6

Trends in Jai Alai Handle, 1974 - 1997

Current Dollars and 1992 Constant Dollars

Current Dollars   —— Constant Dollars

1992 constant dollars are developed by using the Gross Domestic Product implicit price deflator.

Source: *Pari-Mutuel Racing, 1997,* Association of Racing Commissioners International, Inc., Lexington, KY, n.d.

The Handle, Government Revenues, and Purses to the Winning Dog Owners

Greyhound racing's serious difficulties are further reflected in the drop in virtually all financial categories during the 1990s. The amount wagered fell from $3.5 billion in 1991 to $2.3 billion in 1997 in constant dollars, which accounts for inflation. Figure 4.4 shows the decline of the greyhound racing handle. With the handle dropping, government revenues fell from $233.7 million in 1991 to $156.8 million in 1995 to $113.6 million in 1997. The purse distribution fell from $131.2 million in 1993 to $115 million in 1995 to $111.2 million in 1997.

Overall, about 82 percent of the handle is returned to the bettors, 6 percent to the government, 4 percent to purses for the winning owners, and 8 percent to the track owners for operating expenses and profit. The average bettor wagered $112.47 at the track.

Fighting to Survive

The dog racing industry is struggling to survive. The Valley Greyhound Park in Harlingen, Texas, and Greenetrack in Alabama have shut down. The Black Hills racetrack in South Dakota, which opened in 1949, closed in 1992, and the Key West track in Florida, opened in 1953, closed in 1991. The Coeur d'Alene Greyhound Park in Post Falls, Idaho, and the Camptown Greyhound Park in Frontenac, Kansas, have closed their doors. The Biscayne Greyhound Track in Miami Shores, Florida, the nation's second oldest track (opened in 1926), went out of business in 1995. Other recent closings include Wisconsin Dells Greyhound Park in Wisconsin and Waterloo Greyhound Park in Iowa (both in 1996).

In 1998, there were 48 greyhound tracks open for live racing in 15 of the 17 states where dog racing is legal. In the last five years, 14 tracks have

TABLE 4.11

JAI ALAI, 1997

	Number of Performances	Number of Games	Live Meet Attendance	Average Attendance	Live Handle ($)	Inter-Track/ Off-Track Handle ($)
Connecticut	548	6,462	271,197	495	44,108,901	31,247,771
Florida	1,915	25,569	1,853,964	968	131,914,544	40,163,628
Rhode Island	185	2,405	N/A		3,649,762	
Totals	2,648	34,436	N/A	N/A	179,673,207	71,411,399

	Total Handle ($)	Total Takeout ($)	Effective Takeout Rate	Total Government Revenue ($)	Pari- Mutuel Tax Revenue ($)	Breakage to Gov't ($)
Connecticut	75,356,672	16,024,814	21.27%	2,076,260	1,975,752	86,142
Florida	172,078,172	40,575,334	23.58%	7,927,296	5,915,177	
Rhode Island	3,649,762	751,827	20.60%	174,191	145,991	2,035
Totals	251,084,606	57,351,975	22.84%	10,177,747	8,036,920	88,177

	Uncashed Tickets to Gov't ($)	Fronton License Revenue ($)	Occupational License Revenue ($)	Admission Tax to Gov't ($)	Miscellaneous Government Revenue ($)	Effective Pari-Mutuel Tax Rate
Connecticut			11,949		2,417	2.74%
Florida	753,090	1,008,560	36,210	199,487	14,772	3.44%
Rhode Island	20,950		5,215			4.06%
Totals	774,040	1,008,560	53,374	199,487	17,189	3.24%

Source: *Pari-Mutuel Racing, 1997,* Association of Racing Commissioners International, Inc., Lexington, KY, n.d.

been closed; four of the 14 (Yuma Greyhound Park in Arizona, Coeur d'Alene in Idaho, Greenetrack in Alabama, and Sodrac in South Dakota) remain open for simulcasting. Greyhound racing is banned in seven states — Idaho, Maine, Nevada, North Carolina, Vermont, Virginia, and Washington.

Like horse tracks, dog tracks have turned to simulcasting and off-track/telephone betting. Figure 4.5 shows the increasing importance of off-site gambling to the industry. In addition to simulcasting other dog racing, most tracks are also showing horse races. Moreover, many dog tracks have turned to casino-type games such as slot machines, video lottery terminals (VLTs), and other games. In virtually every state in which greyhound tracks operate, owners are appealing, if not begging, state legislatures to permit their tracks to operate casino games, most notably slot machines.

Without simulcasting and casino games, many dog tracks will not survive. Marketing attempts to make dog racing more attractive to younger gamblers have generally failed, and if dog tracks do not somehow incorporate the more successful forms of gambling, they will continue to suffer grave economic difficulties.

Like the owners of horse tracks, the owners of dog tracks will have to become more innovative. Lincoln Park (formerly Lincoln Greyhound Park) in Rhode Island has successfully introduced video lottery terminals (VLTs) at their facility. The income from the VLTs has attracted more customers and has allowed the track to increase the purses. The track has upgraded the facility to make it more attractive to visitors. Nonetheless, despite its success, Lincoln remains threatened by the opening of more Native American casinos in the area, which can offer more casino gambling alternatives than just the VLTs that Lincoln provides. One day the ownership of Lincoln may have to turn to the state government and ask permission to introduce other casino games, such as slot machines, so that it can compete.

Bluffs Run Greyhound Park in Council Bluffs, Iowa, has been virtually converted into a casino as a 52,000 square-foot addition offers over 1,000 slot machines to gamblers. Without this addition, it is unlikely the track would have survived.

Animal Rights Movement

The dog racing industry has also run afoul of the animal rights movement. Alleged mistreatment of the dogs, to include the killing of dogs that cannot win, has led to protests and the lobbying of state legislatures. Disclosures by animal rights activists of harmful treatment of the animals have led many track owners to improve the conditions for the animals and try to find more homes for the dogs who can no longer race. Many animal rights activists, however, believe the sport itself is barbaric and call for its abolition.

These activists have convinced legislators in Maine and Virginia to ban any future greyhound racing and legislators in Vermont to rescind their existing laws permitting it. Animal rights protesters often picket at dog racing tracks, and their efforts probably played a role in the closing of the Coeur D'Alene Greyhound Track in Post Falls, Idaho. However, the deteriorating financial situation was probably the major consideration as it has been for the numerous tracks that have recently shut down.

JAI ALAI

Jai alai means "merry festival." It is a fast-paced game in which the players, using a large curved basket (called a "cesta") strapped to their arms, whip a small hard ball ("pelota") made of goat skin against the three walls and floor of a huge playing court ("fronton") in much the same manner as handball or racquetball. Jai alai was invented in

TABLE 4.12
JAI ALAI REVENUE TO GOVERNMENT 1978 - 1997

Year	Revenue
1997	10,177,747
1996	11,934,999
1995	12,960,049
1994	21,534,496
1993	26,585,724
1992	30,137,047
1991	35,031,585
1990	38,608,321
1989	38,898,706
1988	43,572,178
1987	51,377,135
1986	50,144,777
1985	50,079,524
1984	48,269,509
1983	45,398,087
1982	45,000,544
1981	44,364,100
1980	35,308,705
1979	36,036,607
1978	34,707,615

Source: *Pari-Mutuel Racing, 1997,* Association of Racing Commissioners International, Inc., Lexington, KY, n.d.

the seventeenth century by the Basques, who live in northern Spain and southern France.

The game has remained popular in Latin America but is in serious trouble in the United States. Figure 4.6 shows a sharp and continuing decline in revenues since 1987, with the handle in 1997 less than half of the 1987 handle in both current and constant (which account for inflation) dollars. Pari-mutuel betting on jai alai is available in just two states, Florida and Connecticut. (The one fronton in Rhode Island indicated for 1997 in Table 4.11 is now offering dog racing.) In 1997, six frontons were operating in Florida and one was functioning in Connecticut. Jai alai has never gained a following in the United States outside of southern New England and Florida.

Number of Performances, Number of Games, and Attendance

During 1997, there were 2,648 performances or events, down from 3,619 in 1990. Florida accounted for 87 percent of total attendance — 1.85 million attendees out of 2.1 million. In 1990, 5.3 million people had attended the games. In 1997, average attendance at the games in Florida (968) was twice the average of Connecticut (495). There are no figures available for Rhode Island, which also offers greyhound racing (Table 4.11).

Handle and Government Revenue

Total pari-mutuel handle for jai alai games in 1997 was $251.1 million, down from $545.5 million in 1990 and $639.2 million in 1988 (See Figure 4.6 and Table 4.11). Total takeout was $57.4 million, and government revenue totaled $10.2 million, one-fifth the $50 to $51 million the government received in 1985, 1986, and 1987 (Tables 4.11 and 4.12).

Trying to Survive

Jai alai suffered through a painful strike from 1988 to 1991. While this hurt the game, the opening of the Foxwoods casino at Ledyard, Connecticut, has been a calamity for jai alai in New England. The frontons in Newport, Rhode Island, and Bridgeport, Connecticut, switched to dog racing, and the Hartford fronton closed down. The fronton in Milford, Connecticut, is the only remaining jai alai-only facility in New England.

Florida has tried to revitalize the jai alai industry in several ways. The state legislature passed a law to change the taxing structure on jai alai profits, and there is a proposed bill in Florida's senate that would permit electronic gambling devices (EGDs) at all pari-mutuel venues, including frontons. Florida also voted not to introduce land-based casino gambling, giving jai alai a respite from the challenge of land-based casino gambling. Nonetheless, the future of the sport in the United States is very uncertain. Tourists in Florida can still take "cruises to nowhere" which offer casino gambling and take customers away from jai alai. The lottery has also drawn considerable money away from the frontons. In Connecticut, the opening of more Indian gambling throughout New England will undoubtedly draw more gamblers away from the shrinking number of frontons.

Virtually every fronton has introduced simulcasting of horse races and even staggered the jai alai games so they will not conflict with horse races. In fact, in many cases the simulcasting has become more important than the jai alai, and the jai alai season is becoming shorter. Jai alai frontons are often open now for simulcast horse races on which gamblers bet, but there is no jai alai game going on. Without simulcasting, many frontons could not make a profit. Perhaps more aggressive marketing might help the jai alai industry, but its future is certainly in doubt.

CHAPTER V

CASINO GAMBLING — LAND-BASED CASINOS

Gambling is now bigger than baseball, more powerful than a platoon of Schwarzeneggers, Spielbergs, Madonnas, and Oprahs. More Americans went to casinos than to major league ballparks in 1993. Ninety-two million visits! — The New York Times Magazine, July 17, 1994

Technically, a casino is any room or rooms in which gaming is conducted. However, when most Americans think of casinos, they picture the gaudy hotel/casino/entertainment complexes seen on TV and movie screens. Up until the 1970s, casinos were associated exclusively with Nevada and especially Las Vegas. However, in 1977, the state of New Jersey legalized casino gambling for Atlantic City.

Over the past decade, local and state governments have increasingly turned to gambling in an effort to increase revenues. Lotteries have been the most popular form of gambling, but a growing number of state and local governments have resorted to casino gambling to raise money without having to do the politically unpopular act of raising taxes. Economically depressed cities, such as Bridgeport, Connecticut, where the state eventually rejected a casino, or Detroit, Michigan, which has approved these facilities, have looked to casinos as a means to improve the ailing local economy.

Although the recent growth of casinos has been most popular in the Midwest, casinos have been introduced throughout the country. Not only are casinos now located in towns such as Deadwood, South Dakota, and Cripple Creek, Colorado, but also casinos float up and down the Mississippi and Missouri Rivers and out into the Gulf of Mexico and the Pacific and Atlantic Oceans. (See Chapter VI for more on gambling on the water.)

In addition, many Native American tribes have opened casino gambling on their reservations in an effort to raise money. These new casinos are a growing source of the total amount earned by casinos, and the management of organizations that operate casinos in Las Vegas and Atlantic City assisted in developing many new casinos on Native American reservations.

CASINOS IN NEVADA — A CENTURY OF GAMBLING

Nevadans adopted gambling long before the state was admitted to the Union. Casinos were located in gold mining camps and were considered a major source of entertainment, but there were few professional gamblers. By 1869, the Nevada legislature had legalized gambling in the state, and except for a few periods of reform (gambling was made illegal in 1909 and reinstated in 1931), casinos and Nevada have been linked ever since.

Within the past 100 years, a pastime that mainly served to separate miners and cowboys from their money has become a respected state industry. Today, casino gambling is the main pillar of Nevada's economy, attracting residents and tourists alike and, with them, many dollars for which neither individuals nor corporations pay any state income taxes.

CASINOS IN NEW JERSEY

At the turn of the twentieth century, Atlantic City, New Jersey, was a famous seaside resort that attracted thousands of tourists to its Boardwalk on the oceanfront. But by the 1950s, its glory had faded. Cars and planes allowed East Coast residents to travel to more exotic shores, and the resort did not have an alternate economy to make up for the lost tourist dollars. In an attempt to rebuild the city's financial base, lower taxes, provide employment for its residents, and subsidize its considerable elderly population, the state of New Jersey legalized gambling in Atlantic City on June 2, 1977. All funds raised from the licensing and taxation of gambling operations were to be used for state and local social programs. As the "East Coast Vegas," Atlantic City once again became a resort — this time for gamblers and East Coast day-trippers.

AND NOW CASINOS
ARE ALMOST EVERYWHERE

During the 1980s, federal funding for state and local projects were cut, and financial demands on state and local governments increased. Many manufacturing companies moved elsewhere in search of cheaper labor and more concessions, while areas dependent on agriculture suffered severe economic reverses. At that time, many states and localities began to consider various forms of gambling to raise money as an alternative to raising taxes. Lotteries had already gotten most state governments into the gambling business, making it easier for other methods of gambling to appear as acceptable alternatives.

By the mid-1990s, card rooms where players could gamble on card games were booming in California, Oregon, Washington, and Montana. Casinos attracted players in South Dakota and Colorado, while gamblers placed wagers on riverboats in Illinois, Iowa, Missouri, Mississippi, and Louisiana. Missouri voters approved an amendment permitting slot machines on the state's riverboats, while South Dakota passed a referendum legalizing video lottery terminals (VLTs). Earlier in 1994, VLTs had been declared unconstitutional. In 1996, Arizona and West Virginia approved limited expansion of gambling, and voters in Michigan said yes to a casino in economically depressed Detroit. By July 1999, 160 tribes

in 24 states were permitted to operate gambling establishments on their reservations (not including bingo). Meanwhile, many cruise lines have added or expanded casino operations in order to earn more money from existing cruises.

Losing Support?

By the mid-1990s, however, the expansion of gambling had slowed. In the November 1994 elections, voters in Florida rejected a referendum that would have permitted land-based casinos. A referendum calling for limited-stakes casinos in Wyoming failed, and Colorado voters said no to expanding casino gambling. Rhode Islanders voted to limit Indian gambling to the town of Charlestown, and Iowa voters denied the city of Des Moines the right to develop riverboat gambling. Voters in Michigan rejected a proposal to permit Indian casino gambling in Port Huron.

Gambling issues did little better in November 1995. Voters in Floyd and Clark counties in Indiana rejected a referendum calling for riverboats. Massachusetts voters said no to a casino in Springfield. Jefferson City, Missouri, residents repealed riverboat gambling, which they had approved in 1992, and voters in Washington state turned down unrestricted gambling on Indian reservations. In October and November, California voters in six of nine communities rejected attempts to introduce card rooms.

The trend continued in the November 1996 elections. A casino proposal was defeated in Arkansas. The voters in Ohio turned down a plan to develop eight riverboat casinos, and Washington state voters rejected the idea for slot machines on Indian land. Colorado, Nebraska, and Iowa defeated limited expansions of gambling in their states. In Louisiana, video poker was ousted from 33 parishes. (See above for a number of proposals that did pass.)

In the past several years, no new territories have been opened up to casino gambling. The failure of several riverboats in Mississippi, corruption scan-

TABLE 5.1
Combined Income Statement — Summary

FISCAL YEAR 1998
STATEWIDE CASINOS
WITH GAMING REVENUE OF $1,000,000 AND OVER

AMOUNTS REPRESENT 235 LOCATIONS

REVENUE	DOLLARS	PERCENT
GAMING	7,743,934,793	55.8%
ROOMS	2,321,374,479	16.7%
FOOD	1,749,854,499	12.6%
BEVERAGE	721,368,846	5.2%
OTHER	1,340,672,935	9.7%
TOTAL REVENUE	13,877,205,552	100.0%
COST OF SALES	1,222,800,583	8.8%
GROSS MARGIN	12,654,404,969	91.2%
DEPARTMENTAL EXPENSES	7,239,438,374	52.2%
DEPARTMENTAL INCOME (LOSS)	5,414,966,595	39.0%
GENERAL AND ADMINISTRATIVE EXPENSES		
ADVERTISING AND PROMOTION	330,389,662	2.4%
BAD DEBT EXPENSE	5,067,919	0.0%
COMPLIMENTARY EXPENSE (not reported in departments)	170,656,187	1.2%
DEPRECIATION - BUILDINGS	373,112,273	2.7%
DEPRECIATION AND AMORTIZATION - OTHER	620,168,588	4.5%
ENERGY EXPENSE (electricity, gas, etc.)	196,156,644	1.4%
EQUIPMENT RENTAL OR LEASE	20,109,316	0.1%
INTEREST EXPENSE	355,016,030	2.6%
MUSIC AND ENTERTAINMENT	88,993,121	0.6%
PAYROLL - TAXES	84,104,529	0.6%
PAYROLL - EMPLOYEE BENEFITS	175,541,301	1.3%
PAYROLL - OFFICERS	44,382,437	0.3%
PAYROLL - OTHER EMPLOYEES	757,465,527	5.5%
RENT OF PREMISES	121,307,873	0.9%
TAXES - REAL ESTATE	123,533,239	0.9%
TAXES AND LICENSES - OTHER	26,662,739	0.2%
UTILITIES (OTHER THAN ENERGY EXPENSE)	51,045,684	0.4%
OTHER GENERAL AND ADMINISTRATIVE EXPENSES	736,925,026	5.3%
TOTAL GENERAL AND ADMINISTRATIVE EXPENSES	4,280,638,095	30.8%
NET INCOME (LOSS) BEFORE FEDERAL INCOME TAXES AND EXTRAORDINARY ITEMS	1,134,328,500	8.2%

Source: *Nevada Gaming Abstract, 1998*, State Gaming Control Board, Carson City, NV, December 1998

dals in Louisiana, and the bankruptcy of Harrah's in New Orleans have all added to the impression that the gambling industry has lost its spark. (Four years after the 1995 closure of Harrah's on the edge of the French Quarter, the company opened a downtown casino, located at the New Orleans Tourist Center.) Recent election victories by more conservative Republicans, many of whom are concerned about "family values," have often made it more difficult to get pro-casino legislation through state legislatures. Grass roots efforts by such anti-gambling organizations as the National Coalition Against Legalized Gambling have mobilized popular opposition. (See Chapter II.)

Some economic observers believe that the market may be saturated or that a natural backlash has occurred as local economies try to absorb the

TABLE 5.2

FISCAL YEAR 1998
STATEWIDE CASINOS
WITH GAMING REVENUE OF $1,000,000 AND OVER

AMOUNTS REPRESENT 235 LOCATIONS

CASINO DEPARTMENT

REVENUE	DOLLARS	PERCENT
PIT REVENUE (INCLUDES KENO AND BINGO)	2,577,314,088	33.3%
COIN OPERATED DEVICES	4,913,670,729	63.5%
POKER AND PAN	62,960,341	0.8%
RACE BOOK	112,493,859	1.5%
SPORTS POOL	77,495,776	1.0%
TOTAL REVENUE	7,743,934,793	100.0%

Source: *Nevada Gaming Abstract, 1998*, State Gaming Control Board, Carson City, NV, December 1998

effects of introducing casino gambling into their areas. The improvement in the economy has made the need for additional sources of income less pressing. Other observers note that this slow period may benefit the industry so that it can consolidate its businesses. Until recently, corporate matters have focused upon expansion. Perhaps it is time, observe some experts, that the gambling business focus upon improving the operations of existing casinos. Finally, it is only natural that at some time the growth in an exploding industry would eventually slow down.

REGULATIONS

For many years, casino gambling in Las Vegas has been associated with organized crime. In 1959, the State of Nevada created the State Gaming Control Board, which is responsible for establishing gambling policy and suspending or revoking licenses for any cause it considers reasonable. In 1976, New Jersey formed the New Jersey Casino Control Commission (NJCCC) to be responsible for monitoring gambling activities, which are permitted only in casino rooms located within approved hotels in Atlantic City. The NJCCC strictly controls the extension of credit to gamblers and the collection of gambling funds.

States new to gambling have set up gambling control boards or commissions to regulate gambling. Many of these new states put limits on how much can be bet in order to make the new gambling operations less attractive to organized crime. However, many of these limitations were changed as competition forced some states to increase gambling limits. For example, Illinois does not limit the amount a person may bet or lose on riverboats based in that state. On the other side of the river in Iowa, the limit was $5 per bet and $200 in losses per day. The Iowa legislature reconsidered its limits since many gamblers chose to spend their money on Illinois-based riverboats. Similarly, many observers in Missouri are worried that the $500 limit will hurt gambling's growth in the state.

Because of the potential risk of stealing by gambling patrons or casino workers, all games are closely monitored. The gambling area is carefully watched and videotaped to guarantee that none of the casino employees steal from either the customers or their employers. State auditors conduct regular, unannounced audits and check the casinos' internal control systems. In every instance where money is counted and transferred from one station to another, two or more people are involved so they can check on each other, thus lessening the likelihood of "skimming" — the practice of reporting less money than is actually collected and stealing the difference.

TABLE 5.3

FISCAL YEAR 1998
STATEWIDE CASINOS
WITH GAMING REVENUE OF $1,000,000 AND OVER

AMOUNTS REPRESENT 235 LOCATIONS

GAMING REVENUE PER SQUARE FOOT OF FLOOR SPACE

AREA	NO. OF CASINOS OPERATING	AVERAGE AREA IN SQUARE FEET	GAMING REVENUE PER SQUARE FOOT
PIT (INCLUDES BINGO AND KENO)	180	7,144	2,000
COIN OPERATED DEVICES	232	20,901	1,011
POKER AND PAN	62	1,755	548
RACE AND SPORTS	98	3,847	500
TOTAL CASINO	235	28,173	1,170

Source: *Nevada Gaming Abstract, 1998*, State Gaming Control Board, Carson City, NV, December 1998

CASINO GAMES

Slot Machines

Slot machines are vending-like machines into which a player drops a coin or dollar bill, pulls a lever or pushes a button, and hopes to "hit the jackpot" that releases a large amount of money from the machine. Bettors can play for as little as 5 cents, 25 cents, or $1. High rollers can bet on the $5, $25, $100, or even $500 machines. The "pay-out" or jackpot, which is set by the casino and displayed on the machine, ranges from 78 percent to 97 percent, with an average of 85 percent being returned as payoff to players, while management and the state take the rest.

Table Games

Table games include twenty-one, craps, roulette, baccarat, keno, and bingo. Not all types of games are available at all gambling establishments. The larger casinos and hotel/casino complexes generally offer the widest variety of table games.

FINANCIAL INFORMATION

All the states with casino gambling have established casino control commissions. As part of the responsibilities, these commissions issue reports (usually annually) indicating casino gambling revenues. The information in this section has been taken from these reports.

Casino Revenues

In 1998, Americans bet $488 billion on casino games and slot machines. Most (65 percent) of that amount was bet on table games ($181.8 billion) and slot machines ($137.5 billion) in Nevada and New Jersey. The total handle (amount wagered) has increased steadily over the past few years. About 72 percent in 1998 was bet at land-based casinos.

The Nevada/New Jersey casinos earned $8.1 billion from slot machines and $3.8 billion from table games. Between 1982 and 1998, the win from slot machines rose 280.6 percent, while the win from table games rose only 77.9 percent. (See Chapter III, Table 3.5.)

A Shift to Slot Machines

Since 1983, casinos have earned more money from slot machines than they have earned from table games. This shift to slot machines is probably the major change that has occurred on the floors of the nation's gambling casinos over the past two decades. In 1982, in Nevada and New Jersey, table games produced 52 percent of all casino revenue; by 1998, these games produced just

64

TABLE 5.4

PER ROOM PER DAY STATISTICS

AVERAGE PIT REVENUE PER ROOM PER DAY	71.07	AVERAGE BEVERAGE SALES PER ROOM PER DAY	19.89
AVERAGE SLOT REVENUE PER ROOM PER DAY	135.49	AVERAGE ROOMS DEPARTMENT PAYROLL PER ROOM PER DAY	18.83
AVERAGE FOOD SALES PER ROOM PER DAY	48.25	AVERAGE ROOM RATE PER DAY	64.01

Source: *Nevada Gaming Abstract, 1998*, State Gaming Control Board, Carson City, NV, December 1998

32 percent. In 1982, Blackjack accounted for 23.5 percent of winnings; by 1996 (latest figures available), it had dropped to 13 percent. Craps dropped from 15 to 5.7 percent over the same period. Baccarat and roulette remained about the same. Casino operators are concerned about craps, which seems to be generation-oriented, with older Americans having grown up with the game and younger people knowing little about it. Some observers believe that unless a greater effort is made to introduce this game to younger people, its decline will likely continue.

Meanwhile, the proportion produced by slot machines in Nevada and New Jersey rose from 47.5 percent in 1982 to 67.8 percent in 1998. For the casino, a slot machine has several advantages. A single machine costs only about $5,000, and it is not likely to complain about working hours or salary. This shift is also occurring in casinos on riverboats and Native American reservations.

This shift in gambling preferences, however, does bring a change to the feel of gambling. Table games involve the participation of the gambler, enough commitment to learn the rules of the game, some degree of thought, and, no matter how impersonal the dealer, some human contact. Playing the slot machines requires little mental commitment by the player, is solitary, and is potentially addictive. The player continually feeds one, two, or three machines until she has lost her money or won enough or until it is time to go home.

Slot machines are more suited than table games for the huge increase in casino gambling. A riverboat can easily be filled with many hundreds of slot machines. The slot machine is the perfect tool to bring gambling to the uninitiated. There is little for the new customer to learn. Furthermore, the new gambler does not have to risk embarrassment because he does not know the rules of craps. In fact, slot machines are so simple they can be placed in bars and bathrooms with no risk that the inexperienced gambler will not know how to play the game.

GAMBLING IN NEVADA

The 235 major casinos operating in Nevada in 1998 (up from 169 locations in 1989, 182 in 1990 and 192 in 1992) produced $13.9 billion in gross revenues (up from $7.3 billion in 1989, $8 billion in 1990, and $9.1 in 1992). Net income (before federal income taxes and extraordinary items) for the year was $1.1 billion, up from $848.6 million in 1992 and $545.9 million in 1990. The casinos' 1998 "Combined Income Statement — Summary" (Table 5.1) shows that gaming accounted for 55.8 percent ($7.7 billion) of total casino revenue. About 64 percent of gambling revenue ($4.9 billion) came from slot machines ("coin-operated devices") and 33.3 percent ($2.6 billion) from pit revenue (blackjack, roulette, etc.). (See Table 5.2.) Table 5.3 shows gaming revenue per square foot of floor space.

TABLE 5.5

COMBINED INCOME STATEMENT - SUMMARY

FISCAL YEAR 1998
PUBLICLY OWNED CASINO OPERATIONS
WITH GAMING REVENUE OF $12,000,000 AND OVER

AMOUNTS REPRESENT 65 LOCATIONS

REVENUE	DOLLARS	PERCENT
GAMING	5,844,797,696	54.7%
ROOMS	1,956,763,990	18.3%
FOOD	1,296,904,631	12.1%
BEVERAGE	514,911,030	4.8%
OTHER	1,075,034,129	10.1%
TOTAL REVENUE	10,688,411,476	100.0%

Source: *Nevada Gaming Abstract, 1998*, State Gaming Control Board, Carson City, NV, December 1998

In fiscal year 1998, 41.9 million rooms (up from 26 million rooms in 1992) were filled in Nevada for a 86.5 percent occupancy rate. Room rates in Nevada are generally inexpensive, running about $64 per day, a far lower rate than that charged by most much less luxurious hotels in other cities, although with the increase of non-gambling visitors, the prices have started to rise somewhat (see below). These low rates are meant to attract potential gamblers who, the hotel hopes, will spend a lot of money at the slot machines and gaming tables.

In fact, the average room produced $71.07 in daily revenues at the tables and $135.49 on the slot machines. Between the room charge, gambling revenues, and food and beverage sales, the hotels brought in an average of $357.54 per room per day in 1998. Table 5.4 shows where that money was earned.

The giant "Super Casinos" or mega-resorts that have developed along the Las Vegas Strip, many in just the past few years, dominate the industry. (See below for a more detailed discussion of these hotels.) Of the 235 Nevada casinos included in the *1998 Nevada Gaming Abstract*, published by the State Gaming Control Board, 65 grossing $12 million or more in gaming revenue were owned by 23 publicly held corporations. These 65 casinos grossed 75.5 percent ($10.7 million) of the total

revenue for fiscal year 1998 in Nevada. (See Table 5.5.)

A Time of Major Changes

The gambling industry presents itself as a business, just like selling cars, reference books, or corn flakes. While the handle in Nevada has continued to grow, there is no guarantee that demand may not slacken in the future. Casinos outside of Nevada and Atlantic City, as small as some of them might be, offer another alternative to potential gamblers who might choose to visit Dubuque, Iowa, or a nearby Native American reservation instead of flying all the way to Las Vegas.

As a result, Las Vegas is going through one of the most interesting metamorphoses (changes in appearance) in the history of the entire gambling industry. While the 1980s were dominated by the spread of lotteries from coast to coast, gambling in the 1990s has been dominated by the growth of casino gambling on Native American Reservations (see Chapter VII) and the development of huge, mega-resort complexes in Las Vegas.

Traditionally, in addition to the opportunity to gamble, famous hotel/casinos like Caesars Palace, Circus World, the Dunes, the Golden Nugget, Harrah's, the Hilton, MGM Grand, and the Sahara offer a resort-type atmosphere with big-name en-

TABLE 5.6

Ten Biggest Numeric Gainers in Population -- 1997 to 1998

Rank	County	State	Number Increase
1	Los Angeles	Calif.	97,027
2	Maricopa	Ariz.	84,977
3	Orange	Calif.	58,140
4	San Diego	Calif.	56,881
5	Clark	Nev.	55,229
6	Harris	Texas	51,953
7	Riverside	Calif.	39,628
8	Broward	Fla.	30,480
9	Dallas	Texas	30,245
10	Tarrant	Texas	29,229

Source: Bureau of the Census, Washington, DC

tertainment, luxurious accommodations, and lavish restaurants. Some also feature tennis, golf, swimming, boxing matches, an occasional cattle auction, and attractions for children.

A Fast Growing Area in a Fast Growing State

Between 1990 and 1996, Nevada became the fastest growing state in the nation with a 33.4 percent increase in population and is expected to continue to grow rapidly through 2000. Clark County, which includes Las Vegas, was ranked fifth in population growth in 1997 and 1998 (Table 5.6). Reflecting the growing interest in gambling and Las Vegas, the city and gambling have played a central role in a number of recent movies, including *Bugsy, Casino, Leaving Las Vegas, Honeymoon in Las Vega*s, and *Indecent Proposal*.

Changing the Image

The image of Las Vegas has benefited from the spread of gambling throughout American society. About three-fourths of the states now operate lotteries. Casino gambling in one form or another is legal (although not necessarily operative) in 24 states and Puerto Rico. At one time, many Americans connected Las Vegas with organized crime — after all, it was the gangster "Bugsy" Siegel who built the Flamingo, one of the first gambling casinos. The current aggressive business in-

terests now controlling gambling in Las Vegas have worked hard to bury this image.

Over the past decade, as gambling has become common throughout the United States and even sanctioned by government, it has tended to lose whatever criminal character may have been attached to it. In 1992, "Bugsy's" Flamingo Hotel was demolished to make way for future development. A year later, in 1993, the Dunes Hotel and Casino, once the pride of the mob, was also dynamited. Perhaps symbolically, at least in the eyes of the new gambling industry financed by Wall Street and big banks, not gangsters, these explosions blew away gambling's tie to its disreputable past.

"Mega-Resorts" with "Mega" Family Entertainment

While gambling is the basis of these giant casinos, it has become only part of the total experience. These new complexes offer opportunities for the whole family. Las Vegas is no longer a place for mother and father to go alone and gamble at the slot machines or casino tables — it is now a complete experience that the whole family can enjoy.

In 1989 and 1990, the huge, 3,000-room Mirage hotel and the even larger, 4,000-room Excalibur, then the biggest hotel in the world,

67

opened in Las Vegas. Rather than billing themselves as casinos, these two new, enormous hotels were presented as resorts that happened to offer casinos as one form of entertainment.

The Mirage hotel has become a "must see" Polynesian-style attraction in the Nevada desert with a $13-million erupting volcano outside and a 20,000-gallon aquarium filled with exotic tropical fish. The Excalibur purports to take guests back to an idyllic medieval time. Medieval-costumed hosts greet arriving guests, and telephone operators tell guests to "have a royal day."

TABLE 5.7

New Las Vegas construction

1997	Estimated cost (in millions)	Rooms	Scheduled open date
Harrah's Las Vegas - Expansion	$150	1,000	2nd Quarter 1997
Desert Inn - Expansion	$114	N/A	3rd Quarter 1997
Sunset Station	$196	467	3rd Quarter 1997
Alexis Park - Expansion	N/A	100	4th Quarter 1997
Reserve	$60	225	4th Quarter 1997
Orleans	$40	N/A	4th Quarter 1997
1998			
Caesars Palace - Expansion	N/A	600	1st Quarter 1998
Bellagio	$1,350	3,000	3rd Quarter 1998
1999			
Paradise	$800	4,000	1999
Paris	$750	3,000	1999
Resort at Summerlin	N/A	300	1999
The Venetian	$1,500	6,000	1999

Christiansen/Cummings Associates, Inc.

Source: "The United States — 96 Gross Annual Wager," *International Gaming and Wagering Business*, New York, NY, August 1997

In 1993, three more gigantic hotels/casinos/tourist attractions opened. The Luxor Las Vegas is a 30-story pyramid covered by 11 acres of glass. In front of the hotel is a huge obelisk and copy of the Sphinx. A Nile River flows inside the hotel, and the atrium is the world's largest. The hotel's 2,526 rooms are done in an ancient Egyptian style. The casino covers more than 100,000 square feet. Another 1,800 rooms became available in 1996.

In keeping with its efforts to attract families with children, the hotel contains a Sega amusement arcade, and Sega has agreed to introduce all its new video products at the hotel before it markets them nationwide. In addition, Sega is operating VirtuaLand, a virtual-reality facility of 20,000 square feet. A huge child-care center allows parents to leave their children under adult supervision while they go off to play the slot machines or visit the roulette tables.

The Treasure Island Resort is loosely based on Robert Louis Stevenson's classic tale of piracy. The three 36-story towers holding 2,900 rooms face onto Buccaneer Bay, a theme park designed to look like a seaport of the 1700s. Every hour, two 90-foot frigates do battle. In addition, the hotel also offers video games and other electronically simulated games.

The MGM Grand Hotel is the largest hotel (5,005 rooms in four 30-story towers) and gambling casino (as big as four football fields) in the world. In front, a seven-story lion guards the hotel. The hotel contains a 33-acre theme park with 12 major attractions, plus a giant swimming complex. Circus Circus was the first to offer child-friendly entertainment, including live circus acts, a carnival midway, and a 5-acre amusement park.

At the Excalibur, children can watch Merlin the Magician battle a fire-breathing dragon. Caesars puts on a laser light show. The 1,149-foot tower of the Stratosphere Tower and Casino is even higher than the Eiffel Tower in Paris. A 70-foot mechanical gorilla reminiscent of King Kong periodically scales the tower, while daring visitors ride the roller coaster down the side. On top of the tower is a restaurant, two observation decks, and four suites with a view for the "high rollers," bettors who wager large amounts of money. The world's largest indoor/outdoor swimming pool (13,500 square feet) is located at the Tropicana Hotel and Casino.

TABLE 5.8

Casino Facility Statistics 1998/1997

	AC HILTON		BALLY'S PARK PLACE		CAESARS		CLARIDGE		HARRAH'S MARINA		RESORTS	
	1998	1997	1998	1997	1998	1997	1998	1997	1998	1997	1998	1997
TABLE GAMES:												
Blackjack	46	51	92	93	74	56	36	36	37	48	39	45
Craps	10	10	12	14	12	13	8	8	9	9	6	9
Roulette	11	10	19	19	13	12	5	5	9	12	8	10
Big Six	1	1	3	4	2	2	1	1	1	1	1	2
Baccarat	2	2	2	2	3	3	2	2	2	1	2	3
Minibacarat	6	6	2	2	4	4	2	3	2	1	2	1
Red Dog	0	0	0	0	0	0	0	0	0	0	0	0
Sic Bo	1	1	1	1	2	3	0	1	0	0	0	1
Pai Gow Poker	4	5	5	5	4	4	2	2	2	2	2	1
Pai Gow	3	3	2	1	1	3	2	0	0	0	1	1
Poker	0	8	16	16	6	7	0	0	8	8	0	17
Caribbean Stud Poker	6	6	6	8	4	4	3	4	5	7	4	4
Let It Ride Poker	4	4	8	10	8	5	2	2	5	6	4	2
Mini-Craps	0	0	0	0	0	0	1	1	0	2	0	0
Three Card Poker	0	0	0	0	0	0	0	0	0	0	0	2
Mini-Dice	0	0	0	0	0	0	0*	0	0	0	0	0
Casino War [a]	0	0	0	0	0	0	0	0	1	0	0	0
Total Table Games	94	107	168	175	133	116	64	65	80	97	69	98
KENO WINDOWS	0	4	4	4	6	6	0	0	4	4	0	4
SLOT MACHINES:												
$.05 Slot Machines	50	0	264	172	0	0	36	15	0	0	0	0
$.25 Slot Machines	1,104	1,088	2,440	2,512	1,991	1,430	1,265	1,288	1,455	1,365	1,525	1,500
$.50 Slot Machines	221	241	472	468	550	482	170	158	229	270	282	359
$1 Slot Machines	396	369	578	671	756	582	247	262	643	708	315	325
$5 Slot Machines	77	80	99	117	123	72	30	27	113	113	55	58
$25 Slot Machines	13	12	11	11	13	13	4	1	9	9	7	4
$100 Slot Machines	10	5	6	3	7	7	0	0	3	3	0	2
Other Slot Machines	25	31	129	152	155	95	0	0	48	61	6	6
Total Slot Machines	1,896	1,826	3,999	4,106	3,595	2,681	1,752	1,751	2,500	2,529	2,190	2,254
Casino Square Footage	58,272	58,124	118,710	118,710	110,540	75,642	58,932	58,705	80,822	80,775	67,655	67,655
Simulcast Square Footage	1,517	1,517	36,124	36,124	9,691	6,765	0	0	0	0	8,058	8,058
Number Of Hotel Rooms	804	801	1,251	1,268	1,144	1,144	507	507	1,174	1,174	662	662
Number of Parking Spaces	1,762	1,848	2,830	2,245	2,148	2,018	1,460	1,460	2,753	2,753	1,485	1,719
Fixed Asset Investment ($ in Millions) [b]	$505.9	$486.7	$989.6	$947.1	$824.0	$735.5	$39.6	$45.4	$496.2	$483.8	$249.6	$228.9
Number of Employees	3,378	3,432	5,447	5,473	4,688	4,126	2,411	2,508	3,477	3,543	3,245	3,526

[a] Casino War was introduced in December 1997.
[b] Represents property and equipment before accumulated depreciation. Fixed asset
    investment for Claridge primarily represents gaming equipment and the parking garage,
    since Claridge leases its hotel property and non-gaming equipment.

(continued)

Since 1989, when the Mirage and Excalibur opened, many of the famous old-line casinos, including the Dunes and the Riviera, have gone bankrupt. While the new casinos hope to attract the many millions of Americans who have never visited Las Vegas (MGM Grand Chief Executive Robert Maxey claims that his studies show that only 15 percent of Americans have ever been to Las Vegas), it is likely that other casinos may not survive.

On the other hand, new hotels or mega-resorts continue to be built. One example is the $350 million New York-New York — opened in 1997 — which recreates the Statue of Liberty, the skyscrapers of the New York skyline, and the Coney Island roller coaster. Another is the $325 million Monte Carlo — opened in 1996 — which has a Victorian theme. The 6-million-square-foot Bellagio Hotel opened in 1998 at a cost of $1.6 billion, making it one of the most expensive hotels ever built. It features an extensive art collection, which includes impressionist, post-impressionist, and modern masterpieces. The collection is located in the Bellagio Gallery of Fine Art (just off the 15,000-square-foot conservatory garden). Admission to the gallery costs $12 per person — more than any major American museum charges.

The Las Vegas Hilton has gone into partnership with Paramount Parks and plans to construct a 40,000-square foot *Star Trek* entertainment area. Mirage Resorts plans to build the Beau Rivage, a $900 million, 3,000-room resort surrounded by a 50-acre lake on which visitors can waterski, parasail, and windsurf. Numerous downtown ho-

TABLE 5.8 (Continued)

Casino Facility Statistics 1998/1997

	SANDS		SHOWBOAT		TROPICANA		TRUMP MARINA		TRUMP PLAZA		TRUMP TAJ MAHAL		INDUSTRY TOTALS	
	1998	1997	1998	1997	1998	1997	1998	1997	1998	1997	1998	1997	1998	1997
	43	57	49	48	56	56	44	46	56	65	70	74	642	675
	8	11	8	10	14	14	12	12	8	10	12	14	119	134
	12	14	13	13	13	13	9	9	13	15	19	18	144	150
	2	2	2	2	1	1	1	1	2	2	3	4	20	23
	4	5	3	5	3	3	3	3	2	2	5	7	32	38
	3	3	2	2	7	8	2	4	6	7	3	3	41	44
	0	0	0	0	0	0	0	0	0	0	0	0	0	0
	1	1	1	1	1	1	1	1	1	2	2	2	11	15
	2	2	2	2	5	5	3	4	3	3	9	8	43	43
	1	1	2	1	6	6	3	2	2	2	6	7	29	27
	12	16	0	0	50	50	0	0	0	0	64	63	156	185
	6	6	6	6	6	6	5	6	5	4	10	10	66	71
	4	4	6	6	4	4	7	6	5	5	7	7	64	61
	1	1	0	0	0	0	0	0	0	0	0	0	2	4
	0	0	0	0	0	0	0	0	0	0	0	0	0	2
	0	0	0	0	0	0	0	0	0	0	1	1	1	1
	0	0	1	0	0	0	1	0	0	0	0	0	3	0
	99	123	95	96	166	167	91	94	103	117	211	218	1,373	1,473
	0	4	0	0	7	7	0	0	0	0	10	10	31	43
	29	0	88	75	144	0	51	35	439	287	266	210	1,367	794
	1,284	1,317	2,674	2,705	2,079	2,144	1,238	1,233	2,601	2,532	2,745	2,752	22,401	21,866
	246	257	261	317	441	463	308	293	513	512	324	322	4,017	4,142
	371	408	569	551	735	771	435	448	514	623	663	694	6,222	6,412
	64	68	48	58	127	143	77	81	84	86	102	106	999	1,009
	6	6	0	2	15	18	13	12	14	8	13	13	118	109
	3	3	0	2	10	9	7	4	4	4	4	4	54	46
	22	17	48	27	149	171	49	46	35	38	94	35	760	679
	2,025	2,076	3,688	3,737	3,700	3,719	2,178	2,152	4,204	4,090	4,211	4,136	35,938	35,057
	57,296	57,812	80,707	80,707	114,320	114,205	73,734	73,734	138,295	138,305	116,199	116,199	1,075,482	1,040,573
	15,963	15,447	20,998	20,998	10,183	10,183	2,150	2,150	0	0	31,521	31,521	136,205	132,763
	532	532	800	800	1,624	1,624	728	728	1,404	1,404	1,250	1,250	11,880	11,894
	1,738	1,738	3,521	3,521	3,265	2,968	2,986	2,986	3,282	3,682	7,180	7,180	34,410	34,118
	$327.1	$320.5	$471.0	$457.3	$710.6	$689.2	$527.1	$521.4	$731.0	$719.1	$1,026.0	$1,007.0	$6,897.7	$6,641.9
	3,037	3,071	3,353	3,551	5,084	5,116	3,482	3,487	5,124	5,275	5,766	6,015	48,492	49,123

Source: *1998 Annual Report*, New Jersey Casino Control Commission, Atlantic City, NJ, 1999

tels are being upgraded, modernized, and expanded. Table 5.7 shows construction scheduled through 1999 for Las Vegas.

There is a Hard Rock Hotel, a spin-off of the Hard Rock Cafes located in every major city in the Western world, where gamblers can enjoy over $2 million in music memorabilia and around-the-clock rock and roll music. The 27-year-old Circus Circus Hotel is adding 1,000 new rooms. Wealthy financiers are considering building a $4 billion Lake Las Vegas project 17 miles east of the city, which would include a half dozen new resorts around the edge of a man-made lake. In addition, as well as offering an alternative to the older gambling casinos, these new hotel/casinos offer an alternative to the family considering a trip to Disneyland in Anaheim, California, or Disney World in Orlando, Florida.

In downtown Las Vegas, a five-block section of Fremont Street, which intersects Las Vegas Boulevard, has been closed to traffic. This five-block-long covered pedestrian mall offers an extraordinary laserlight and music show with 2.1 million lights. Street performers entertain, sidewalk cafes offer food and the opportunity to watch passersby, while merchants sell their wares in pushcarts or kiosks.

Not surprisingly, 9 of the 10 largest and costliest hotels in the world are located in Las Vegas. The Luxor cost an estimated $390 million; the Treasure Island, $450 million; and the MGM Grand, $1.03 billion. The Bellagio opened in 1998 and the Venetian and Paris Hotel and Casino in 1999, each costing well over $1 billion. The Holiday Inn Casino Boardwalk has been expanded to make it the largest hotel in the Holiday Inn chain. Openings scheduled for 2000 include the Marriott

TABLE 5.9

THE NEW JERSEY CASINO INDUSTRY

GROSS REVENUE STATISTICS

FOR THE YEARS ENDED DECEMBER 31, 1998 AND 1997

($ IN THOUSANDS)

Casino Hotel	Casino Win	Daily Average Casino Win	Adjustment for Uncollectibles	Gross Revenue	Tax	Market Share of Casino Win
AC Hilton						
1998	256,703	703	1,464	255,239	20,419	6.4%
1997	248,939	682	1,479	247,460	19,797	6.4%
Bally's Park Place						
1998	466,867	1,279	1,455	465,412	37,233	11.6%
1997	406,627	1,114	1,155	405,472	32,438	10.4%
Caesars						
1998	424,695	1,164	9,078	415,617	33,249	10.5%
1997	383,537	1,051	4,046	379,491	30,359	9.8%
Claridge						
1998	164,705	451	1,101	163,604	13,088	4.1%
1997	165,424	453	196	165,228	13,218	4.2%
Harrah's Marina						
1998	349,216	957	1,798	347,418	27,793	8.7%
1997	322,976	885	1,404	321,572	25,726	8.3%
Resorts						
1998	235,493	645	643	234,850	18,788	5.8%
1997	245,950	674	786	245,164	19,613	6.3%
Sands						
1998	221,901	608	2,021	219,880	17,591	5.5%
1997	236,274	647	2,788	233,486	18,679	6.0%
Showboat						
1998	357,064	978	1,179	355,885	28,471	8.9%
1997	353,380	968	2,075	351,305	28,104	9.0%
Tropicana						
1998	388,576	1,065	7,473	381,103	30,488	9.6%
1997	371,703	1,018	3,882	367,821	29,426	9.5%
Trump Marina						
1998	264,825	726	984	263,841	21,107	6.6%
1997	265,572	728	1,488	264,084	21,127	6.8%
Trump Plaza						
1998	379,604	1,040	1,866	377,738	30,219	9.4%
1997	377,637	1,035	1,579	376,058	30,084	9.7%
Trump Taj Mahal						
1998	523,348	1,434	12,323	511,025	40,882	13.0%
1997	528,121	1,447	5,409	522,712	41,817	13.5%
TOTALS						
1998	**4,032,997**	**11,049**	**41,385**	**3,991,612**	**319,328**	
1997	**3,906,140**	**10,702**	**26,287**	**3,879,853**	**310,388**	

Note: These statistics do not include simulcasting, since revenue from simulcasting is not subject to the casino revenue tax.

Source: *1998 Annual Report*, New Jersey Casino Control Commission, Atlantic City, NJ, 1999

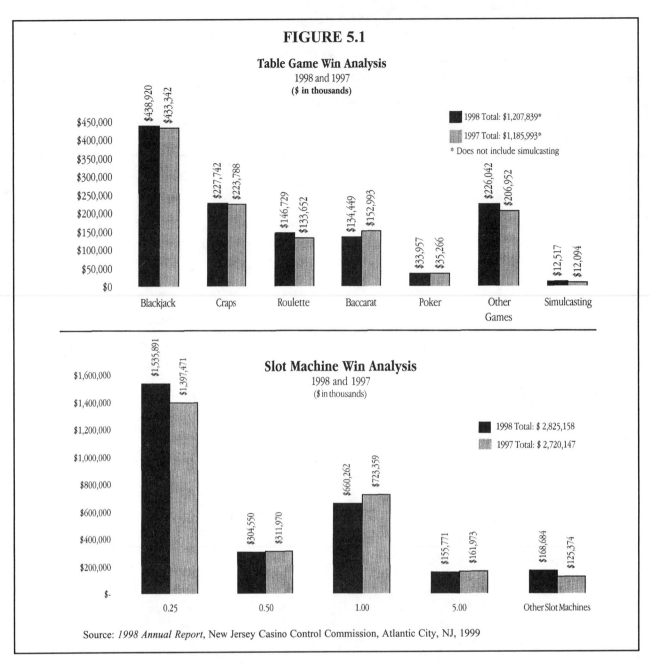

FIGURE 5.1

Table Game Win Analysis
1998 and 1997
($ in thousands)

1998 Total: $1,207,839*
1997 Total: $1,185,993*
* Does not include simulcasting

	Blackjack	Craps	Roulette	Baccarat	Poker	Other Games	Simulcasting
1998	$438,920	$227,742	$146,729	$134,449	$33,957	$226,042	$12,517
1997	$433,342	$223,788	$133,652	$152,993	$35,266	$206,952	$12,094

Slot Machine Win Analysis
1998 and 1997
($ in thousands)

1998 Total: $ 2,825,158
1997 Total: $ 2,720,147

	0.25	0.50	1.00	5.00	Other Slot Machines
1998	$1,535,891	$304,550	$660,262	$155,771	$168,684
1997	$1,397,471	$311,970	$723,359	$161,973	$125,374

Source: *1998 Annual Report*, New Jersey Casino Control Commission, Atlantic City, NJ, 1999

Marquis at MGM and The New Aladdin. These huge investments are changing the way the gambling business is done in Las Vegas. It may no longer be enough to offer only a hotel and gambling casino. Certainly that is what the owners of many of the mega-hotels described above believe.

Bringing Malls to the Hotels

Several of the hotels are increasingly referring to themselves as "mega-resorts" to emphasize the changing nature of the Las Vegas experience. These "mega-resorts" are opening retail outlets in the hotels to offer the growing number of visitors yet another opportunity to spend their money. Many of the newer tourists do not have the commitment to gambling that visitors a decade ago did. These shops give them the opportunity to purchase things they would buy on a visit to any other vacation spot, such as elegant clothing or T-shirts and sweatshirts with Las Vegas images on them.

The entrance to the MGM Grand is part minimall. The expansion at Caesars World is mainly to increase the size of its shopping mall. Even the Foxwoods Resort Casino, the gambling facility owned by the Mashantucket Pequot Indians in Ledyard, Connecticut, has incorporated retail sales spaces. Retail sales may also play a significant role in expansion plans for Atlantic City. While not all casinos are transforming gambling space into malls, the change reflects the ongoing transformation of Las Vegas.

New Image Seems to Be Working

The new image for Las Vegas appears to be successful. In 1991, 21.3 million people visited Las Vegas; by 1994, 28 million people came, and an estimated 29.6 million arrived in 1998. Of course, the changing image of Las Vegas is not all positive for the visitor. Despite adding 45,000 rooms in the past decade, the average room occupancy rate has been around 85 to 90 percent, a very high rate for hotels. Hotel rooms and meals in Las Vegas used to be cheap because the casino owners looked on food and lodging as just part of the business of getting people to bet their money in the casinos. The money earned at the tables and slot machines subsidized the rooms and meals.

Today, many visitors coming to Las Vegas are spending less time in the casinos and, instead, are visiting the other attractions. With the increase in such visitors, more of the hotel and meal expenses have to be paid for by the tourist. As a result, hotels and meals cost more. Lodging and food in Las Vegas are now moderately priced — the $79 dollar room is far nicer than a similarly priced room in New York or San Francisco — but they are no longer the inexpensive deal they once were. The famous low-priced buffets that used to cost just a few dollars may run $10, still inexpensive by any standards, but not as cheap as before.

Not all casino operators are happy with the changing situation. After all, they believe, the main point of coming to Las Vegas is to gamble, and all of the new attractions and amusements distract visitors from the casinos. On the other hand, those supporting the change note that these people could be somewhere else spending their money. Since they have come to Las Vegas, and many have never been exposed to gambling, savvy casino operators can draw them into the casinos and make gambling part of their entertainment.

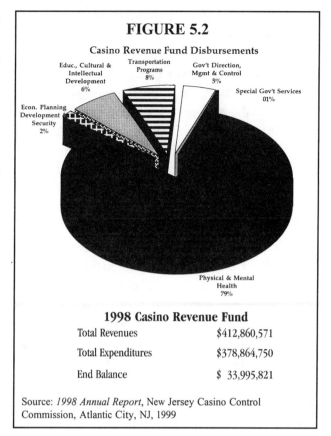

FIGURE 5.2

Casino Revenue Fund Disbursements

1998 Casino Revenue Fund	
Total Revenues	$412,860,571
Total Expenditures	$378,864,750
End Balance	$ 33,995,821

Source: *1998 Annual Report*, New Jersey Casino Control Commission, Atlantic City, NJ, 1999

Finally, the gambling industry, like all other industries, is learning to market every aspect of the business. Any business that does not take advantage of every possibility to increase revenues in the current competitive world economy is destined to fall behind and not survive.

GAMBLING IN ATLANTIC CITY

All 12 casinos operating in Atlantic City in 1998 were of the hotel/casino variety. (Table 5.8 shows statistics for the individual resorts.) Together, the casinos grossed $4 billion in 1998, up from $3.2 billion in 1992. Gross revenue and related taxes for each facility are shown in Table 5.9. The State of New Jersey took in $319.3 million worth of taxes from the casinos. In 1998, the Taj Mahal had the largest market share of all the hotel/casinos in Atlantic City, followed by Bally's Park Plaza and Caesars (Table 5.9).

Blackjack was the most profitable table game, followed by craps and roulette. The 25-cent slot machines accounted for the largest casino win by game in 1998, followed by $1.00 and 50-cent slot machines (Figure 5.1).

State of New Jersey Casino Control Fund

When the New Jersey legislature implemented legalized gambling in New Jersey, it established the Casino Revenue Fund to finance assistance programs for New Jersey's elderly and disabled. To finance the fund, the 12 operating casinos are taxed 8 percent of their gross revenues, or "win," each month. In 1998, the fund spent $378.9 million. To be eligible for the programs supported by the Casino Revenue Fund, a person must be at least 65 years old or receiving Social Security disability benefits. The maximum income limit is $13,650 for single persons and $16,750 for married couples. More than three-fourths (79 percent) of the money went to physical and mental health — mainly to pay for medicine and medical services. (See Figure 5.2 for a breakdown of how the Casino Revenue Fund was allotted.)

Growing Competition

As noted in the 1992 *Annual Report of the New Jersey Casino Control Commission*,

Despite this steady climb [in revenues], state and local officials are no longer so sanguine (optimistic) about the notion that such growth is inevitable. Atlantic City, which long had a monopoly on casino gambling in the eastern half of the United States, now faces competition for that gaming dollar. From an Indian reservation in Connecticut to riverboats on the Mississippi, gamblers now have more options. And, with the likely prospect that even more jurisdictions will legalize casino gambling in coming years, that trend will only accelerate.

The new gambling casino opened in Ledyard, Connecticut, in 1992 by the Mashantucket Pequot (see Chapter VII) has definitely cut into the number of visitors to Atlantic City. For New Englanders, it is much easier to go to Ledyard than it is to travel all the way to Atlantic City. This is particularly important because most people who go to Atlantic City are day visitors who do not stay overnight. Saving three or four hours means more time to have fun, less time spent driving, and a chance to get home earlier.

Nonetheless, while recognizing the drop in the number of arrivals by bus, mostly day visitors, casino managers point out that earnings from these arrivals are the least profitable. They say that future development has to court other visitors who spend more and stay longer.

Revitalizing Atlantic City

In response to these concerns, recent chairmen of the Casino Control Commission have brought a less adversarial relationship than had previously existed between the Casino Control Commission and the gambling industry in Atlantic City. They have introduced several major changes to improve the financial situation of the casinos. Gambling can now take place 24 hours a day. Additional space can be used for casinos, and more of that space can be used for more financially profitable slot machines. More and different types of games, such as poker, keno, and Caribbean Stud Poker, have been allowed. Simulcasting of horse races is now shown in the Atlantic City casinos. In addition, the New

---

TABLE 5.10

AVERAGE NUMBER OF EMPLOYEES FOR THE YEAR

CASINO DEPARTMENT	55,614
ROOMS DEPARTMENT	27,225
FOOD DEPARTMENT	46,041
BEVERAGE DEPARTMENT	12,163
G & A DEPARTMENT	29,932
OTHER DEPARTMENTS	11,646
TOTAL	182,621

Source: *Nevada Gaming Abstract, 1998*, State Gaming Control Board, Carson City, NV, December 1998

Jersey legislature further deregulated gambling, permitting one person or company to own more than three casinos (such as Trump Taj Mahal, Trump Plaza, and Trump Marina). In addition, the state no longer requires Casino Control Commission approval of marketing programs and allows hotels to increase the size of their casinos.

A new convention center, the largest between New York and Washington, DC, has been built. The convention center will be tied to a new 500-room (non-gambling) hotel. A new airport has opened. A $225 million Corridor Project has widened and remade the approaches to the Boardwalk. Seven casinos invested $580 million to add another 3,000 hotel rooms. The city has even signed a minor league baseball team.

While the changes in Atlantic City do not equal those occurring in Las Vegas, they are nonetheless significant. Furthermore, it is important to understand that Atlantic City is not Las Vegas. Las Vegas attracts visitors from all over the country and the world. Atlantic City is a regional attraction that draws visitors from the East Coast. It has gambling, a boardwalk, and a beach that can attract Easterners for a vacation weekend. Few people, however, are going to fly in from Paris or San Francisco to tour Atlantic City. As a result, comparisons between the two gambling centers should be made carefully.

Increased Community Participation

Casino owners have increased their participation in the community over the past few years. The casinos have begun to help local schools and provide food for the homeless. Casino revenues have underwritten the construction of new, subsidized housing. Atlantic City is only one deteriorating city among many in New Jersey. It had not appeared to benefit from the arrival of gambling and was often cited as an illustration that casino gambling does little, if anything, to benefit a community. While gambling did not cause the problems confronting Atlantic City, casino gambling had done little to slow the decline of the city. As casino gambling

FIGURE 5.3

Casino Hotel Employment

Other 8%

Part Time 8%

Full Time 84%

Casino Hotel Employment by License Category

Key Employees 4%

Casino Employees 43%

Hotel Employees 36%

Casino Service Employees 17%

Source: *1998 Annual Report*, New Jersey Casino Control Commission, Atlantic City, NJ, 1999

began to spread across the country, it became imperative for the casino companies to show that gambling could help local communities. In the past few years, Atlantic City has benefited from this.

EMPLOYMENT

The gambling industry is the major employer in Nevada, with the 235 major casinos employing an average 182,621 Nevada residents in 1998 (Table 5.10). Gamblers may tip casino employees, but all tips are pooled and divided equally among the employees to prevent any collusion between employees and customers. Many workers in the larger casinos earn more in tips than they do from their base salaries.

In New Jersey, the casino industry employed 41,000 full-time people in 1998. About one-third (36 percent) worked in the hotel section, while 43 percent worked in the casino gaming. The major-

TABLE 5.11

SOUTH DAKOTA COMMISSION ON GAMING
RECAP OF COMMISSION ACTIVITY
11/1989 — 06/1999

GAMING ACTION	FY 96 (07/95-6/96)	FY 97 (07/96-6/97)	FY 98 (07/97-6/98)	FY 99 (07/98-6/99)	CUMULATIVE TOTALS (11/89 - 6/99)	
TOTAL GAMING ACTION	$482,164,324.44	$471,762,901.37	$490,377,425.38	$498,330,933.03	$4,145,099,580.27	
% INCREASE	-1.28%	-2.16%	3.95%	1.62%		
WON BY BETTORS	$437,582,257.64	$429,082,249.74	$446,480,408.38	$453,701,269.41	$3,750,897,839.31	
% OF $ WAGERED	90.75%	90.95%	91.05%	91.04%	90.49%	
TOTAL GROSS REVENUES	$44,582,066.80	$42,680,651.63	$43,897,017.00	$44,629,663.62	$394,201,740.96	
LESS: CITY SLOT REVENUES	$1,127,119.55	$1,104,904.57	$1,406,766.59	$1,687,468.37	$10,212,273.52	
ADJUSTED GROSS REVENUES	$43,454,947.25	$41,575,747.06	$42,490,250.41	$42,942,195.25	$383,989,467.44	
% INCREASE	-5.07%	-4.32%	2.20%	1.06%		
NUMBER OF LICENSED DEVICES	2252	2420	2444	2220		
APPROXIMATE # OF ACTIVE SUPPORT AND KEY LICENSEES	1634	1492	1308	1361		
NUMBER OF LOCATIONS (06/30)	89	99	90	92		
COMMISSION FUND ACTIVITY						
DEVICE TAX	$4,504,000.00	$4,840,000.00	$4,888,000.00	$4,440,000.00	$41,002,000.00	51.67%
GROSS REVENUE TAX	$3,507,707.00	$3,323,850.91	$3,390,421.07	$3,446,908.00	$30,667,074.61	38.65%
CITY SLOT TAX	$546,091.50	$500,001.00	$465,910.00	$534,092.00	$4,076,778.43	5.14%
APPLICATION FEE	$174,554.00	$154,035.00	$218,030.00	$156,960.00	$1,672,318.51	2.11%
LICENSE FEE	$66,010.00	$99,370.00	$91,110.00	$90,180.00	$995,825.05	1.26%
DEVICE TESTING FEE	$20,437.16	$13,059.74	$4,530.09	$10,835.00	$150,283.58	0.19%
PENALTIES	$15,679.25	$18,140.00	$30,220.00	$11,250.00	$132,682.80	0.17%
INTEREST	$59,671.03	$79,754.43	$78,819.66	$86,647.00	$634,069.73	0.80%
MANUAL SALES	$1,887.90	$255.40	$506.85	$149.00	$16,637.41	0.02%
TOTAL	$8,896,037.84	$9,028,466.48	$9,167,547.67	$8,777,021.00	$79,347,670.12	100.00%
SDCG OPERATING EXPENSES:	$974,696.45	$984,252.39	$1,005,792.89	$1,031,951.10	$9,235,801.26	
% OF REVENUES	10.96%	10.90%	10.97%	11.76%	11.64%	
REFUND OF PRIOR YEARS REVENUE:			$971.85	$5,521.00	$6,492.85	
DISTRIBUTIONS TO LOCAL GOVERNMENTS						
LAWRENCE COUNTY	$354,955.23	$334,183.84	$336,447.67	$342,696.53	$2,988,089.96	
(10% OF 8% TAX ON AGR)	-2.33%	-5.85%	0.68%	1.86%		
STATE OF SOUTH DAKOTA % INCREASE					$5,025,549.16	
SD TOURISM **	$1,402,961.32	$1,329,315.10	$1,356,005.15	$1,376,504.99	$7,142,926.81	
(40% OF 8% TAX ON AGR)	-16.40%	-5.25%	2.01%	1.51%		
STATE HISTORICAL PRESERVATION ** ($100,000 ANNUALLY)	$100,000.00	$100,000.00	$100,000.00	$100,000.00	$500,000.00	
CITY OF DEADWOOD	$6,112,167.06	$6,321,341.44	$6,336,470.98	$5,912,053.43	$53,946,531.77	
(COMM FUND - OPER. COSTS)	-0.96%	3.42%	0.24%	-6.70%		
TOTAL TO LOCAL GOVERNMENTS:	$7,970,083.61	$8,084,840.38	$8,128,923.80	$7,731,254.95	$69,603,097.70	
% OF TOTAL COMM FUND REV:	89.59%	89.55%	88.67%	88.09%	87.72%	

NOTE: THIS REPORT IS FOR INFORMATIONAL PURPOSES ONLY. DUE TO TIMING DEFERENCES, THERE ARE ADJUSTMENTS NECESSARY TO PROVIDE MEANINGFUL CASH FLOW STATEMENTS FOR THE COMMISSION FUND.

Source: *Annual Report Fiscal Year 1999*, South Dakota Commission on Gaming, Pierre, SD, 1999

ity of these employees (84 percent) worked full-time; 8 percent worked part-time (Figure 5.3).

PROMOTING GAMBLING

The largest expenditure for any casino is the cost of promoting itself. These outlays include direct advertising and promotion, as well as the junket and complimentary expenses (which can include free airline tickets, lodging, food, and drinks). Complimentary flights and rooms offered to preferred customers, the so-called "high-rollers," usually account for about 10 to 15 percent of the larger hotels' budgets.

Junkets, where a hotel/casino offers complimentary transportation, room, food, and drinks to groups of eight or more people, can be very risky for the casino, as each customer must gamble at least $2,500 in order for the hotel to cover the costs of accommodating the junketeers. Both junketeers and complimentary visitors who do not gamble enough to provide the hotel with a profit are usually not invited to return.

In order to get and hold the high-rollers, or "whales," as the very top tier of gamblers is called, many casinos are introducing private luxury suites, often furnished with original artwork by such mas-

ters as Renoir, Cezanne, and Picasso. "Whales" typically bet $100,000 to $250,000 to $1,000,000 per visit. Other incentives are special programs similar to the airline mileage programs. Individuals who bet large amounts of money for at least 3 to 4 hours a day can earn complimentary benefits ranging from free rooms and meals to the best seat in the house at a show, free air travel, and, for the really high rollers, a private jet to bring them to the casinos. It all depends on how much and how long the person gambles.

RECREATING THE OLD WEST

South Dakota

As many areas of the Midwest and West began to suffer from a changing and often declining economy, some states and localities looked for alternative ways to raise money and attract tourists. The voters of South Dakota approved casino gambling in the historic town of Deadwood, where Wild Bill Hickock was killed. Almost all of the town's gambling houses are located in buildings that date from the late 1800s or early 1900s. In fact, the town of Deadwood has been designated as a National Historical Landmark.

The town has been transformed into a gambling center, but the town's citizens now debate whether gambling will have to grow in order to remain successful. Currently, there can be no more than 30 slot machines in a single building, and a single business can have no more than 90 machines. The betting limit is $5.

Many residents prefer the quaint nature of the town, especially since much of the town's revenues from gambling have been used to restore the older, formerly rundown buildings. Gambling interests have tried to increase the number of machines permitted in each establishment, but Governor William Janklow vetoed the proposed bill in 1997. The major drive behind the proposed increases

FIGURE 5.4

"What are your own personal views of casino gambling?"

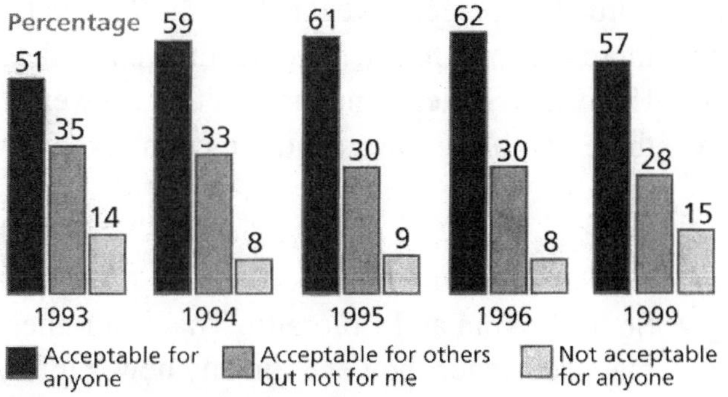

Among those expressing an opinion, only a small fraction of the U.S. population believes casino gambling is not acceptable for anyone.
Source: Hart/Luntz

Source: *State of the States: The AGA Survey of Casino Entertainment*, American Gaming Association, Washington, DC, 1999

was the 1997 construction, by actor Kevin Costner and his brother, of a 635-acre, 320-room resort just outside town. The Costner brothers already run a casino in Deadwood.

While promoters of casino gambling expected gamblers to bet around $4 million in Deadwood the first year, bettors wagered over $145 million in 1990. This figure more than doubled to $330 million in 1991 and has increased ever since, reaching $498 million in 1999.

Meanwhile, revenues for the South Dakota gambling casinos rose from $14.3 million in 1990 to $33 million in 1991 and $42.9 million in 1999. However, there was some decrease in revenues from 1996 to 1997. Figures for 1998 and 1999 increased slightly (Table 5.11). The government collected an 8 percent tax on the revenues. About 9 of 10 dollars are produced by the slot machines, mainly the $0.25 machines. Of the $7.7 million distributed to local governments, the City of Deadwood got about $5.9 million, and the South Dakota Department of Tourism received about $1.4 million. (See Table 5.11.)

Colorado

In Colorado, the casinos in the historic mining towns of Central City, Black Hawk, and Cripple Creek have already gone through a shakeout. The number of casinos peaked at 75 in September of 1992. Since then the number has dropped slowly but steadily, reaching 49 as of October 1, 1998.

Single bets in both South Dakota and Colorado are limited to $5, but at $5 a throw, large amounts of money can still be lost rather quickly. In 1999, gamblers in the 49 casinos wagered $475 million, far more than the $244.2 million bet at 67 casinos in 1993 and the $307.6 million bet at 61 casinos in 1994. The number of gambling devices increased from 10,567 in 1993, to 13,376 in 1998.

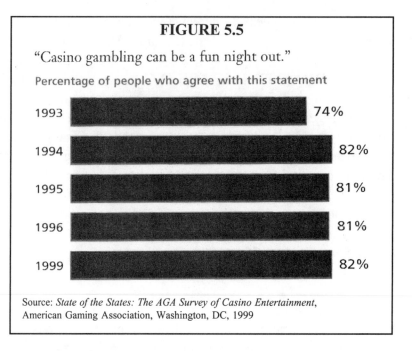

FIGURE 5.5

"Casino gambling can be a fun night out."

Percentage of people who agree with this statement

Year	Percentage
1993	74%
1994	82%
1995	81%
1996	81%
1999	82%

Source: *State of the States: The AGA Survey of Casino Entertainment,* American Gaming Association, Washington, DC, 1999

In 1998, Black Hawk had 18 casinos producing $270 million in revenues, Central City had 11 casinos making $91.9 million in revenues, and Cripple Creek had 20 casinos earning $113 million in revenues. Fewer casinos are producing more money. Some of the money earned from the casinos is used to restore some of the dilapidated buildings in these former mining towns.

The State of Colorado taxes 2 percent of the first $2 million, 4 percent from $2 to $4 million, 14 percent from $4 to $5 million, 18 percent from $5 to $10 million, and 20 percent thereafter. In 1998, the state collected $58.9 million, up from only $13.5 million in 1992. Approximately one-third (36.6 percent) went to the State General Fund, more than one-fourth (28 percent) went to the State Historical Society, and most of the rest went to the three gambling towns and the counties they were in.

Some turnover has occurred in the casinos in South Dakota and Colorado. This is a rather normal occurrence, however, in any new, rapidly expanding area of business in which large numbers of entrepreneurs, many of them inexperienced, scramble for a piece of the action. Nonetheless, there is little question that gambling is here to stay in the historic mining towns.

CARD ROOMS

Card rooms are small gambling parlors where individuals can play cards, usually poker and blackjack, with other people for money. The parlor usually earns its revenues by charging the players for every hour or every hand they play. Currently, card rooms are legal, although not necessarily operative, in 13 states. Public card rooms have been legal in California since the Gold Rush days. While card games have always been part of the state's western tradition, the passing of Proposition 13 limiting property taxes left many cities and counties in difficult financial straits. As a result, cities like Bell Gardens, Commerce, and Huntington Park legalized card clubs in an effort to raise revenue. Nonetheless, in recent voting, about half the California communities considering the introduction of card rooms voted them down.

Eugene Martin Christiansen and Will E. Cummings, in "The Gross Annual Wager of the United States, 1997" (*International Gaming and Wagering Business,* August, 1998), reported that betting in card rooms has increased tenfold from an estimated $1 billion in 1982 to an estimated $10.4 billion in 1997. Well over 90 percent of this amount was bet in California. Over the same period, revenues grew from $50 million to $700.2 million. (Figures for card rooms are only estimates, since these rooms are privately owned and need not report their earnings.)

Christiansen and Cummings report that at least 229 card rooms, and perhaps as many as 330, with at least 2,164 tables, are currently operating in California. Traditionally, card clubs have been small establishments, often with only one or two tables. Only 13 clubs have 26 or more tables. Some of the more recently developed clubs, however, have been considerably larger. The largest card clubs in California are the Commerce Club in Commerce with 223 tables, the Bicycle Club in Bell Gardens with 180 tables, and the Hollywood Park

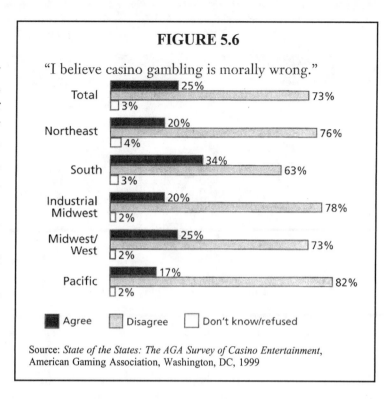

FIGURE 5.6

"I believe casino gambling is morally wrong."

Region	Agree	Disagree	Don't know/refused
Total	25%	73%	3%
Northeast	20%	76%	4%
South	34%	63%	3%
Industrial Midwest	20%	78%	2%
Midwest/West	25%	73%	2%
Pacific	17%	82%	2%

Source: *State of the States: The AGA Survey of Casino Entertainment,* American Gaming Association, Washington, DC, 1999

Casino with 140 tables. About 42 percent of all card tables are in Los Angeles County.

Card clubs in California, Las Vegas, and Atlantic City, got a boost from the introduction of games of Asian origin, often called the "Asian Games." Games such as Pai Gow and Super Pan Nine are much faster and, for many people, more exciting. With the introduction of these games, more people have begun visiting these card rooms and giving the industry a real boost.

The State of Washington has more than 80 clubs and limits wagers to $10 per bet. Montana has over 50 small clubs and limits the action to $300 per pot. North Dakota has about 20 clubs, with most of the proceeds going to charity. While these small clubs provide a source of revenue for the operators, they also provide a social setting for the players. The players may know each other and consider playing poker a form of recreation and a chance to get together with friends and acquaintances. Players know there will always be a game going on at the local card room. Oregon permits "social gambling" — small-stakes poker and blackjack — in taverns and bars. Card rooms can also be found in Deadwood, South Dakota, and in Central City, Black Hawk, and Cripple Creek, Colo-

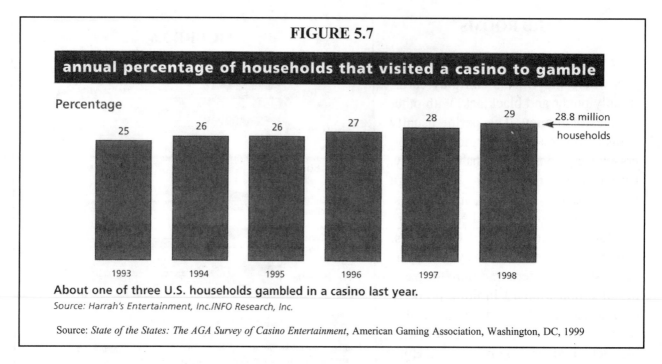

FIGURE 5.7

annual percentage of households that visited a casino to gamble

Percentage

28.8 million
households

1993	1994	1995	1996	1997	1998
25	26	26	27	28	29

About one of three U.S. households gambled in a casino last year.

Source: *Harrah's Entertainment, Inc./INFO Research, Inc.*

Source: *State of the States: The AGA Survey of Casino Entertainment*, American Gaming Association, Washington, DC, 1999

rado. Card rooms are now legal in Florida as well. In 1996, the Florida House passed Bill 337 authorizing card rooms at licensed pari-mutuel facilities beginning January 1, 1998.

While card tables are available in Nevada and Atlantic City, casino operators do not see them as very profitable. In Nevada, the house take is limited to about 2.5 percent of the pot. Consequently, the per-square-foot income does not come near the output of other types of gambling. As a result, the casinos in Las Vegas have only about 300 tables, and there are only about 500 tables in all of Nevada. Generally, the big casinos see card games as a method of attracting gamblers to other games.

NON-CASINO DEVICES

Eugene Christiansen and Will Cummings (see above) reported that, in Louisiana, an estimated 16,239 video gambling devices have been placed in restaurants and other retail establishments throughout the state. These video games may be poker, keno, or dozens of other possible games, although the games are often referred to generally as "video poker machines." In Louisiana, until recently, for example, to play a legal non-casino device, the bettor inserted $0.25, $1, $5, or $10, up to a maximum of $200, with a maximum payout of $500. If the player won, the machine printed out a ticket that could be cashed in at a nearby bar or grill.

Non-casino gambling devices did about $1.7 billion in sales in 1997. Not including Nevada and Maryland, there were 64,600 non-casino gambling devices in the United States in 1997. Montana accounted for 18,000 machines and South Carolina for 34,000. These machines have led to the creation of mini-casinos in Louisiana, Montana, South Carolina, and Maryland, mainly at truck stops and restaurants.

While returns have been considerable, many observers have expressed concern about the allegedly addictive nature of these machines. In Louisiana, it is also suspected that earnings from such machines have been used to influence politicians. Furthermore, a recent scandal concerning organized crime has further tainted the Louisiana devices. Members of the Gambino and Genovese crime families have been accused of conspiring with members of two suppliers of video poker games to skim profits from the devices. In July 1999, Louisiana shut down 4,874 of the state's 15,000 poker machines, and banned them in 33 of the state's 64 parishes (counties).

In October 1999, the South Carolina Supreme Court ruled that all the 34,000 video poker machines in the state would be unplugged by midnight June 30, 2000. The issue pitted the gambling industry against much of the public, which did not want the machines. Some church groups even referred to the machines as the crack cocaine of gambling because they are allegedly so addictive. The state's business community and many politicians also favored closing down the industry.

A GENERALLY
POPULAR ALTERNATIVE

In only a few short years, casino gambling has spread from two states to the point where it has been approved, in some form, in a total of 24 states. (This does not include gambling on Indian reservations, which is discussed in Chapter VII.) With the adoption of lotteries by the vast majority of states, the inhibitions often tied with gambling have been dropping — after all, if the state government urges that a person gamble, how bad can it be?

In addition, increasing financial demands on state and local governments, coupled with a strong voter resistance to increased taxes and, in some areas, a declining economy, have forced them to look for other alternatives to raising money. Like lotteries, casino gambling has been seen as a painless way of raising money, a "fun" or a "voluntary" form of taxation.

But Some Have Turned It Down

That does not mean that every state or locality has supported casino gambling. Floridians have periodically voted casino gambling down, but it will likely return to the ballot. Casino supporters in Arkansas saw their proposal defeated. Alaskans rejected casino gambling by a margin of almost 2 to 1, while Ohio voters also refused casino gambling by a similar proportion. Chicago decided against casino gambling, although riverboats from neighboring Indiana fulfill some Chicagoans' desire to gamble.

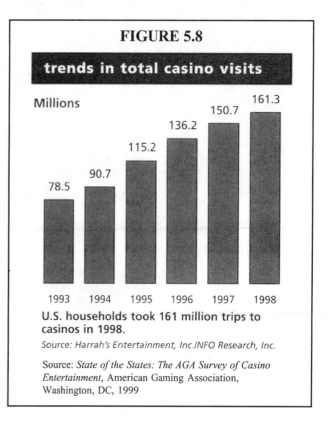

FIGURE 5.8

trends in total casino visits

Millions

Year	Visits
1993	78.5
1994	90.7
1995	115.2
1996	136.2
1997	150.7
1998	161.3

U.S. households took 161 million trips to casinos in 1998.

Source: Harrah's Entertainment, Inc./NFO Research, Inc.

Source: *State of the States: The AGA Survey of Casino Entertainment*, American Gaming Association, Washington, DC, 1999

Nonetheless, for many states and localities, casino gambling is considered a way to reverse economic decline and raise revenue. From an economic standpoint, the expansion of the opportunity to introduce casino gambling is seen as a growing business opportunity. Those in the gambling business believe there is a large, unmet demand for casino gambling throughout the United States. The successes of gambling in South Dakota and Colorado, of riverboat gambling on the Mississippi and other waterways, at Ledyard in Connecticut, in casinos on Native American reservations throughout the country, and the increases in casino gambling on cruise ships would seem to indicate they are right. Like any other business, gambling will continue to grow until the needs of the consumer are met. It may be some time before that need is completely filled.

THE AMERICAN GAMING
ASSOCIATION'S SURVEY OF
CASINO ENTERTAINMENT

The American Gaming Association (AGA), an industry trade group, published the first annual *State of the States: The AGA Survey of Casino*

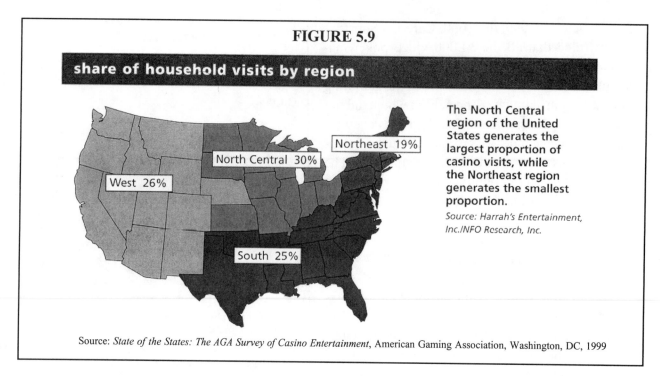

FIGURE 5.9

share of household visits by region

North Central 30%

West 26%

Northeast 19%

South 25%

The North Central region of the United States generates the largest proportion of casino visits, while the Northeast region generates the smallest proportion.

Source: Harrah's Entertainment, Inc./NFO Research, Inc.

Source: *State of the States: The AGA Survey of Casino Entertainment*, American Gaming Association, Washington, DC, 1999

Entertainment in 1999. The survey is modeled after the longtime Harrah's surveys of U.S. casino gaming entertainment and gathers information from a number of sources, including Harrah's Entertainment, Inc., Christiansen Capital Advisors, Peter D. Hart Research Associates, Inc./The Luntz Research Companies, and The Evans Group, in addition to information from state gaming commissions. More than 80,000 people were polled, and the findings for the AGA survey are based on their responses.

General Acceptance of Casino Gambling

The *AGA Survey* found that the public generally accepted casino gambling. In 1999, about 57 percent of all those questioned thought casino gambling was "acceptable for anyone," while 28 percent believed it was "acceptable for others, but not for me." Only 15 percent thought casino gambling was "not acceptable for anyone." (See Figure 5.4.)

The general acceptance of gambling has been increasing rapidly. In 1992, 39 percent said they "would favor the introduction of casino gaming in many local communities because of its benefits to the local economy"; by 1999, 52 percent would. Three of five (59 percent) of those asked thought

"legalized casino gaming brings money into a local economy without hurting existing business." A large majority (73 percent) thought "a casino can be an important part of a community's entertainment and tourism offering." Even more people (82 percent) believed "casino gaming can be a fun night out." (See Figure 5.5.)

About three-fourths (73 percent) disagreed with the sentence, "I believe casino gambling is morally wrong." One-fourth (25 percent) agreed that casino gambling was morally wrong. More people living in the South (34 percent) agreed that casino gambling was wrong than those living in any other section of the country. (See Figure 5.6.)

Not surprisingly, with the increased availability of casino gambling, more people have visited casinos. *AGA's Survey* found that people from about 29 percent of U.S. households had gambled at a casino at some time during 1998 (Figure 5.7), up dramatically from 17 percent in 1990.

These people had made an estimated 161 million trips to casinos in 1998 (Figure 5.8). A lot of the increase was attributable to the new casino destinations. The largest proportion (30 percent) of casino visits was made by people in the north central portion of the country; the smallest proportion (19 percent) from people in the Northeast. (See Figure 5.9.) While 70 million trips were made to either Nevada or Atlantic City, 106 million were made to the new casino destinations. Again, reflecting the increased availability of gambling, the number of trips to the casino made by each casino household rose from 3.3 per year in 1993 to 5.6 per year in 1998 (Figure 5.10).

Demographics

According to the *AGA Survey*, there was not much difference in demographic information between the typical gambling household and other households. The biggest variation was in the earnings of the typical casino-gambling household ($46,000) and the general household ($39,000). Another difference was that the average casino customer (45 percent) was more likely than the average American (40 percent) to hold a white-collar job. (See Figure 5.11.)

CASINOS AROUND THE WORLD

Casino gambling is very common around the world. The casinos in Monte Carlo are probably the most famous. Although there are four casinos in Monte Carlo, the elegant Casino of Monte Carlo is almost certainly the most well-known. There are 12 casinos in Austria and eight in Belgium. France has more than 150 casinos, many of them as beautiful as the Casino of Monte Carlo, and many are located in such exotic places as Biarritz and Cannes. Until 1996, French casinos were restricted to small towns. Starting in 1997, they may be established in tourist cities with populations of over 500,000.

Many of Germany's 48 casinos are located in spas, probably the most famous of which is the luxurious casino at Baden-Baden. The more than 115 casinos in the United Kingdom are called "private clubs." Portugal has 8 casinos. Spain has 26 casinos, and several autonomous regions in Spain are beginning to act on their own authority to establish more casinos.

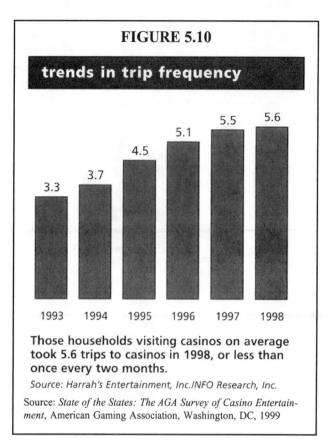

FIGURE 5.10

trends in trip frequency

1993	1994	1995	1996	1997	1998
3.3	3.7	4.5	5.1	5.5	5.6

Those households visiting casinos on average took 5.6 trips to casinos in 1998, or less than once every two months.

Source: Harrah's Entertainment, Inc./INFO Research, Inc.

Source: *State of the States: The AGA Survey of Casino Entertainment*, American Gaming Association, Washington, DC, 1999

In April 1998, four new casino licenses were granted in Gauteng Province (Johannesburg) in South Africa. The four licenses will account for more than 4,000 slot machines and 160 table games in temporary casinos, increasing to 5,700 slots and 220 tables at the four permanent facilities. The licenses were awarded to Sun International; London Clubs International; MGM Grand, Inc.'s Tsogo Sun Gaming and Entertainment; and Caesars World, Inc. Most of the developers plan to have temporary casinos up in 1999 and permanent facilities in 2000.

In the Caribbean, people may gamble at the hotel casinos of Puerto Rico or Aruba. Almost all tourists who fly to the Bahamas visit that country's casinos, and Sun International Hotels plans to build a new casino on Paradise Island in the Bahamas.

Latin America has a fairly healthy gambling market, but problems exist due to a lack of coordination among countries. Regulations that apply in one country do not necessarily apply in another. Furthermore, within a specific country, regulations

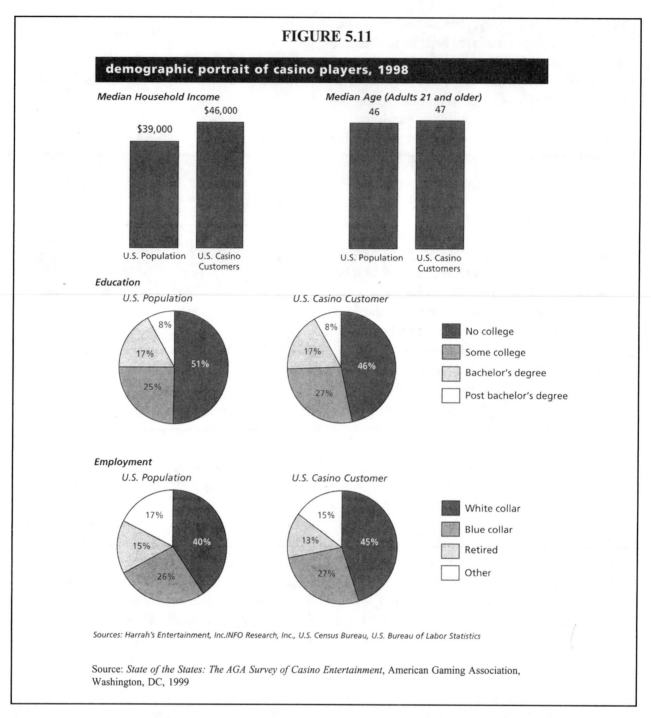

FIGURE 5.11

demographic portrait of casino players, 1998

Median Household Income

$39,000 — U.S. Population

$46,000 — U.S. Casino Customers

Median Age (Adults 21 and older)

46 — U.S. Population

47 — U.S. Casino Customers

Education

U.S. Population

8%
17%
51%
25%

U.S. Casino Customer

8%
17%
46%
27%

- No college
- Some college
- Bachelor's degree
- Post bachelor's degree

Employment

U.S. Population

17%
15%
40%
26%

U.S. Casino Customer

15%
13%
45%
27%

- White collar
- Blue collar
- Retired
- Other

Sources: Harrah's Entertainment, Inc.INFO Research, Inc., U.S. Census Bureau, U.S. Bureau of Labor Statistics

Source: *State of the States: The AGA Survey of Casino Entertainment*, American Gaming Association, Washington, DC, 1999

may vary from state to state and within each state from town to town. Therefore, two new gaming organizations have joined forces to share information in order to coordinate the Latin American markets. The Latin American Gaming Association (Asociaciún Latinoamericana de Juegos de Azar; ALAJA) and the Institute for International Research S.A., both based in Buenos Aires, Argentina, met in October 1999. Their goals include, but are not limited to, improving the gambling sector's image, establishing a code of conduct for gambling operators, and creating institutes to train gambling and lottery personnel.

In April 2000, Halifax, Nova Scotia, Canada, will become host to the new 140,000-square-foot Halifax Casino. The casino was financed, built, and will be operated by Caesars World. The 32,900-square-foot gaming floor will offer 39 table games and 650 slot machines.

Like many late twentieth-century industries, the gambling business has become international. A casino opening up in Cambodia or Australia might receive financial investment from, or even be owned by, an American or European gambling corporation. A new casino opening in Great Britain might involve investment money from Singapore or Hong Kong. The leading gambling companies like Harrah's, Caesars (which is owned by ITT Corp.), and Mirage are international corporations whose interests now extend far beyond America's shores.

CHAPTER VI

CASINO GAMBLING — ON THE WATER

Once baseball was considered America's favorite pastime. Nothing could beat the crack of the bat, the smell of a hot dog.... But that's changing. These days people are more into the clank of quarters dropping in slot machines and the thrill of drawing a royal flush or four-of-a-kind. — *Knight-Ridder Newspapers,* November 20, 1994

RIVERBOAT GAMBLING

Many states that forbid casino gambling on dry land take a more liberal view of gambling on water, as if, by putting gambling on the water, it somehow separates the state from any problems that might be associated with gambling. On April 1, 1991, the State of Iowa brought back riverboat gambling to the Mississippi River. Since then five more states (Missouri, Illinois, Indiana, Mississippi, and Louisiana) have passed laws permitting riverboat casinos. In 1998, 90 vessels were operating in six states and producing more than $6 billion in revenues.

The growth in riverboats, however, has slowed, and no additional state has introduced riverboat gambling since 1993. In fact, the industry suffered major defeats in two potentially lucrative markets, Philadelphia and Chicago. Proposals in Alabama, Kentucky, Massachusetts, Ohio, South Carolina, Texas, Maryland, Virginia, and West Virginia died. On the other hand, existing facilities are being expanded and developed to make them more attractive to visitors. The next few years are likely to be a shakeout period, as weaker companies either succumb or are bought out by the larger players, many of whom have come from either Las Vegas or Atlantic City.

Often More a Barge Than a Riverboat

Most riverboats range in size from 200 to 300 feet long and 45 to 95 feet wide. The *President,* sailing out of Davenport, Iowa, is 300 feet long, has a 27,000-square foot casino, 700 slot machines, and 30 gaming tables. The smaller *Par-A-Dice* out of Peoria, Illinois, is 228 feet long, has 12,500 square feet of casino space with 478 slot machines and 40 tables. The *Casino Queen* out of East St. Louis offers 896 slot machines and 62 tables, while Harrah's *Vicksburg* has 525 slot machines and 38 tables.

Not all the riverboats must be seaworthy. Illinois demands that the riverboats cruise in the rivers, while Missouri and Louisiana require the ships to cruise an ill-defined "certain extent." Mississippi does not require the ships to sail; in fact, many of the ships docked in Mississippi are not really capable of sailing — they are giant buildings constructed on barges. Mirage Resort subsidiary Golden Nugget's $650 million casino resort in Biloxi makes few pretenses to seaworthiness. Barry Shier, president of Golden Nugget, observed, "We don't consider this to be a riverboat project. We consider this to be a major resort destination." When the complex opened in March 1999, the Beau Rivage Hotel adjoining the "riverboat" boasted

TABLE 6.1
ALL IOWA EXCURSION BOAT TOTALS

	1997	1998
Admissions	12,226,277	12,523,215
Slot Drop	$1,075,899,358	$1,339,553,185
Coin In	$5,530,187,830	$6,558,673,012
Slot Revenue	$346,055,831	$399,638,801
Table Drop	$444,074,455	$443,665,837
Table Revenue	$95,847,145	$96,376,503
Adjusted Gross Revenue	$441,902,976	$496,015,304
Tax to City	$2,209,514	$2,480,075
Tax to County	$2,209,514	$2,480,075
Tax to Gambler's Treatment	$1,325,707	$1,488,047
Tax to General Fund (Gaming)	$79,485,853	$89,604,864
Admission Fee	$2,526,930	$2,693,970

Source: *1998 Annual Report of the Iowa Racing and Gaming Commission*, Des Moines, IA, December 31, 1998

1,780 rooms, making it the largest hotel in the state. At 364 feet in height, it is the tallest building in Mississippi.

Iowa

When Iowa introduced riverboat gambling, individual bets were limited to $5, and betting losses on the Iowa riverboats were limited to $200 per cruise. The gambler bought up to $200 worth of scrip before getting on board. When the bettor got on board, he could then change the scrip into tokens or chips for gambling. If a player took four cruises in one day, he could lose up to $800. If someone simply wanted to enjoy a brief cruise on the Mississippi and not bet money, he or she could usually buy a cruise-only ticket for $10 or less. The $200 limit, however, led many riverboat casinos to sail for more profitable shores. For example, the *Diamond Lady* and the *Emerald Lady* steamed to Mississippi, and some observers feared for the future of riverboat gambling in Iowa if the limit were maintained.

Consequently, the Iowa legislature removed betting and loss limits, restrictions on space on the riverboat devoted to gambling, and requirements that the boat actually cruise. As a result, the total revenues, which had tumbled from $69.9 million in 1992 to $45.5 million in 1993, rose sharply to $104.9 million in 1994 and reached $496 million in 1998. Most (81 percent) of the revenues were produced by slot machines.

Gambling revenues in Iowa are taxed on the basis of 5 percent for the first $1,000,000, 10 percent for the next $2,000,000, and 20 percent thereafter. This tax is distributed 2 percent each to the city and county, 1.3 percent to Gambler's Assistance (intended to help compulsive gamblers), and the remainder to the state general fund. In 1998, the State of Iowa received $89.6 million, while the cities and counties each got $2.5 million and Gambler's Assistance received $1.5 million. (See Table 6.1.) Ten boats were operating in Iowa in 1998.

TABLE 6.2

Illinois Five-Year Summary

	1994	1995	1996	1997	1998
No. of Licensees	10	10	10	10	* 10
AGR	$979,551,111	$1,178,311,827	$1,131,491,531	$1,054,573,793	$1,106,751,600
Table Games	$334,304,445	$368,380,581	$322,007,802	$275,399,950	$260,038,232
EGD	$645,246,666	$809,931,246	$809,483,729	$779,173,843	$846,713,368
Patrons	N/A	14,787,836	14,075,884	13,274,264	13,327,477
AGR Per Patron	N/A	$79.68	$80.39	$70.44	$83.04
Admissions	20,367,119	24,835,833	25,211,329	24,972,139	24,813,818
AGR Per Adm	$48.09	$47.44	$44.88	$42.23	$44.60
Total Tax	$236,644,461	$285,334,031	$276,720,964	$260,859,037	$336,899,568
Wagering Tax	$195,910,223	$235,662,365	$226,298,306	$210,914,759	$287,271,932
Admissions Tax	$40,734,238	$49,671,666	$50,422,658	$49,944,278	$49,627,636
State Share	$167,299,786	$201,582,607	$194,935,059	$183,158,208	$256,782,080
Local Share	$69,344,675	$83,751,424	$81,785,905	$77,700,829	$80,117,488

Jo Daviess Silver Eagle ceased operations July 29, 1997.

Source: *1998 Annual Report*, Illinois Gaming Board, Springfield, IL, no date

Nonetheless, although gambling seems to have recovered in Iowa, the state's cities are being more careful this time around. Earlier, when profits did not develop because of the gambling limit, the riverboats were quick to sail off and leave many communities high and dry. This time, many of the communities are demanding that the gambling companies develop the land around the riverboat to include hotels and restaurants. Such development would make it harder for the boat owners to lift anchor and sail away if revenues decline.

Illinois

Meanwhile, across the river in Illinois, gamblers have had the opportunity to bet without limit. Illinois believed that gamblers would come to their state instead of Iowa because of this policy. They were correct, and gamblers continued to visit the Illinois riverboats even after Iowa had lifted its limits on gambling. Nonetheless, the *Silver Eagle* in East Dubuque closed because of the increased competition from across the river.

In 1998, 13.3 million people visited the state's riverboats, down from 14.8 million in 1995. Gross receipts fell from $1.2 billion in 1995 to $1.1 billion in 1996, 1997, and 1998. In 1998, the casinos earned about $45 for every visitor. About $336.9 million was collected in tax revenues. The state received $256.8 million and the local communities, $80 million. (See Table 6.2.) Ten boats were operating in 1998.

Missouri

Missouri, located across the river from Illinois, was the fifth state to introduce riverboat gambling. By June 1999, 13 vessels were operating. For the fiscal year ending June 30, 1999, adjusted gross receipts totaled $898 million, and there were 40.8 million paid admission fees to gamble on the riverboats. The total gambling tax amounted to $179.6 million — $161.6 million was the state's portion, and $18 million remained locally. (See Table 6.3.)

TABLE 6.3

Fiscal Year 1999 Project Summary

BOAT NAME LOCATION	LICENSE DATE	FY 1999 ADMISSIONS	ADMISSION FEES	ADMISSION FEE STATE & LOCAL PORTION**	ADJUSTED GROSS RECEIPTS	GAMING TAX	GAMING TAX LOCAL PORTION	GAMING TAX STATE PORTION	ESTIMATED CAPITAL INVESTMENT***	EMPLOYEES	TABLE GAMES	ELECTRONIC GAMING DEVICES	GAMING POSITIONS	GAMING SPACE (SQ FT)
ADMIRAL ST. LOUIS	27-May-94	3,125,669	6,251,338	3,125,669	59,253,097	11,850,619	1,185,062	10,665,557	63,300,000	788	59	1,230	1,422	58,000
CASINO ST. CHARLES I & II ST. CHARLES	27-May-94 28-Dec-94	4,779,516	9,559,032	4,779,516	111,379,893	22,275,979	2,227,598	20,048,381	166,000,000	1,296	62	1,986	2,107	47,000
ARGOSY RIVERSIDE CASINO RIVERSIDE	22-Jun-94	3,425,104	6,850,208	3,425,104	77,390,591	15,478,118	1,547,812	13,930,306	87,748,690	769	39	1,064	1,173	30,000
ST. JO FRONTIER CASINO ST. JOSEPH	24-Jun-94	924,300	1,848,600	924,300	20,105,239	4,021,048	402,105	3,618,943	25,008,000	323	18	466	519	18,000
NORTH STAR & MARDI GRAS NORTH KANSAS CITY	22-Sep-94 15-May-96	6,515,864	13,031,728	6,515,864	169,067,703	33,813,541	3,381,354	30,432,187	172,649,000	2,095	76	2,174	2,387	61,600
CASINO AZTAR CARUTHERSVILLE	27-Apr-95	624,945	1,249,890	624,945	21,527,134	4,305,427	430,543	3,874,884	57,849,000	419	23	634	701	10,400
SAMS TOWN KANSAS CITY	13-Sep-95	39,299	78,598	39,299	635,836	127,167	12,717	114,450	n/a	n/a	n/a	n/a	n/a	n/a
FLAMINGO HILTON KANSAS CITY	18-Oct-96	3,564,558	7,129,116	3,564,558	66,211,268	13,242,254	1,324,225	11,918,028	119,800,000	856	44	1,029	1,166	30,000
RIVER KING & QUEEN KANSAS CITY	16-Jan-97	7,883,179	15,766,358	7,883,179	162,671,060	32,534,212	3,253,421	29,280,791	303,000,000	2,224	146	3,317	3,785	140,000
PLAYERS ISLAND														
KOKOMO & GRAND CAYMEN MARYLAND HEIGHTS	11-Mar-97	4,716,520	9,433,040	4,716,520	96,583,305	19,316,661	1,931,666	17,384,995	134,716,323	864	48	1,586	1,697	52,000
MARDI GRAS & EASY STREET MARYLAND HEIGHTS	11-Mar-97	5,189,475	10,378,950	5,189,475	113,190,577	22,638,115	2,263,812	20,374,304	143,334,204	1,147	49	1,671	1,779	52,000
GRAND TOTALS:		40,788,429	81,576,858	40,788,429	898,015,703	179,603,141	17,960,314	161,642,827	1,273,405,217	10,781	564	15,157	16,736	499,000

** Amount of admission fees paid to each entity.

*** Formulas used by the Licensees to arrive at total capital investment vary.

The figures published in this report are subject to adjustment.

1) Boyd Gaming closed casino operations on July 15, 1998

Source: Kevin P. Mullally, *Annual Report to the General Assembly, Fiscal Year 1999*, Missouri Gaming Commission, Jefferson City, MO, no date

Just as Iowa had done earlier, and then rescinded, Missouri has set a limit to gambling losses. Bettors may lose no more than $500, a restriction that chafes the Missouri Gaming Commission, which

> finds that the $500 loss limit places Missouri riverboat gaming operations at a competitive disadvantage as opposed to similar operations in adjoining states. The net effect appears to be a significant decrease in state revenue.

In fact, the *Missouri Gaming Commission Annual Report 1999* includes an entire section showing "The Effect of the Loss Limit on Competitiveness." Not surprisingly, the section concluded that the cap on the amount that may be lost limits the return. Many Missouri gamblers are willing to travel to other states to gamble in a friendlier environment that will allow them to lose more money. Casual surveys of license plates on cars in parking lots of riverboat casinos in Illinois show this to be true. Moreover, Missouri riverboat operators are less likely to draw out-of-state customers because of the loss limit.

Mississippi

Farther down the river, Mississippi has promoted the development of riverboat gambling more than any other state. While most other states have tried to closely control the expansion of casino gambling, Mississippi has opened the state up to riverboats and let the free market decide which casinos will survive. By the end of 1999, 30 boats were operating.

Revenues from riverboat gambling have been increasing dramatically over the past few years, rising from $790 million in 1993 to $1.72 billion in 1995 and $2.1 billion in 1999. (See Table 6.4.) The state of Mississippi receives 8 percent of this total or about $168 million.

Concern has developed for the Gulf Coast casinos at Biloxi. As late as July 1994, revenues from the Gulf Coast counties exceeded those from the river counties. Since then, however, the river counties have produced increasingly more revenues (Table 6.4), while several casinos on the Gulf Coast have gone bankrupt. Some believe the shakeout was to be expected with over a dozen and a half casinos competing for gamblers' attention. In addition, the development of riverboat gambling in neighboring Louisiana probably has affected attendance. Observers hope that quality hotels, like the new Beau Rivage, a $650 million, 1,780-room hotel, casino, and marina on Biloxi Beach, will provide incentive for visitors to stay for more than a day.

Louisiana

Louisiana approved riverboat gambling in 1991. The law allows 15 riverboats on its 11 rivers and lakes. (As of December 1998, there were 13 riverboat casinos in the state.) While the law limits the number of riverboats per parish (county) to six, most of the riverboats sail out of New Orleans or nearby parishes. The New Orleans metropolitan area spreads out over Orleans, Jefferson, St. Tammany, and St. Bernard parishes, so it is possible that all 15 riverboats could serve the New Orleans region.

Many optimistic state political leaders and residents had hoped that riverboat gambling would turn around Louisiana's seriously ailing economy and perhaps transform New Orleans into the next Las Vegas. Unfortunately, after only two months of operation, the *Grand Palais* and *Crescent City Queen*, the two riverboats that made up the River City Complex in New Orleans, ceased operation because of poor performance in 1994 and eventually went bankrupt. This disappointment was compounded a year later by the bankruptcy of Harrah's Jazz Co., whose attempt to develop a land-based casino also foundered on poor revenues. (Harrah's opened a new casino in downtown New Orleans at the Tourist Center in October 1999.)

While the executives at Harrah's complained about inefficiency and corruption, it appears that

TABLE 6.4

MISSISSIPPI STATE TAX COMMISSION
MISCELLANEOUS TAX DIVISION
CASINO GROSS GAMING REVENUES

POST OFFICE BOX 1033
JACKSON, MS 39215
November 19, 1999

TELEPHONE: (601)923-7175
FAX: (601)923-7188
www.mstc.state.ms.us

MONTH	YEAR	GULF COAST COUNTIES	MISSISSIPPI RIVER COUNTIES	TOTALS
JANUARY	1999	$76,232,974.76	$116,429,342.01	$192,662,316.77
FEBRUARY		75,450,129.25	119,948,021.97	$195,398,151.22
MARCH		88,450,841.08	134,690,898.96	$223,141,740.04
APRIL		92,247,225.51	125,695,886.03	$217,943,111.54
MAY		87,642,275.45	121,089,605.97	$208,731,881.42
JUNE		85,839,372.97	127,998,367.50	$213,837,740.47
JULY		102,582,591.02	144,128,821.04	$246,711,412.06
AUGUST		87,351,834.16	130,772,218.29	$218,124,052.45
SEPTEMBER		88,374,078.94	118,736,305.13	$207,110,384.07
OCTOBER		86,552,177.28	120,134,786.77	206,686,964.05
NOVEMBER				
DECEMBER				
TOTALS 1999		$870,723,500.42	$1,259,624,253.67	$2,130,347,754.09
JANUARY	1998	$69,979,276.83	$113,324,733.85	$183,304,010.68
FEBRUARY		67,563,516.28	109,184,714.58	176,748,230.86
MARCH		74,530,958.92	119,543,407.96	194,074,366.88
APRIL		64,313,822.88	108,338,989.67	172,652,812.55
MAY		67,695,901.70	113,527,117.24	181,223,018.94
JUNE		68,127,833.32	110,705,452.53	178,833,285.85
JULY		77,962,369.95	129,843,215.72	207,805,585.67
AUGUST		73,636,474.29	122,271,082.56	195,907,556.85
SEPTEMBER		57,378,217.83	108,757,402.79	166,135,620.62
OCTOBER		59,682,649.85	112,046,006.71	171,728,656.56
NOVEMBER		65,715,501.25	111,568,554.37	177,284,055.62
DECEMBER		67,082,078.07	101,421,906.61	168,503,984.68
TOTALS 1998		$813,668,601.17	$1,360,532,584.59	$2,174,201,185.76
JANUARY	1997	$59,184,096.95	$91,805,085.04	$150,989,181.99
FEBRUARY		60,505,861.62	98,907,400.04	159,413,261.66
MARCH		65,818,688.10	110,713,231.46	176,531,919.56
APRIL		61,598,935.83	97,192,944.21	158,791,880.04
MAY		64,419,783.77	107,785,860.45	172,205,644.22
JUNE		64,162,328.21	104,944,736.44	169,107,064.65
JULY		68,506,249.08	104,952,518.55	173,458,767.63
AUGUST		70,580,030.23	112,360,855.89	182,940,886.12
SEPTEMBER		61,789,882.00	97,884,789.49	159,674,671.49
OCTOBER		62,697,913.69	100,265,064.57	162,962,978.26
NOVEMBER		59,929,657.50	103,822,608.05	163,752,265.55
DECEMBER		58,375,073.91	96,163,249.73	154,538,323.64
TOTALS 1997		$757,568,500.89	$1,226,798,343.92	$1,984,366,844.81
JANUARY	1996	$57,077,789.77	$84,052,770.69	$141,130,560.46
FEBRUARY		60,963,023.41	83,633,806.34	144,596,829.75
MARCH		69,349,125.68	104,634,959.51	173,984,085.19
APRIL		62,849,810.02	89,805,317.47	152,655,127.49
MAY		62,181,216.41	90,398,796.06	152,580,012.47
JUNE		63,232,689.51	90,176,186.82	153,408,876.33
JULY		70,608,566.44	101,228,611.98	171,837,178.42
AUGUST		66,249,144.24	96,420,866.94	162,670,011.18
SEPTEMBER		61,132,630.90	93,899,014.56	155,031,645.46
OCTOBER		57,962,553.89	93,139,661.80	151,102,215.69
NOVEMBER		59,505,894.82	94,295,404.16	153,801,298.98
DECEMBER		58,226,642.77	91,021,846.40	149,248,489.17
TOTALS 1996		$749,339,087.86	$1,112,707,242.73	$1,862,046,330.59
JANUARY	1995	$57,169,532.06	$76,323,989.57	$133,493,521.63
FEBRUARY		56,467,578.82	72,761,743.57	129,229,322.39
MARCH		62,368,506.62	80,836,898.95	143,205,405.57
APRIL		61,404,213.27	84,341,784.45	145,745,997.72
MAY		59,062,692.92	85,671,861.27	144,734,554.19
JUNE		58,613,777.34	80,215,782.97	138,829,560.31
JULY		70,565,494.28	98,268,060.31	168,833,554.59
AUGUST		59,724,279.79	84,759,463.33	144,483,743.12
SEPTEMBER		60,160,592.99	86,232,083.46	146,392,676.45

(continued)

TABLE 6.4 (Continued)

MISSISSIPPI STATE TAX COMMISSION
MISCELLANEOUS TAX DIVISION
CASINO GROSS GAMING REVENUES

POST OFFICE BOX 1033
JACKSON, MS 39215
November 19, 1999

TELEPHONE: (601)923-7175
FAX: (601)923-7188
www.mstc.state.ms.us

MONTH	YEAR	GULF COAST COUNTIES	MISSISSIPPI RIVER COUNTIES	TOTALS
OCTOBER		55,334,961.20	87,283,609.06	142,618,570.26
NOVEMBER		58,044,360.84	83,256,655.58	141,301,016.42
DECEMBER		57,100,563.49	88,374,519.77	145,475,083.26
TOTALS 1995		$716,016,553.62	$1,008,326,452.29	$1,724,343,005.91
JANUARY	1994	$53,322,302.81	$46,644,364.91	$99,966,667.72
FEBRUARY		58,170,877.18	48,207,480.72	106,378,357.90
MARCH		60,329,742.81	59,840,790.11	120,170,532.92
APRIL		64,221,626.70	56,862,105.90	121,083,732.60
MAY		66,784,833.35	58,015,781.54	124,800,614.89
JUNE		62,332,691.62	57,532,709.35	119,865,400.97
JULY		72,102,661.68	69,809,172.31	141,911,833.99
AUGUST		60,317,077.43	68,631,094.73	128,948,172.16
SEPTEMBER		61,470,651.01	66,869,527.80	128,340,178.81
OCTOBER		58,208,055.46	68,520,808.05	126,728,863.51
NOVEMBER		56,904,454.66	65,536,547.80	122,441,002.46
DECEMBER		53,161,725.90	68,997,562.00	122,159,287.90
TOTALS 1994		$727,326,700.61	$735,467,945.22	$1,462,794,645.83

MONTH	YEAR	GROSS REVENUE	MONTH	YEAR	GROSS REVENUE
JANUARY	1993	$40,118,994.77			
FEBRUARY		42,595,656.72			
MARCH		51,243,878.09			
APRIL		52,421,280.15			
MAY		58,752,131.66			
JUNE		61,396,051.85			
JULY		74,695,230.42			
AUGUST		78,017,867.75	AUGUST	1992	$10,616,710.10
SEPTEMBER		77,061,720.61	SEPTEMBER		18,455,071.10
OCTOBER		80,490,318.35	OCTOBER		26,987,123.62
NOVEMBER		82,836,509.43	NOVEMBER		32,427,489.77
DECEMBER		90,206,070.60	DECEMBER		33,321,575.70
TOTAL 1993		$789,835,710.40	TOTAL 1992		$121,807,970.29

NOTE: ALL NUMBERS ARE SUBJECT TO AMENDMENT DUE TO ADJUSTMENTS MADE FOR PRIOR PERIODS.

Source: Mississippi State Tax Commission, Jackson, MS, no date

there are just too many other things for tourists to do in New Orleans. New Orleans is one of the more unusual cities in the United States, and few visitors go there to gamble. Time is better spent walking around the French Quarter and enjoying the unique food and authentic American jazz. Finally, a recent video poker scandal involving the slot machine producer, Bally, did not benefit the image of gambling in a state with a long history of corruption.

Nonetheless, during the 1997-98 fiscal year, Louisiana casinos took in $1.27 billion, and the state collected $235.3 million in taxes. The big winners were the gambling establishments in the Texas-area markets of Shreveport, Bossier City, and Lake Charles.

OTHER PLACES TO GAMBLE ON THE WATER

Regular Cruises

A generation ago, if there was a casino on a cruise ship, the traveler had to make a determined effort to find it. Today, virtually all major cruise lines include gambling as an attraction for their passengers along with entertainment, dining, dancing, and shuffleboard. Growing competition in the cruise industry has made the money earned from casinos more important. The Carnival Cruise Lines' *Ecstasy*, a particularly large cruise ship, has 234 slots, 16 blackjack tables, 3 roulette wheels, 2 crap tables, and 3 Caribbean stud poker tables. The cruise lines emphasize that gambling is just one among many attractions. They further stress that they are a hospitality business, not a gambling business.

Virtually all cruise passengers are there to enjoy the cruise experience, not to gamble. As a result, most cruise ships have a limit of $100 to $200 in order to control losses. After all, a cruise passenger would not have a pleasant voyage if she or he lost huge amounts of money at the gaming tables. Eugene Christiansen and Will Cummings, in their "United States Gross Annual Wager, 1997" (*International Gaming and Wagering Business*, August 1998), estimated that cruise ship companies earned an estimated $244 million in 1997 in gross gambling revenue.

The cruise business has been expanding. In addition, federally mandated safety regulations that went into effect in 1997 will lead to many older ships being moved out of the American market and into other markets where the requirements are not as strict. Therefore, in order to handle the expected passenger growth and to replace older vessels, cruise ship companies have ordered 31 ships worth about $8.5 billion over the next several years. Virtually all of these ships will offer gambling facilities. Cruise operators believe that many cruise vacationers have never been exposed to casino gambling, so there is a significant opportunity for increased revenues in this area.

Cruises to Nowhere

"Cruises to nowhere" or "day trips" are gambling opportunities offered from several coastal ports in Florida, Georgia, Massachusetts, New York, South Carolina, and Texas. In order to create a day-cruise ship, the cruise company generally purchases an older, smaller cruise ship. Workers strip out the cabins and replace them with dining and dancing facilities and, of course, casinos. The ship travels three to nine miles into international waters, where neither state nor federal laws apply, and sails around for about six hours. A typical day-trip ship may make two or three trips a day. About a dozen ships operate out of Dade and Broward Counties in southern Florida.

With the exception of those out of Florida, day cruises have either failed or met with limited success. An estimated 23 cruise ships operate out of Florida where day-cruise trips have proven quite profitable. In Florida, the weather is more predictable and generally pleasant year-round, and there is already a large tourist base looking for something else to do, enabling the "day-cruise" industry to succeed. Should land-based casinos ever be introduced to South Florida, the day-trip industry would probably be devastated, but Florida voters have already voted down one casino initiative, and they do not appear likely to approve a casino initiative in the near future.

Until recently, attempts at developing a "cruise to nowhere" industry in other states have failed. In 1997, a casino ship — *Liberty I* — in Brooklyn, New York, offered short, offshore, daytime gambling cruises. However, the New York City government, leery of possible ties to organized crime, opposed the gambling cruise ship. Mayor (Rudy) Giuliani's administration set up several temporary roadblocks to halt the Bay Cruise Company from operating. These included forced employee background checks, charges of violating local zoning laws, and city tax requirements. Ultimately, New York City found a loophole in federal law to force day cruises to travel 12 miles out to sea before gambling could begin. In late 1997, the Bay Cruise Company was forced to close the city's first gambling vessel.

In December 1997, a Brooklyn federal district court restored the three-mile limit, bringing a great sigh of relief from all "cruise to nowhere" operators. In 1998, the 32,753-ton, 713-foot, 1,000-passenger *Edinburgh Castle* began to carry passengers out to the three-mile limit to gamble.

In the past five years, the day-cruise gambling industry has more than tripled, growing from 10 to 35 vessels. In 1997, the industry generated nearly $220 million in revenues, according to *International Gaming and Wagering Business* (August 1998). In addition to Florida and New York, ships are presently operating out of Georgia, South Carolina, Massachusetts, and Texas. Such cruises not only appeal to local consumers, but also permit modern casino entrepreneurs to enter the industry relatively inexpensively.

On the other hand, some state and local governments are not happy with the growth of this industry. Day-cruise casinos are unique in that they are the only form of gambling that does not need voter approval in order to operate. Some communities have fought the industry as New York City did when it tried to use a loophole in federal law to force day cruises to travel 12 miles out to sea.

In 1999, Rep. Frank Wolf (R-VA) proposed a congressional bill that would permit casino cruises only if states specifically allowed it. Currently, state approval is not required. In addition, in June 1999,

Florida's Governor Jeb Bush and the state cabinet voted not to renew state submergible land leases to day-cruise operators. The vote could evict 17 of the 23 day-cruise casinos in Florida from their berths. The governor and the cabinet also voted not to renew three dock leases designated to casino cruise ships.

The National Gambling Impact Commission Report, released in June 1999, sided with the individual states on the issue of day cruises to nowhere. The Commission recommended ... "gambling 'cruises to nowhere' should be prohibited unless the state from which the cruise originates adopts legislation specifically legalizing such cruises consistent with existing law."

CHAPTER VII

CASINO GAMBLING — NATIVE AMERICAN RESERVATIONS

As discussed in Chapter II, the Indian Gaming Regulatory Act of 1988 (IGRA; PL 100-497) permits Native American tribes to introduce gambling on their reservations. Many tribes had already been holding bingo games, but the new law opened up the possibility that other forms of gambling could be played on Native American lands. It also meant that the Native American tribes could play a major role in the large expansion of gambling throughout the country.

A NEW OPPORTUNITY

As returns from bingo — the major form of gambling on reservations — were beginning to level off, many Native American tribes recognized that casino games were being offered in more places throughout the United States. (See Chapter III.) They saw this as an opportunity to bring some prosperity to their reservations.

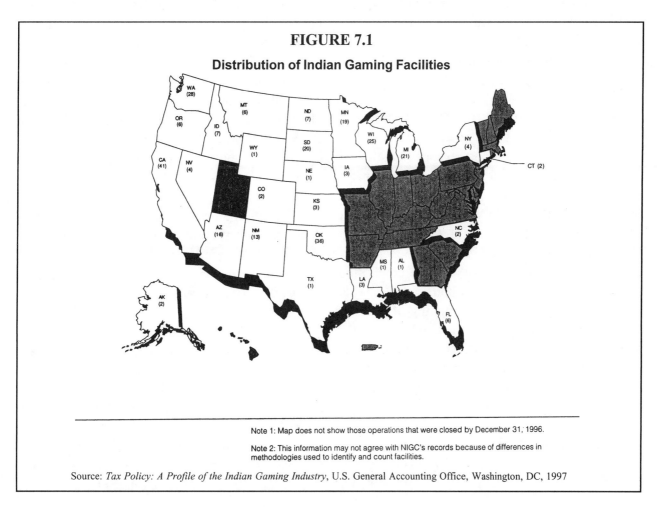

FIGURE 7.1

Distribution of Indian Gaming Facilities

Note 1: Map does not show those operations that were closed by December 31, 1996.

Note 2: This information may not agree with NIGC's records because of differences in methodologies used to identify and count facilities.

Source: *Tax Policy: A Profile of the Indian Gaming Industry*, U.S. General Accounting Office, Washington, DC, 1997

TABLE 7.1

1995 Revenues, Costs and Expenses, and Net Income for Class II and III Indian Gaming Facilities

| Income statement item | Dollars in millions | | | Percentage of total | | |
	Class II (N=66)[a]	Class III (N=112)[a]	Total (N=178)[a]	Class II	Class III	Total
Revenue						
Gaming	$568	$3,979	$4,547	12%	88%	100%
Other[b]	35	306	341	10	90	100
Total	603	4,285	4,888	12	88	100
Costs and expenses	367	2,644	3,011	12	88	100
Net income	236	1,641	1,877	13	87	100

[a]The "N" represents number of facilities.

[b]Other revenues include, for example, revenues from food, beverages, hotel rooms, and interest.

Source: GAO analysis of 1995 financial statements that were filed with NIGC as of November 22, 1996.

Source: *Tax Policy: A Profile of the Indian Gaming Industry*, U.S. General Accounting Office, Washington, DC, 1997

IGRA permitted the tribes to conduct any type of gambling on their reservation that was permitted in the state within which the reservation was located. The law also called for the tribe and the state to negotiate agreements or "compacts" that would allow this gambling. The states were required to bargain with the tribes in good faith. If they did not, or if a tribe was not satisfied with the process, the law permitted the tribe to take the issue to court, an option that has frequently been used.

FIRST FINANCIAL INFORMATION

Until 1997, wagering and revenue statistics for Native American gambling casinos were estimates since these facilities were not required to report their returns. However, in May 1997, at the request of Rep. Bill Archer (R-Texas), Chairman of the Committee on Ways and Means, the General Accounting Office (GAO) provided the committee with a profile of the Indian gambling industry. This report was the first public accounting of Class II and Class III gambling. (Class II gambling includes bingo, lotto, and other games similar to bingo. It does not include baccarat, chemin de fer, or blackjack. Class III gambling includes casinos, slot machines, and horse and dog racing.)

As of December 31, 1996, 184 tribes were operating 281 gambling facilities. The GAO obtained 1995 financial statements for 178 establishments operated by 126 tribes in 28 states. (See Figure 7.1.) Gambling revenues (dollars bet less payouts) amounted to $4.5 billion, with eight of the largest operations accounting for 40 percent of the revenues. The gambling facilities reported earning over $300 million in revenues from sales of food, beverages, and hotel rooms. Net income (total revenues less expenses) for the 178 establishments was about $1.9 billion (38 percent of the total revenues.) (See Table 7.1 and Figure 7.2.) Approximately $1.6 billion went to 106 tribes in 1995. (Some tribes received additional monies for taxes, fees, rent, and other reimbursements.) More than 50 percent of the $1.6 billion went to 10 tribes. None of the financial statements showed how the tribes used the money.

In 1996, the amount of money bet on Native American reservations reached $6.5 billion, up from $4.5 billion in 1995, $1.6 billion in 1992 and $125 million in 1985. (See Figure 7.3.) The casinos retain about 10 percent of the handle (money bet).

In 1997, *International Gaming and Wagering Business* (IGWB) magazine estimated that the revenues from Class III gambling on Native American reservations amounted to $5.8 billion and revenues from Class II came to $899 million, for a total of $6.7 billion. When sales of food, beverages, and hotel rooms are added in, the total amount of money spent on Native American reservations topped $7 billion. IGWB estimates that, in 1997,

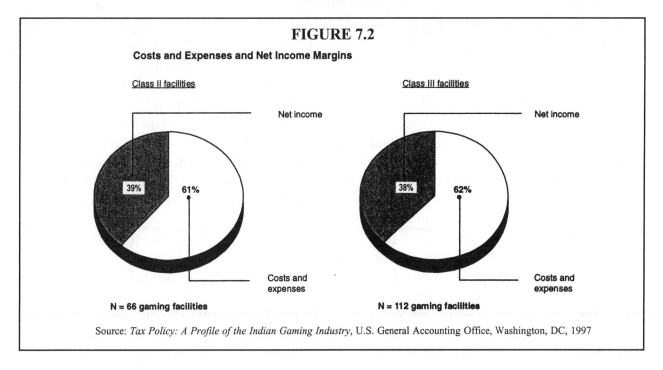

FIGURE 7.2

Costs and Expenses and Net Income Margins

Class II facilities

Net income

39% 61%

Costs and expenses

N = 66 gaming facilities

Class III facilities

Net income

38% 62%

Costs and expenses

N = 112 gaming facilities

Source: *Tax Policy: A Profile of the Indian Gaming Industry*, U.S. General Accounting Office, Washington, DC, 1997

148 tribes received $2.5 billion in direct tribal revenues from their gambling businesses. (Direct tribal revenues include tribes' shares of distributable profits, tribal gambling taxes, non-gambling revenues, and IGRA benefits.)

A GROWING NUMBER OF CASINOS

By July 30, 1999, 160 tribes in 24 states had reached 179 compacts with the governments in the states where their lands were located. Table 7.2 indicates which tribes have reached compacts with each state. Undoubtedly the most successful Native American casino is the Mashantucket Pequot Foxwoods facility in Ledyard, Connecticut. The 79,000-square foot building offers gamblers blackjack, roulette, the big-six money wheel, baccarat, poker, and electronic video games. The well-run, well-regulated casino has been so successful that lines form to play the games and dealers must work double shifts. Foxwoods earned an estimated $800 to $900 million in 1995. The eight largest facilities with gross gaming revenues (GGR) of at least $100 million — including Foxwoods, Mohegan Sun (in Connecticut), and the Hinckley and Mille Lacs Grand Casino operation (in Minnesota) — accounted for over 40 percent of all Class III GGR.

Foxwoods had an unusual arrangement with the State of Connecticut. The tribe agreed to pay 25 percent of the revenue from the slots or $100 million, whichever was greater, for exclusive rights to operate a casino in the state. (The arrangement has since been modified. See below.) In 1993, the Mashantucket Pequot tribe paid $113 million, and in 1997, it contributed $208 million to the state. The success of Foxwoods has contributed to the recent investment and development down the Atlantic Coast in Atlantic City, New Jersey. Casino operators there have been very concerned about customers being drawn away from the once aging casinos in Atlantic City.

Meanwhile, Foxwoods has expanded into a resort to encourage people to stay awhile and gamble longer. In addition, the tribe plans to open a new casino in the near future. The management recognizes that it will not have a monopoly on Indian gambling forever and it must try to use its early entry into the field to best advantage. In addition to investments in the casino, the tribe has been making other investments, including buying local land for future development, a printing plant, and an historical colonial inn. It has also contributed to local schools and churches. The tribe contributed $10 million to the Smithsonian Institute in Washington for a new American Indian building and even paid $500,000 to buy a stadium for the local minor league baseball team.

GROWING COMPETITION

Diversification is important; Foxwoods is no longer the only major casino in the region. In 1995, the 1,000-person Mohegan tribe, after a lengthy process of documenting its continued existence, opened a casino in Montville, Connecticut. The tribe agreed to contribute a minimum of $80 million or 25 percent of slot revenues to the state. Foxwoods, which had been given exclusive rights to slot machines in the state, agreed to a special exemption to allow the Mohegan casino to have slot machines. In return, Foxwood's minimum contribution to the state dropped to $80 million or 25 percent of slot revenues.

In neighboring Rhode Island, the Narragansett tribe has a casino in West Greenwich, only 17 miles from Ledyard. The Aquinnah Wampanoag Tribe of Gay Head, Massachusetts, would like to build a casino in New Bedford, although this project has run into serious political difficulties. In upstate New York, the Oneida tribe has opened a new 90,000-square foot casino. The Oneidas are now considering opening a second casino in Sullivan County in the Catskills, just 60 miles from New York City.

CASINOS AROUND THE COUNTRY

The St. Regis Mohawk tribe of northern New York State is planning a $500 million casino at Monticello Raceway in Monticello, New York. The United States Bureau of Indian Affairs (USBIA) has approved the tribe's proposal for the property. The plan calls for the construction of a 700,000-square-foot casino and convention center at the Raceway site and will create approximately 3,000 new jobs. The tribe, in partnership with three New York developers, will build the casino and convention center, which is expected to generate 4.4 million day trips to the area.

In Minnesota, 11 tribal compacts have led to the development of 14 high-stakes casinos. The Mille Lacs band of Chippewa Indians, for example, has built a $25 million casino gambling complex near Hinckley, Minnesota. The 102,000-square-foot casino contains 1,000 to 1,500 video slot machines, 60 blackjack tables, a 500-seat bingo hall, and a 100- to 150-seat keno hall. The 2,000-member Pokagon Band of Potawatomis are planning to build a $50 million facility in Dowagiac, Michigan. On the other hand, the Mohawks on the Kahnawake lands near Montreal, Quebec, voted down having a casino.

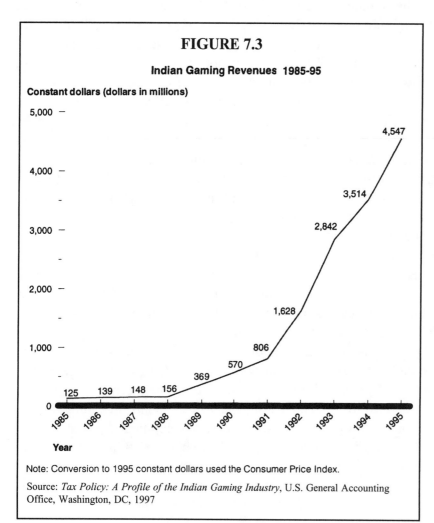

FIGURE 7.3

Indian Gaming Revenues 1985-95

Constant dollars (dollars in millions)

Note: Conversion to 1995 constant dollars used the Consumer Price Index.

Source: *Tax Policy: A Profile of the Indian Gaming Industry*, U.S. General Accounting Office, Washington, DC, 1997

98

In 1995, in Philadelphia, Mississippi, the Chocktaw Indians upgraded their successful Silver Star Casino Hotel by adding 400 rooms, a swimming pool, a health spa, and a golf course to induce visitors to stay longer. Since then, the tribe has added 500 rooms and an 85,000-square-foot casino. In 1998, the Silver Star Resort and Casino added an additional 15,000 square feet. In Colorado, the Southern Utes tribe and the Mountain Utes tribe have opened casinos. In the State of Washington, the Tulalip tribe reached an agreement with the state that eventually permits 31 gaming tables with $10 and $20 bets. The 7 Cedars Casino in Blyn, Washington, built by the Jamestown S'Klallam tribe, at a cost of $9, contains an on-site art gallery.

In South Dakota, the Santee Sioux tribe offers table games and slot machines. Until recently, the complex in Flandreau, South Dakota, was popular for one-day excursions. However, by 1995, the tribe decided that it could increase its revenues and bring in more people if the casino could offer customers an entertainment facility and a convenient place to spend the night. The tribe chose to build a new casino. They spent $17.5 million on a new structure that includes a 60-room hotel, showroom/ conference center, and 450-seat bingo hall. The new Royal River Casino, opened in 1997, is an 82,000-square-foot entertainment center that is open 24 hours a day, seven days per week. It is the largest Las Vegas-style casino in South Dakota.

The Sault Sainte Marie tribe will be the first tribe to own and operate a casino in a major U.S. city. In 1996, Michigan voters approved casino gambling for the city of Detroit, and the Sault Sainte Marie tribe has won one of the three sites that will feature a casino in downtown Detroit. The complex is expected to open in 2003 or 2004 and will include a 1,000-room hotel with twin towers more than 40 stories tall, 100,000 square feet of gambling space, a children's center, a 1,600-seat theater, restaurants, and stores. The project will cost $525 million and will employ approximately 4,000 people. Annual casino revenues are expected to reach $400 million. Until the project is complete, the tribe has set up temporary facilities totaling 62,369 square feet housing 2,200 slot machines and 94 tables. The tribe currently owns and operates five casinos in Michigan's Upper Peninsula.

In Wisconsin, 11 tribes have reached agreement with the state to offer blackjack and electronic games of chance. The Winnebago tribe of Wisconsin opened a new $8.5 million casino at Black River Falls. The Chippewa tribe has three casinos in Wisconsin. In San Diego, California, the 95-member Sycuan tribe operates a $3 million, 58,000-square foot casino offering poker, bingo, off-track betting, and lottery-type games on their reservation. In Louisiana, the Tunica-Biloxi tribe plans to build a $25 million casino, while the Coushatta tribe intends to construct a $35 million facility.

How Some of the Profits Are Spent

The Indian Gaming Regulatory Act (IGRA) specifies that the revenues from gambling must be used by the tribes for economic development and welfare of the people. Some tribes, like the 1,200-member Morongo Band of Mission Indians of Banning, California, have used the revenues from their successful Casino Morongo to end welfare on their reservation. They have also upgraded and repaired their water system. Before the 1960s, much of the tribe's drinking and household water came from open ditches. Now, the tribe has new storage tanks and over seven miles of increased capacity water lines.

Approximately one-third of American Indian tribes have invested some of the money earned from their casinos to improve health services. The Sandia Pueblo in New Mexico, for example, now has a $3 million medical complex on the pueblo. This saves the residents long drives to distant clinics that provide medical and dental care through the Indian Health Service. The 10,400-square-foot health care center includes seven examination rooms, three dental rooms, and state-of-the-art equipment. There is also a wellness and education center. After the health complex was built, the Sandia Pueblo used federal funds to hire a part-time doctor and a full-time nurse. Other medical personnel help staff the facility.

TABLE 7.2

TRIBAL-STATE COMPACT LIST
TRIBAL INFORMATION FOR THOSE WITH APPROVED
TRIBAL-STATE COMPACTS AS OF JULY 30, 1999
160 TRIBES - 24 STATES - 179 COMPACTS
115 AMENDMENTS/ADDENDA
24 SUPERSEDED COMPACTS

This list is maintained and updated as new compacts/amendments are published in the FEDERAL REGISTER by the Indian Gaming Management Staff, Bureau of Indian Affairs, Office of the Commissioner (202) 219-4066.
*Tribe has compact with more than one state.
**Tribe has more than one compact for different types of games.
† Compact deemed approved.

ARIZONA - 17 TRIBES
- AK-CHIN INDIAN COMMUNITY
- COCOPAH TRIBE OF ARIZONA
- COLORADO RIVER INDIAN TRIBES
- FORT MCDOWELL MOHAVE-APACHE INDIAN COMMUNITY
- FORT MOJAVE INDIAN TRIBE*
- GILA RIVER PIMA-MARICOPA INDIAN COMMUNITY
- HUALAPAI INDIAN TRIBE
- KAIBAB BAND OF PAIUTE INDIANS
- PASCUA YAQUI INDIANS
- QUECHAN TRIBE
- SALT RIVER PIMA-MARICOPA INDIAN COMMUNITY
- SAN CARLOS APACHE TRIBE
- TOHONO O'ODHAM NATION
- TONTO APACHE TRIBE
- WHITE MOUNTAIN APACHE TRIBE
- YAVAPAI-APACHE NATION
- YAVAPAI-PRESCOTT TRIBE

CALIFORNIA - 13 TRIBES
- BARONA GROUP OF THE CAPITAN GRANDE BAND OF MISSION INDIANS**
- BIG SANDY RANCHERIA OF MONO INDIANS
- CABAZON BAND OF CAHUILLA MISSION INDIANS
- CHER-AE HEIGHTS INDIAN COMMUNITY OF THE TRINIDAD RANCHERIA
- JACKSON RANCHERIA OF ME-WUK INDIANS
- MOORETOWN RANCHERIA OF MAIDU INDIANS
- PALA BAND OF LUISENO MISSION INDIANS
- REDDING RANCHERIA
- RUMSEY INDIAN RANCHERIA
- SAN MANUEL BAND OF SERRANO MISSION INDIANS
- SYCUAN BAND OF DIEGUENO MISSION INDIANS**
- TABLE MOUNTAIN RANCHERIA
- VIEJAS GROUP OF CAPITAN GRANDE BAND OF MISSION INDS.**

COLORADO - 2 TRIBES
- SOUTHERN UTE INDIAN TRIBE
- UTE MOUNTAIN TRIBE

CONNECTICUT - 2 TRIBES
- MASHANTUCKET PEQUOT TRIBE
- MOHEGAN INDIAN TRIBE

IDAHO - 3 TRIBES
- COEUR D'ALENE TRIBE
- KOOTENAI TRIBE
- NEZ PERCE TRIBE

IOWA - 3 TRIBES
- OMAHA TRIBE OF NEBRASKA
- SAC AND FOX TRIBE OF MISSISSIPPI IN IOWA
- WINNEBAGO TRIBE OF NEBRASKA

KANSAS - 4 TRIBES
- IOWA TRIBE OF KANSAS AND NEBRASKA
- KICKAPOO TRIBE OF INDIANS, KANSAS
- PRAIRIE BAND OF POTAWATOMI INDIANS, KANSAS
- SAC AND FOX NATION OF MISSOURI IN KANSAS AND NEBRASKA

LOUISIANA - 3 TRIBES
- CHITIMACHA TRIBE OF LOUISIANA
- COUSHATTA TRIBE OF LOUISIANA
- TUNICA-BILOXI INDIAN TRIBE OF LOUISIANA

MICHIGAN - 11 TRIBES
- BAY MILLS INDIAN COMMUNITY
- GRAND TRAVERSE BAND OF OTTAWA AND CHIPPEWA INDS.
- HANNAHVILLE INDIAN COMMUNITY
- HURON POTAWATOMI, INC †
- KEWEENAW BAY INDIAN COMMUNITY
- LAC VIEUX DESERT BAND OF LAKE SUPERIOR CHIPPEWA INDS.
- LITTLE RIVER BAND OF OTTAWA INDIANS OF MICHIGAN †
- LITTLE TRAVERSE BAY BANDS OF ODAWA INDIANS †
- POKAGON BAND OF POTAWATOMI INDIANS †
- SAGINAW CHIPPEWA INDIAN TRIBE
- SAULT STE. MARIE TRIBE OF CHIPPEWA INDIANS

MINNESOTA - 11 TRIBES
- BOIS FORTE (NETT LAKE) BAND OF MINNESOTA CHIPPEWA **
- FOND DU LAC BAND OF MINNESOTA CHIPPEWA**
- GRAND PORTAGE BAND OF MINNESOTA CHIPPEWA**
- LEECH LAKE BAND OF MINNESOTA CHIPPEWA**
- LOWER SIOUX INDIAN COMMUNITY**
- MILLE LACS BAND OF MINNESOTA CHIPPEWA**
- PRAIRIE ISLAND INDIAN COMMUNITY **
- RED LAKE BAND OF CHIPPEWA INDIANS**
- SHAKOPEE MDEWAKANTON SIOUX COMMUNITY**
- UPPER SIOUX INDIAN COMMUNITY**
- WHITE EARTH BAND OF MINNESOTA CHIPPEWA**

MISSISSIPPI - 1 TRIBE
- MISSISSIPPI BAND OF CHOCTAW INDIANS

MONTANA - 6 TRIBES
- ASSINIBOINE & SIOUX TRIBES OF THE FORT PECK RESERVATION
- BLACKFEET TRIBE
- CHIPPEWA-CREE INDIANS OF THE ROCKY BOY'S RESERVATION
- CONFED. SALISH & KOOTENAI TRIBES OF THE FLATHEAD RES.
- CROW TRIBE
- NORTHERN CHEYENNE TRIBE

NEBRASKA -1 TRIBE
- OMAHA TRIBE OF NEBRASKA *

NEVADA - 6 TRIBES
- FORT MOJAVE INDIAN TRIBE *
- LAS VEGAS TRIBE OF PAIUTE INDIANS
- MOAPA BAND OF PAIUTE INDIANS
- PYRAMID LAKE PAIUTE TRIBE
- RENO-SPARKS INDIAN COLONY
- WALKER RIVER PAIUTE TRIBE

NEW MEXICO - 16 TRIBES
- JICARILLA APACHE TRIBE †
- MESCALERO APACHE TRIBE †
- PUEBLO OF ACOMA †
- PUEBLO OF ISLETA †
- PUEBLO OF LAGUNA
- PUEBLO OF NAMBE †
- PUEBLO OF PICURIS
- PUEBLO OF POJOAQUE †
- PUEBLO OF SANDIA †
- PUEBLO OF SAN FELIPE †
- PUEBLO OF SAN ILDEFONSO
- PUEBLO OF SAN JUAN †
- PUEBLO OF SANTA ANA †
- PUEBLO OF SANTA CLARA †
- PUEBLO OF TAOS †
- PUEBLO OF TESUQUE †

(continued)

The St. Regis Mohawks, whose Akwesasne Mohawk Casino opened in 1999, in Monticello, New York, plan to use their casino earnings to banish poverty from their reservation, install 20 miles of water lines and 10 miles of sewer lines. The tribe also plans to provide guaranteed health

TABLE 7.2 (Continued)

NEW YORK - 2 TRIBES . . . .
   ONEIDA NATION . . . .
   ST. REGIS BAND OF MOHAWK INDIANS . . . .

NORTH CAROLINA - 1 TRIBE . . . .
   EASTERN BAND OF CHEROKEE INDIANS . . . .

NORTH DAKOTA - 5 TRIBES . . . .
   SPIRIT LAKE TRIBE (FORMERLY DEVILS LAKE SIOUX) ** . . . .
   SISSETON-WAHPETON SIOUX TRIBE* ** . . . .
   STANDING ROCK SIOUX TRIBE* . . . .
   THREE AFFILIATED TRIBES OF FORT BERTHOLD** . . . .
   TURTLE MOUNTAIN BAND OF CHIPPEWA INDIANS** . . . .

OKLAHOMA - 8 TRIBES . . . .
   CHOCTAW NATION OF OKLAHOMA . . . .
   CITIZEN POTAWATOMI NATION . . . .
   COMANCHE INDIAN TRIBE . . . .
   IOWA TRIBE OF OKLAHOMA . . . .
   MIAMI TRIBE OF OKLAHOMA . . . .
   MODOC TRIBE OF OKLAHOMA . . . .
   OTOE-MISSOURIA TRIBE OF OKLAHOMA . . . .
   TONKAWA TRIBE OF INDIANS OF OKLAHOMA . . . .

OREGON - 9 TRIBES . . . .
   BURNS-PAIUTE TRIBE . . . .
   CONFEDERATED TRIBES OF THE COOS, LOWER UMPQUA AND
      SIUSLAW INDIANS . . . .
   COQUILLE TRIBE . . . .
   COW CREEK BAND OF UMPQUA INDIANS . . . .
   CONFEDERATED TRIBES OF THE GRAND RONDE COMMUNITY. . . .
   KLAMATH INDIAN TRIBE . . . .
   CONFEDERATED TRIBES OF THE SILETZ RESERVATION . . . .
   CONFEDERATED TRIBES OF THE UMATILLA RESERVATION . . . .
   CONFEDERATED TRIBES OF THE WARM SPRINGS RESERVATION

RHODE ISLAND - 1 TRIBE . . . .
   NARRAGANSETT INDIAN TRIBE . . . .

SOUTH DAKOTA - 9 TRIBES . . . .
   CHEYENNE RIVER SIOUX TRIBE . . . .
   CROW CREEK SIOUX TRIBE . . . .
   FLANDREAU SANTEE SIOUX TRIBE . . . .
   LOWER BRULE SIOUX TRIBE . . . .
   OGLALA SIOUX TRIBE . . . .
   ROSEBUD SIOUX TRIBE . . . .
   SISSETON-WAHPETON SIOUX TRIBE* ** . . . .
   STANDING ROCK SIOUX TRIBE* . . . .
   YANKTON SIOUX TRIBE OF SOUTH DAKOTA . . . .

WASHINGTON - 19 TRIBES . . . .
   CONFED. TRIBES OF THE CHEHALIS RESERVATION . . . .
   CONFED. TRIBES & BANDS OF THE YAKAMA INDIAN NATION . . .
   JAMESTOWN S'KLALLAM TRIBE . . . .
   KALISPEL INDIAN COMMUNITY OF THE KALISPEL RESERVATION
   LOWER ELWHA TRIBAL COMM. OF THE LOWER ELWHA RES. . . . .
   LUMMI TRIBE OF THE LUMMI RESERVATION . . . .
   MUCKLESHOOT INDIAN TRIBE OF THE MUCKLESHOOT RES. . . . .
   NISQUALLY INDIAN TRIBE OF THE NISQUALLY RESERVATION . .
   NOOKSACK INDIAN TRIBE . . . .
   PORT GAMBLE INDIAN COMMUNITY OF THE PORT GAMBLE RES.
   PUYALLUP TRIBE OF THE PUYALLUP RESERVATION . . . .
   QUILEUTE TRIBE OF THE QUILEUTE RESERVATION . . . .
   QUINAULT TRIBE OF THE QUINAULT RESERVATION . . . .
   SKOKOMISH INDIAN TRIBE OF THE SKOKOMMISH RES. . . . .
   SQUAXIN ISLAND TRIBE OF THE SQUAXIN ISLAND RES. . . . .
   SUQUAMISH INDIAN TRIBE OF THE PORT MADISON RES. . . . .
   SWINOMISH INDIANS OF THE SWINOMISH RESERVATION . . . .
   TULALIP TRIBES OF THE TULALIP RESERVATION . . . .
   UPPER SKAGIT INDIAN TRIBE . . . .

WISCONSIN - 11 TRIBES . . . .
   BAD RIVER BAND OF LAKE SUPERIOR TRIBE OF CHIPPEWA . . . . .
   FOREST COUNTY POTAWATOMI COMMUNITY . . . .
   HO-CHUNK NATION (FORMERLY WISCONSIN WINNEBAGO) . . . .
   LAC COURTE OREILLES BAND OF LAKE SUPERIOR CHIPPEWA . . .
   LAC DU FLAMBEAU BAND OF LAKE SUPERIOR CHIPPEWA . . . . . .
   MENOMINEE INDIAN TRIBE . . . .
   ONEIDA TRIBE OF INDIANS . . . .
   RED CLIFF BAND OF LAKE SUPERIOR CHIPPEWA . . . .
   ST. CROIX CHIPPEWA INDIANS . . . .
   SOKAOGAN CHIPPEWA COMM. OF THE MOLE LAKE BAND OF
      CHIPPEWA . . . .
   STOCKBRIDGE-MUNSEE COMMUNITY OF MOHICAN INDIANS . . . .

Source: Indian Gaming Management Staff, U.S. Bureau of Indian Affairs, Office of the Commissioner, Washington, DC, 1999

---

care for every tribal member, a youth center, and a nursing home. The St. Regis Mohawks would like to do what the Mille Lacs Band of Chippewa Indians did — use the income from their casino to build the reservation's first schools.

STRENGTHENING THE NATIONAL INDIAN GAMING COMMISSION

The Indian Gaming Regulatory Act of 1988 (IGRA) has given a growing number of Native American tribes, many of which are very poor, the opportunity to "cash in" on the gambling boom of the last several years. Like any new business venture, the budding tribal gambling establishments have run into some problems. It took three years to appoint the three members of the National Indian Gaming Commission (NIGC) created by the IGRA. The Commission was to prepare the policies and procedures necessary to help develop and regulate the tribal gaming projects.

When the National Gambling Impact Commission began their study, they learned that, until 1997, the NIGC had been underfunded and understaffed. However, in 1997, federal legislation amended IGRA, and since then, NIGC has been authorized to impose fees on both Class II and Class III gambling activities. (Prior to this, NIGC was regulating Class II gambling only.) Because of this change, NIGC has received more funding and has been able to hire more field investigators and compliance officers. The additional funds and personnel have resulted in bringing more than 95 percent of all the tribal gambling facilities into compliance with federal law. (Prior to the increases, tribes were operating gambling facilities without compacts in some states.)

NICG's new responsibilities concerning Class III gambling include conducting background investigations on individuals and entities with a financial interest in, or a management responsibility for, a Class III gambling contract. NIGC also reviews and approves Class III management contracts.

A FEW PROBLEMS

Gambling sometimes attracts disreputable individuals, and some tribal leaders have made unwise financial deals. A report prepared by the Department of the Interior noted a number of tribes had signed contracts in which the tribes had been overcharged for administrative services and gambling equipment. Several bills have already been proposed in Congress to limit the development of casino gambling on Native American reservations. (See Chapter II.)

In Minnesota, the chairman of the White Earth Band of Chippewa was charged with stealing hundreds of thousands of dollars from a casino project. In Clearlake Oaks, California, two factions of the Elem Indian Colony got into a shooting war over who should control their casino. State and local police had to be called out to end the conflict.

Many tribal leaders recognize that some tribal managers may be victimized or that some gambling operations may expand beyond their ability to handle the growth. Nonetheless, they note, these are typical business problems that often develop in any new industry, and they wonder why their growing pains are being singled out.

Proposition 5

In California, Proposition 5 proposed the expansion of legalized gambling on Indian land by requiring the state to sign a gambling compact with any tribe that wanted one. In November 1998, California voters passed Proposition 5 with 63 percent of the vote. In August 1999, however, the California Supreme Court overturned the measure, saying that it violated the state constitution's ban on Nevada-style casinos. Nevada casino operators opposed Proposition 5 because it could potentially take away thousands of their customers.

The California Supreme Court held that, by legalizing games like 21 or blackjack and slot machine-style video games, Proposition 5 had improperly voided the California constitution's prohibition against such games. In the opinion of the Court, because Proposition 5 was a statute "and because in a conflict between statutory and constitutional law, the constitution must prevail, we conclude Proposition 5's authorization of casino gambling is invalid and inoperative."

Indian tribes, anticipating the Court's decision, have collected signatures to place a new measure on the ballot in California's presidential primary election to amend the state constitution to permit casino gambling. Since they approved the earlier measure, it seems likely that the voters will approve the constitutional amendment. In November 2000, the amendment passed, and the number of slot machines at Indian casinos around California could more than double to 43,000, as could the number of jobs in an industry that currently employs about 16,000 people around the state.

Politics v. Economics

In 1995, three bands of Chippewa Indians suggested turning a failing dog track into a gambling casino in Hudson, Wisconsin, on the Minnesota border. Five rival tribes already operating casinos in the region opposed the proposal. The Bureau of Indian Affairs (BIA) in the Interior Department must issue a permit before a casino can be opened, and the Minneapolis regional office of the BIA initially ruled in favor of issuing the permit. However, the ruling was overturned in Washington, in July 1995, after the tribes opposing the permit contributed nearly $300,000 to the Democratic Party. (Both sides had hired lobbyists to promote their cases, and the losers accused the winners of pressuring the White House and Interior Department to oppose the permit through the donation.)

This led to allegations (claims) that the decision was political rather than economic. Interior Department officials declared that the donation had nothing to do with their decision. They insisted that their ruling was a result of strong local opposition from area lawmakers, the City of Hudson, Wisconsin, where the casino was to be located, and from other tribes already operating profitable gaming establishments.

Secretary of the Interior Bruce Babbitt was accused of influencing the decision and then lying to Congress about it. Secretary Babbitt's office said that the decision to reject the request "was reached on the merits, not on the basis of any alleged political influence." However, following a Justice Department review, Attorney General Janet Reno said that there was "specific and credible evidence indicating that Secretary Babbitt may have testified falsely." In February 1998, Reno recommended that an independent counsel should decide whether Babbitt lied to the Senate.

In October 1999, following 19 months of investigation, Independent Counsel Carol Elder Bruce announced that she and her staff had found insufficient evidence to seek criminal indictments against Mr.Babbitt or anyone else involved in the 1995 decision to reject the permit for the casino sought by the three Wisconsin Indian tribes. She announced that she would not seek criminal charges against the Interior Secretary. She also concluded "that the evidence was insufficient" to prove that Mr. Babbit committed perjury in statements he made to a Senate hearing on the casino decision.

CAN REGULATION BE BENEFICIAL?

During his tenure in the early 1990s, Tony Hope, the former Chairman of the National Indian Gaming Commission (NIGC), the Native American trade organization, tried to convince tribal authorities that regulation would benefit their casinos because it would increase visitors' confidence in the integrity of their casinos. His successor, Harold Monteau, has also indicated his desire to take "a leadership role in encouraging the development of strong tribal regulatory structures." In Foxwoods, the casino works closely with the state of Connecticut to insure that the rules are followed.

Many tribal leaders are concerned about regulation because they fear it would violate their tribal sovereignty. Tim Wapato, executive director of the NIGC, is also concerned about sovereignty, but recognizes that the tribes must have some form of regulation to guarantee the integrity of the games.

He suggests tribal self-regulation. He feels that a tribal-federal relationship is less violative of American Indian sovereignty than a tribal-state relationship, which he believes degrades Indian sovereignty.

Native American tribes are now getting a "piece of the action" of which they have so often been left out. Gambling has provided employment for Native Americans and for other people living near the casinos, revenues for investment for the future, and monies for investment in education, housing, health care, and other needs on reservations.

THE NATIONAL GAMBLING IMPACT STUDY COMMISSION

President Bill Clinton signed the National Gambling Impact Study Commission Act (PL 104-169) into law on August 3, 1997. The legislation created a nine-member federal commission to investigate all facets of gambling in America, including Indian gambling.

The Charge

The National Gambling Impact Study Commission Act (PL 104-169 provides

1. IN GENERAL — it shall be the duty of the commission to conduct a comprehensive legal and factual study of the social and economic impacts of gambling in the United States on (A) ... Native American tribal governments,

2. MATTERS TO BE STUDIED — The matters to be studied by the Commission under paragraph (1) shall at a minimum include (A) a review of existing federal, state, local, and Native American tribal government policies and practices with respect to the legalization or prohibition of gambling, including a review of the costs of such policies and practices ... (E) an assessment of the extent to which gambling provided revenues to state, local, and Native American tribal governments, and the extent to which possible alternative revenue sources may exist for such governments....

Findings

The Commission found that only a few independent studies exist regarding the economic and social impact of Indian gambling. Some studies, including the General Accounting Office Report, *Tax Policy: A Profile of the Indian Gaming Industry*, (GAO/GGD-97-91, May 1997), reported both positive and negative results of the impact of gambling on reservations. Others, such as *The Connecticut Economy* (Department of Economics, University of Connecticut, Spring, 1998), found a positive economic impact on the tribes and surrounding communities. Although the NGISC stressed that this area needs further research, the Commission concluded that revenues from Indian gambling have had a significant and generally positive impact on a number of reservations.

Recommendations

The Commission made a number of recommendations that include, but are not limited to, the following. The Commission acknowledged the central role of the National Indian Gaming Commission (NIGC) as the major federal regulator of tribal governmental gambling and encouraged Congress to assure adequate funding so NIGC can properly regulate and ensure integrity and fiscal accountability throughout the industry. The Commission recommended that IGRA's classes of gambling be clearly defined and that Class III gambling should not include any activities that are not available to other organizations in the state. Indian gambling, according to the Commission, should be consistent with the individual state's overall gambling policies.

The Commission advised that labor organizations, tribal governments, and states work together to ensure the right to organize and bargain collectively for employees of tribal casinos. Furthermore, employees of tribal casinos should have the same or equivalent (or superior) protections that are available to comparable state or private sector employees through federal and state employment laws as those of the state in which the casino is located.

The Commission recognized that, under IGRA, Indian tribes must report certain proprietary (privately held) and non-proprietary tribal governmental gambling financial information to the NIGC, annually, through certified, independently audited financial statements. Moreover, the Commission recommended that certain financial data collected from Indian gambling be consistent with financial data published by commercial casinos (such as those in Nevada and New Jersey) wherever comparable by class and should be published by NIGC annually. The Commission also recommended that independent auditors should review and comment on each tribal gambling operation's compliance with the Minimum Internal Control Standards ordered by NIGC.

The Commission reported that it had heard considerable testimony from tribal and state officials that uncompacted tribal gambling has led to extensive litigation, and that federal enforcement has, until recently, been mixed. The Commission recommended that the federal government fully and consistently enforce all provisions of the IGRA. IGRA permits tribes and states to negotiate any issues related to gambling, and the Commission recommended that the federal government leave such issues to the states and tribes to decide.

The Commission recommended that tribal governments be encouraged to use some of the net revenues earned from Indian gambling to diversify tribal economies and to reduce their dependence on gambling. (For more information on the National Gambling Impact Study Commission Report, see individual chapters.)

CHAPTER VIII

LOTTERIES — LEGAL AND ALLURING

Lotteries are different from any other gaming product. Lottery players risk a small amount of money against very long odds to win a large prize, with the net proceeds going to the public good. — Michael Jones, "Lotteries Must Strike Balance Between Letter of the Law and Unwritten Contract with Players," *Gaming Law Review*, vol. 2, no. 1, n.d.

The lottery is unique in the gambling industry for several reasons — it is the most extensive form of gambling in the United States, it is the only form of commercial gambling that a majority of adults report having played, and it is the only form of gambling in America that is a government monopoly. State lotteries have the worst odds of any common form of gambling (about 1 in 12 to 14 million for most present-day lotto games), but they promise the greatest potential payoff to the winner, with prizes often amounting to tens of millions of dollars.

DEFINITION

A lottery is a game in which people purchase numbered tickets in the hope of winning a prize. A person wins if the number on his or her ticket is the one drawn from a pool of all the tickets purchased for that particular event. In the case of instant lotteries, the bettor wins if the ticket contains a pre-determined winning number. Raffles are a form of lottery in which the prize is usually goods rather than cash. Raffles are most often conducted by churches or charitable organizations and are relatively small in size. As of 1999, lotteries were legal in 37 states, Washington, DC, the Virgin Islands, and Puerto Rico. Lotteries were also legal in the 10 provinces and two territories of Canada.

A PART OF OUR HERITAGE

Lotteries have been a part of American life since the settlement of Jamestown by the Virginia Company of London. Prior to the establishment of a regular tax system, lotteries were the most effective means of raising money to finance public works, churches, schools, and universities. Even after the American Revolution, lotteries remained the most popular form of fund-raising for public services for another generation. Former lottery managers who were able to make enough money to open banks founded some of the nation's most prestigious banks, including the Chase Manhattan Bank and First City National Bank of New York.

The discovery during the 1830s of corruption and fraud among some lottery managers and public officials resulted in a flurry of reform laws. Continued opposition to lotteries was voiced by a small number of newspapers through their editorials and by the Society of Friends (Quakers). Other religious groups did not object to lotteries because they used them to finance new church construction. Most newspapers did not object to lotteries because lottery operators were big newspaper advertisers.

Eventually, however, many newspapers joined the anti-lottery crusade. By 1840, lotteries were abolished in most northern states. During the next 20 years, the number of lottery operations in the South and West also decreased, but some were revived after the Civil War to finance reconstruction efforts. Corruption and fraud continued to be a problem, however, forcing the federal government to enact a number of anti-lottery bills between 1860 and 1895, which ultimately banished lotteries (except for the Louisiana Lottery; see Chapter I) for the next 40 years.

THE MODERN LOTTERY

During the Depression Era of the 1930s, the United States was flooded with lottery tickets from the Caribbean, Latin America, and the Irish Sweepstakes, reviving interest in lottery gambling. Following hearings on organized crime before the Special Senate Committee to Investigate Organized Crime in Interstate Commerce (Kefauver Hearings, 1950), Congress approved the Revenue Act of 1951, which called for the purchase of a $50 occupational tax stamp and a 10 percent excise tax on gross receipts from wagering businesses. Although designed to tax and control other forms of gambling, the Revenue Act opened the door for the establishment of legal lottery games.*

In 1964, New Hampshire became the first state in the twentieth century to legalize lottery games. New Hampshire's funds were to be used for educational programs in local municipalities. New York followed with a state lottery in 1967, but the real revitalization of lottery games occurred in 1971. In that year, New Jersey introduced a computer-based, 50-cent weekly game and increased the size of the prize pool to 45 percent of the gross amount wagered. New Hampshire and New York later adopted the New Jersey system.

In 1974, the federal Commission on the Review of the National Policy Toward Gambling (hereafter referred to as the National Gambling Commission) held hearings to investigate the nineteenth century anti-lottery statutes. State lottery directors claimed that these statutes did not allow states to develop their own policies on gambling or to conduct business and raise revenues as they wished without undue federal regulation or interference. As a result of the Commission's findings, the 93rd Congress passed legislation allowing states to advertise on radio and television and to send lottery information and tickets through the mail within their own states.

Lotteries did not develop nationwide until the 1980s. The federal government was transferring more financial responsibilities to the states at the same time that citizens were becoming increasingly reluctant to pay more taxes. As state and local governments became desperate for money, lotteries were seen as an easy way to raise large sums of revenues without upsetting most voters. The lotteries were often presented as a form of voluntary taxation, and many states have directed that money gained from lotteries be used for purposes with which few voters could quarrel, such as education or aid to the elderly.

The nationwide adoption and promotion of lotteries by the states have contributed to a major change in attitude towards gambling throughout the United States. Gambling has generally lost the image of sin or immorality with which it had once been connected. With the strong public acceptance of lotteries, gambling is now more likely to be seen as entertainment and fun rather than a violation of generally accepted morality. For most people, the connection it once had with corruption and fraud has been forgotten. This change in attitude has been a major factor in the recent boom of huge casino/hotels in Las Vegas designed to attract families to a complete entertainment experience of which gambling, while still the dominant driving engine, is only a part. (See Chapter V.)

---

* Few local gamblers would buy the federal occupational tax stamp because it would indicate to local authorities that the person was a gambler. Paying the excise tax would also expose the gambler. Since gambling was illegal in all but one state, this law virtually made gambling a federal as well as a state crime.

TYPES OF LOTTERY GAMES

Instant Lottery

Instant lotteries were first introduced in Massachusetts in 1974. For $1, a player buys a ticket and immediately finds out if he or she has picked a winning number. Instant tickets have a coating that the player scratches off to uncover the number or symbol underneath that reveals whether or not the ticket is a "winning ticket." Instant lotteries are commonly the first type of lottery established by previously non-lottery states. Every state that has legalized lotteries has an instant lottery.

Numbers — or Pick 3, Pick 4

In 1975, New Jersey was the first state to legalize numbers, a formerly illegal game (see Chapter X). In the most common form of numbers, a bettor puts money on a two- or three-digit number from 00 to 999. The winning number is determined by an arbitrary mechanism, such as numbered Ping-Pong™ balls rising in an air-filled tank. State lottery administrators have found that games must be flexible to keep pace with the interests and demands of the public, and some states have expanded to a four-digit weekly numbers game. In 1999, 32 states, the District of Columbia, and Puerto Rico offered numbers.

Lotto

Lotto was first played in the 1520s in Italy, using hand-painted game pieces and game boards carved from wood. In 1978, Massachusetts became the first state to offer lotto games. In 1999, 37 states, the District of Columbia, and Puerto Rico permitted lotto games. To play lotto, a bettor selects five to six numbers from a pool of 40 to 44 numbers and wagers between $1 and $4. Winning numbers are selected at random from a weekly drawing. If no player has the same set of numbers (in any sequence), the prize is not awarded that week, and the prize money is carried forward to the next week's drawing. Sometimes huge jackpots of many millions of dollars can develop, generating intense interest in the lottery.

Powerball

Twenty-two states, generally states with smaller populations, and the District of Colombia have combined in a Multi-State Lottery Association (MSLA) to offer their citizens *Powerball*, a lotto game that can offer huge jackpots. It is not hard for large states like California, New York, Texas, and Florida to be able to offer multi-million dollar jackpots to players. In these smaller population states, however, *Powerball* offers players the chance to win multi-million-dollar jackpots. Most of the states participating in *Powerball* believe that the multi-state lotto game benefits their state games since people often buy tickets to the state lotto games when they go in to buy a *Powerball* ticket.

Video Lottery

Many gaming industry observers see video lottery terminals (VLTs) as the future of the lottery industry. Unlike most video games played on computers, video lottery games have little to do with skill, so that winning or losing is mainly a matter of chance.

Video games are particularly attractive to young people because of their appealing graphics. Some people are concerned about the addictive nature of video lotteries, and in fact, opponents of gambling often refer to VLTs as the "crack cocaine of gambling." In addition, operators of other forms of gambling, most notably the regular lottery and pari-mutuel operations, fear that VLTs will cut into how much they earn.

Unlike most lottery games, in which only about 50 percent is paid back to the players, VLTs return about 90 percent. If VLTs paid back only 50 percent, players would likely lose interest quickly. However, with a 90 percent return, players win often enough that, for some gamblers, it can become addictive.

For these reasons, VLTs have had a hard time getting approval in most states. VLTs have been legalized in Delaware, Louisiana, Oregon, Rhode Island, South Dakota, and West Virginia. In Louisiana, it is suspected that earnings from such machines have been used to influence politicians. A recent scandal concerning organized crime has further tainted the Louisiana devices. Members of the Gambino and Genovese crime families have been accused of conspiring with two suppliers of video poker games to skim profits from the devices. In July 1999, Louisiana shut down 4,874 of 15,000 poker machines in 33 of 64 parishes (counties).

VLTs were declared unconstitutional in South Dakota, but the issue was immediately put on the ballot, and in November 1995, the voters approved their use in the state. In 1997, in the five states that reported VLT sales separately, VLT sales represented a major proportion of all lottery sales — Delaware (89 percent), Oregon (68 percent), Rhode Island (69 percent), South Dakota (94 percent), and West Virginia (77 percent).

In Rhode Island and West Virginia, VLTs are permitted in racetracks to improve the racetracks' sagging income. Racetracks are a good place to put VLTs because there is considerable time between races during which nothing happens as horse and dog handlers prepare for the next race. During this period, many people who have come to gamble become bored. VLTs give them something to do while they are awaiting the next race. It also gives someone who came along to the races to be with a friend or a spouse, but who has no interest in racing, an opportunity to do something else. Finally, it limits the number of minors who would have access to these games, since some states ban minors from the track.

LOTTERY SALES

Lotteries are big business. According to the *International Gambling and Wagering Business* (IGWB) annual survey, sales for fiscal year (FY) 1999 totaled $37.4 billion, up from $36.6 billion in FY 1998 and $21.8 billion wagered in 1992.

(See Table 8.1 and Figure 8.1.) On the other hand, lottery sales in 1999 were lower than they were in 1996 ($38.9 billion) and 1997 ($42.8 billion). According to IGWB, this may be due to lower state prize distributions and increased interest in multistate games that have huge payouts. Moreover, some of the country's largest state lotteries turned in poor performances, depressing overall industry gains. Texas dropped 16 percent ($500 million), and New York fell 6 percent ($245 million) in sales.

On average, the states paid back about 58 percent of sales in winnings to players. About one-third (32 percent) went into government revenues, while the rest was used to administer the lotteries. Government profits ranged from 43 percent in Pennsylvania to 18 percent in Rhode Island and South Dakota.

LOTTERY REVENUES

In 1997, lotteries produced $16.6 billion in revenues, up 3 percent from the year before. (See Figure 8.1.) Lotteries keep a much higher percentage of the money bet (45.5 percent of all non-VLT bets) than any other type of gambling. (For example, horsetracks retain 20.5 percent; slot machines, 6 percent; casino tables, 2 percent; and bingo, 24.5 percent.) Therefore, while lotteries account for only 7 percent of all monies bet on gambling, they bring in 35 percent of all revenues.

Where Do the Revenues Go?

Until recently, all state lottery revenue went into state programs. However, in 1991, New York State approved a small lottery that would benefit New York City. Proceeds from this instant lottery game are used to help fund a crime-reduction program within the city of New York.

Most revenues from lotteries are put into the general state funds. (In 15 states, all or a portion of lottery profits go into general funds.) Initially, the earnings of many of the lotteries were earmarked for beneficial state programs, most notably educa-

TABLE 8.1

United States Lottery Sales–Fiscal 1999

Unaudited Results
(dollars in millions)

	Instant & Pulltabs	Lotto	5-number/ Cash Lotto	4-number Lotto (1)	Powerball	Big Game	Daily Numbers	Keno	VLTs(2)	Other	FY1999 Total Lottery Sales	FY1998 Total Lottery Sales	Percent Change
Ariz.	$109.4	$48.7	$9.0		$93.7		$7.5				$268.3	$250.7	7.0%
Calif.	959.4	1,036.1	160.6				79.7	$256.0		$9.9	2,501.7	2,294.4	9.0%
Colo.	233.9	119.7	12.1							2.7	368.4	374.3	-1.6%
Conn.	474.0	51.3	48.4		124.6		172.7				871.0	805.6	8.1%
Del.	20.1	10.6			73.2		45.1		$377.6	0.8	527.4	447.2	17.9%
D.C. (3)	29.4		8.7	$1.7	35.9		133.7				209.3	226.4	-7.6%
Fla.	676.1	737.7	241.8				508.7			14.8	2,179.1	2,131.1	2.3%
Ga.	796.2	117.0	84.7			$199.2	777.8	59.4			2,034.3	1,736.1	17.2%
Idaho	57.9	3.2	2.1		27.3						90.5	89.6	0.9%
Ill.	568.6	168.7	113.8			193.5	479.9				1,524.4	1,577.0	-3.3%
Ind.	348.4	103.8	9.8	5.7	156.5		57.1				681.4	648.2	5.1%
Iowa	119.6		4.8	4.2	51.8		3.8				184.1	173.9	5.9%
Kan.	87.8		17.2	4.6	50.4		4.9	34.0			198.9	192.0	3.6%
Ky.	277.8	33.8	16.7	5.1	117.7		132.0				583.1	585.0	-0.3%
La.	109.7	30.1	2.6	7.0	96.8		50.1				296.2	292.9	1.1%
Maine	106.5	24.7	4.7				8.6				144.5	148.9	-2.9%
Md.	177.0	48.2	26.3			52.4	496.0	280.3			1,080.3	1,072.6	0.7%
Mass.	2,165.1	128.1	53.7			96.0	376.7	538.3			3,358.0	3,199.4	5.0%
Mich. (3)	642.7	167.4	29.0			192.9	730.8	11.7			1,774.5	1,637.6	8.4%
Minn.	265.5		19.3	6.4	85.8		13.0				390.0	372.9	4.6%
Mo.	277.8	25.0	23.5		132.7		54.4				513.3	494.3	3.9%
Mont.	7.3	2.7	4.4	1.0	14.6						30.0	29.8	0.7%
Neb.	35.1	0.3	4.8	2.2	30.0						72.4	73.8	-2.0%
N.H.	119.9	14.1	4.5	2.3	48.8		9.3				199.0	183.7	8.3%
N.J.	528.3	283.4	101.9	44.2		10.9	689.4				1,658.2	1,630.3	1.7%
N.M.	46.5		5.0	1.9	35.8						89.2	84.9	5.1%
N.Y.	911.5	749.2	360.9				1,142.8	533.2			3,697.6	3,943.1	-6.2%
Ohio	1,128.9	421.7	69.9				524.5				2,144.9	2,195.8	-2.3%
Ore.	137.2	41.7			43.3			92.2	952.8	11.5	1,278.7	1,173.0	9.0%
Pa.	448.5	243.6	209.6				767.0				1,668.7	1,668.4	0.0%
R.I.	51.6		5.9		52.6		28.2	57.6	545.5		741.4	634.1	16.9%
S.D.	13.2	1.0	1.9	0.7	9.1				528.8		554.6	555.2	-0.1%
Texas (4)	1,436.8	742.7	197.0	87.2			185.6				2,649.3	3,153.4	-16.0%
Vt.	57.1	8.8	2.2				2.3				70.4	74.1	-4.9%
Va.	337.7	121.3	32.1			79.6	355.5			8.3	934.5	914.2	2.2%
Wash.	236.6	140.0	44.1	24.2			18.0	10.5			473.4	454.7	4.1%
W. Va.	79.2		6.6	1.9	81.8		16.3	16.3	741.6		943.6	704.8	33.9%
Wis.	230.8	21.3	31.7	7.0	101.6		35.8				428.2	418.6	2.3%
Total U.S.	$14,309.2	$5,646.1	$1,970.9	$207.4	$1,463.8	$824.5	$7,907.1	$1,889.8	$3,146.3	$48.1	$37,413.1	$36,641.9	2.1%

(1) Includes the multistate online game Cash4Life, and other similar four-number games.
(2) Video lottery sales indicated are cash-in figures for all states except Delaware, which reports only net machine income.
(3) District of Columbia and Michigan figures are lottery estimates for the fiscal year ending 9/30/99.
(4) Texas Lottery sales are for the 12 months ending July 31, 1999 (and July 31, 1998, for comparison).

Canada Lottery Sales-Fiscal 1999

Unaudited Results
Figures in millions, Canadian dollars.
(C$1 = US$0.66)

	Instant & Pulltabs	Lotto	Spiel	3-digit	4-digit	Sports Lottery	Passive	Keno	VLTs/slots (1)	Other	FY1999 Total Lottery Sales	FY1998 Total Lottery Sales	Percent Change
Alberta	$97.5	$182.9	$45.9	$6.6		$30.7	$2.6				$366.0	$331.3	10.5%
British Columbia	292.4	347.7	63.4	4.7		22.8	6.0	$173.7	$146.8		1,057.4	924.1	14.4%
Manitoba	39.5	65.8	16.4	2.8		14.3	0.8				139.6	129.4	7.9%
New Brunswick (2)	55.2	47.5	11.2		$1.0	2.9		2.5	120.7		241.0	236.4	1.9%
Newfoundland (2)	105.9	35.8	8.2		0.5	2.6		2.2	84.5		239.7	230.3	4.1%
Northwest Territories	2.9	2.7	0.6	0.1		0.9	0.0				7.3	7.3	-0.1%
Nova Scotia (2)	91.2	71.8	12.7		1.3	6.0		4.7	129.2		316.9	302.3	4.8%
Ontario	689.9	946.4	158.5	52.1		197.6		64.5	17.5		2,126.5	2,039.0	4.3%
Prince Edward Island (2)	15.5	8.4	1.9		0.2	1.1		0.4	11.4		38.9	40.2	-3.4%
Quebec	546.7	698.7	135.2	24.1		46.5	106.1	111.2	768.0		2,436.6	2,182.4	11.6%
Saskatchewan	42.2	56.2	17.8	1.5		7.6	1.0	0.7		0.1	127.1	117.7	8.0%
Yukon	1.6	2.2	0.5	0.1		0.4	0.0				4.9	4.6	5.3%
Total Canada	$1,980.6	$2,466.1	$472.3	$91.9	$3.0	$333.3	$116.6	$359.9	$1,278.0	$0.1	$7,101.8	$6,545.0	8.5%

(1) All video lottery figures in Canada represent net machine income only. VLT revenues for Alberta, Manitoba and Saskatchewan were not available at press time; for comparative purposes, VLT revenues for these provinces have been removed from FY1998 sales.
(2) The hybrid passive/instant games offered by the Atlantic Lottery Corporation are included this year under "instant and pulltabs." In prior years, they were included separately under "passive."

Source: Patricia McQueen, "Mixed Results in North America," *International Gaming and Wagering Business*, vol. 20, no. 9, September 1999

tion. (Seventeen states allocate revenue for education programs.) In many cases, however, instead of adding lottery revenues to their existing budgets for these programs, states cut their budgets by the amount of lottery funds received. Thus, the net benefit to the programs was zero. The most prominent example was Florida, which had introduced the lottery as a way to increase state funding for schools. However, the state then reduced educational funding by the amount of the revenues received from the lottery.

On the other hand, the neighboring state of Georgia is cited as a laudatory example of the financial possibilities of the lottery. The Helping Outstanding Pupils Educationally program (HOPE) began in 1993 and has provided free tuition to more than 250,000 college students. HOPE has bought new computers and satellite dishes for the state's public schools, upgraded vocational and technical schools, and introduced new preschools for children from low-income families. HOPE costs approximately $200 million per year and is financed entirely through the state lottery. As long as the Georgia governor and legislature keep their promise to use lottery returns for additional educational programs, rather than basic educational needs, the Georgia lottery will likely remain an example of how the lottery can benefit a state.

In New Jersey, revenue goes to homes for disabled veterans. Wisconsin revenues are earmarked for property tax relief.

A MARKETING CHALLENGE

With lotteries directly available to about 88 percent of the nation's population, competition becomes quite keen. Lottery directors must con-

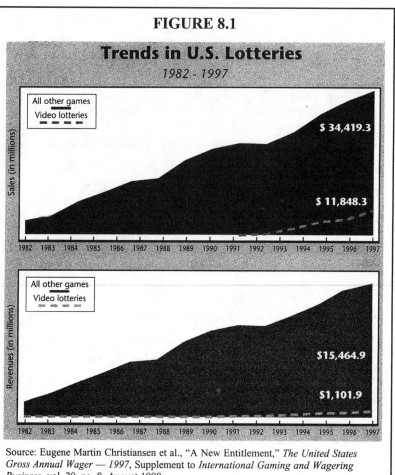

FIGURE 8.1

Trends in U.S. Lotteries
1982 - 1997

All other games
Video lotteries

Sales (in millions)

$ 34,419.3

$ 11,848.3

1982 1983 1984 1985 1986 1987 1988 1989 1990 1991 1992 1993 1994 1995 1996 1997

All other games
Video lotteries

Revenues (in millions)

$15,464.9

$1,101.9

1982 1983 1984 1985 1986 1987 1988 1989 1990 1991 1992 1993 1994 1995 1996 1997

Source: Eugene Martin Christiansen et al., "A New Entitlement," *The United States Gross Annual Wager — 1997*, Supplement to *International Gaming and Wagering Business*, vol. 20, no. 8, August 1998

tinually develop new lottery games to maintain players' interest. To attract more players, lotteries have tied their games with the game Monopoly, the movie *Rocky*, the Winning Spirit of the Olympics, the singer Buddy Holly, and the soft drink 7-UP.

The Search for Younger Players

Most lottery players are currently older than 40 years of age. Marketers for the state lotteries have to figure out ways to attract younger adult players to ensure the future growth of the game. Younger adults seem to be attached to games of skill or games in which they think skills are involved — games that involve more than scratching a single space.

Some marketers believe the best chance to attract younger adult players (at least male adult players) is to tie the lottery to sports. At the same time, the lotteries do not want to alienate older players.

Finally, a program to attract younger players must not appear to be aimed at attracting people less than 18 years. Any marketing campaign that appears to be designed to attract children to gambling would likely cause a negative public reaction.

A NATIONAL LOTTERY

Thomas Jefferson, author of the Declaration of Independence and third president of the United States, thought "the lottery is a wonderful thing; it lays taxation only on the willing." Recent successes in state lotteries have inspired several congressmen to introduce national lottery bills, but to date, none has succeeded.

Some of the major arguments in support of a national lottery are

- It would be a voluntary method of raising money.

- Revenues, estimated at between $6 and $50 billion a year, could help reduce the national debt, bolster the nation's Social Security system, or supplement education and child-welfare programs.

- A lottery is no more regressive (in which a larger portion of revenue is taken from the poor than from middle- and upper-income groups) than sales taxes, which affect everyone equally, regardless of income.

- Studies indicate that state-operated lotteries decrease activity in illegal numbers games.

Some of the major arguments against a national lottery include

- Better methods of balancing the federal budget should be used.

- It is not a productive revenue-raiser and would make only a small dent in the total national debt.

- It is immoral, creating an environment where the "chance ethic" is more important than the "work ethic."

- It promotes compulsive gambling.

- It is a regressive form of taxation.

- It contributes to organized crime.

- A national lottery would become a direct competitor to state lotteries.

Politically Unlikely

Probably the most important reason that a national lottery is unlikely is that it would draw money away from the state lotteries. The North American Association of State and Provincial Lotteries (NASPL), a trade organization that represents the state and provincial lotteries in North America, strongly opposes a federal lottery and has vowed to fight it. NASPL claims that it will be easy for state lottery officials to convince the representatives and senators from their states that a national lottery would have a devastating impact on their state incomes. This would be especially true for small states whose jackpots could never compete with that of a national lottery. Furthermore, it is easier to convince voters that lottery money should help out at the state and local level, rather than be sent to Washington, DC.

LOTTERIES — A WORLDWIDE PASSION

Lotteries are as popular in other parts of the world as they are in the United States. There are lottery games in countries on every continent. In 1996, a lottery in the United Kingdom with a jackpot of $65 million resulted in the sale of $100 million in tickets. The lottery administrators reported that tickets were selling at the rate of 5,000 per minute, and an estimated 90 percent of all adults in the United Kingdom had purchased a ticket. According to *International Gaming and Wagering Business,* worldwide lottery sales (including the United States) in 1998 reached $125 billion,

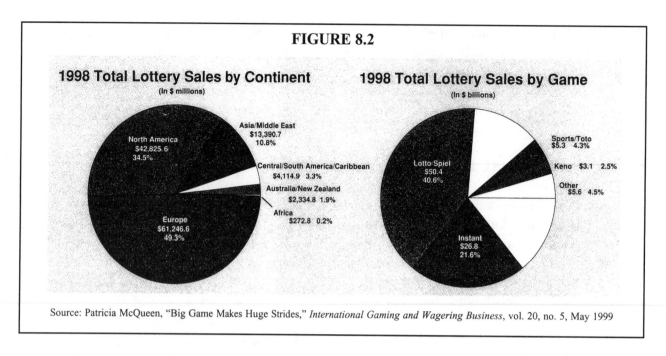

FIGURE 8.2

1998 Total Lottery Sales by Continent
(In $ millions)

North America $42,825.6 34.5%

Asia/Middle East $13,390.7 10.8%

Central/South America/Caribbean $4,114.9 3.3%

Australia/New Zealand $2,334.8 1.9%

Africa $272.8 0.2%

Europe $61,246.6 49.3%

1998 Total Lottery Sales by Game
(In $ billions)

Lotto/Spiel $50.4 40.6%

Sports/Toto $5.3 4.3%

Keno $3.1 2.5%

Other $5.6 4.5%

Instant $26.8 21.6%

Source: Patricia McQueen, "Big Game Makes Huge Strides," *International Gaming and Wagering Business*, vol. 20, no. 5, May 1999

almost double the $64.4 billion in 1990. Europe had the most lottery sales ($61.2 billion), followed by North America ($42.8 billion), Asia and the Middle East ($13.4 billion), Central and South America ($4.1 billion), Australia and New Zealand ($2.3 billion), and Africa ($272.8 million). (See Figure 8.2.)

By country, the United States sold the most lottery tickets ($36.7 billion), followed by Italy ($12.3 billion), the United Kingdom ($9.9 billion), Spain ($9.7 billion), Germany ($9.4 billion), and France ($6.1 billion). (See Table 8.2.)

The largest international lottery organizations in 1998 were the United Kingdom's National Lottery ($9.1 billion in sales), the Italian national lottery ($8.1 billion), the Spanish national lottery ($7 billion), the French lottery ($6.1 billion), and Japan's Dai-Ichi Kangyo Bank Lottery ($6 billion). (See Table 8.2.)

NATIONAL GAMBLING IMPACT STUDY COMMISSION

Lotteries are unique in that they are the province of state governments, and individual states have monopolies on their lotteries. Originally, lotteries were set up in this manner to exclude crimi-

nal activity, and there is still no competition within the state. Lotteries and the officials who run them report to state elected officials, who are responsible for the goals and operations of lotteries.

This means that the lottery director is under pressure from the state politicians to maintain or increase revenues, and the interest in public welfare is often put in second place. Some state governments push lotteries by constant advertising and by placing lottery machines in neighborhood stores everywhere.

Lottery wagering is easily accessible and minors are attracted to it, even though ticket sales to minors are illegal in every state. In Minnesota and Connecticut, anyone may purchase a lottery ticket through self-service vending machines. The Massachusetts attorney general's office reported that 9-year-olds in that state are able to purchase a lottery ticket 80 percent of the time they try, 66 percent of minors have bet on keno games, and 75 percent of Massachusetts high school seniors claim to have played the lottery. In Minnesota, 27 percent of 15- to 18-year-olds reported that they had purchased lottery tickets. In Louisiana, 32 percent; in Texas, 34 percent; and in Connecticut, 35 percent of 15- to 18-year-olds claimed to have purchased lottery tickets.

TABLE 8.2

Top Ten World Lottery Organizations by 1998 Sales

Rank	Lottery	Country	1998 Sales (in billions)
1	The U.K. National Lottery	U. K.	$9.1
2	Amministrazione Autonoma dei Monopoli di Stato	Italy	$8.1
3	Organismo Nacional de Loterías y Apuestas	Spain	$7.0
4	La Francaise des Jeux	France	$6.1
5	Dai-Ichi Kangyo Bank Lottery	Japan	$6.0
6	New York State Lottery	U.S.	$3.9
7	Massachusetts State Lottery	U.S.	$3.2
8	Texas State Lottery	U.S.	$3.1
9	Organización Nacional de Ciegos de España*	Spain	$2.6
10	Sisal Sport Italia	Italy	$2.4

Top Ten Countries by 1998 Lottery Sales

Rank	Country	Total 1998 Sales (in billions)
1	United States	$36.7
2	Italy	$12.3
3	United Kingdom	$9.9
4	Spain	$9.7
5	Germany	$9.4
6	France	$6.1
7	Japan	$6.0
8	Canada	$5.1
9	Malaysia	$5.1

Source: Patricia McQueen, "Big Game Makes Huge Strides," *International Gaming and Wagering Business*, vol. 20, no. 5, May 1999

The National Gambling Impact Study Commission (NGISC) concluded that much of state lottery advertising is overly aggressive and deceptive, is often glitzy, and can be misleading. State advertisements are no longer put forth in the spirit of public service announcements. In 1997, according to *International Gaming and Wagering Business*, the states spent $400 million, or approximately 1 percent of total sales, on advertising. Advertisers acting as agents of the government are not held to the same truth-in-advertising standards as commercial advertisers, and some of their advertising stresses luck over hard work, instant gratification over careful investing, and entertainment over savings.

On the other hand, some states restrict the kinds of advertising the lottery agency can do. Minnesota, Virginia, and Wisconsin ban advertisements that induce people to play. Other states require the odds of winning be prominently displayed and that advertisements be accurate, not misleading. As part of their research, NGISC received a list of advertising standards from the North American Association of State and Provincial Lotteries (NASPL). (See Table 8.3.)

Recommendations

Having considered all the above issues, NGISC recommends the following.

• States with lotteries should publicly develop and review model regulations for their lottery and adopt them legislatively.

TABLE 8.3

NASPL ADVERTISING STANDARDS

The North American Association of State and Provincial Lotteries (NASPL) approved a list of advertising standards for their members on March 19, 1999.[79] These standards address the content and tone of lottery advertising, including the use of minors in ads, the inclusion of game information and a clear listing of lottery revenue beneficiaries. According to the NASPL, signatory NASPL members "will conduct their advertising and marketing practices in accordance with the provisions of these standards."[80] These advertising standards are outlined below:

Content:

- Advertising should be consistent with principles of dignity, integrity, mission, and values of the industry and jurisdictions.

- Advertising should neither contain nor imply lewd or indecent language, images or actions.

- Advertising should not portray product abuse, excessive play, nor a preoccupation with gambling.

- Advertising should not imply nor portray any illegal activity.

- Advertising should not degrade the image or status of persons of any ethnic, minority, religious group nor protected class.

- Advertising by lotteries should appropriately recognize diversity in both audience and media, consistent with these standards.

- Advertising should not encourage people to play excessively nor beyond their means.

- Advertising and marketing materials should include a responsible play message when appropriate.

- Responsible play public service or purchased media messages are appropriate, especially during large jackpot periods.

- Support for compulsive gambling programs, including publications, referrals and employee training is a necessary adjunct to lottery advertising.

- Advertising should not present, directly nor indirectly, any lottery game as a potential means of relieving any person's financial or personal difficulties.

- Advertising should not exhort play as a means of recovering past gambling nor other financial losses.

- Advertising should not knowingly be placed in or adjacent to other media that dramatize or glamorize inappropriate use of the product.

---

[79]In addition to the national standards provided by NASPL, many state lotteries have created their own guidelines for advertising. The advertising codes for 24 lottery states were forwarded to the NGISC on April 20, 1999.

[80]See NASPL Advertising Standards, sent to NGISC by George Anderson, April 1999.

(continued)

- States with lotteries should not permit instant games that are simulations of live card and other casino-type games.

- Each state lottery should willingly agree to follow enforceable advertising rules. The rules should avoid clear or understood appeals to at-risk populations, including youth and low-income neighborhoods. Enforcement should include ways to recognize and address citizen complaints that may arise from advertising.

- Congress should modify the federal truth-in-advertising laws to include state-sponsored lotteries.

- Congress should delegate, to an appropriate federal agency, the task of annually gathering

TABLE 8.3 (Continued)
NASPL Advertising Standards

Tone:

- The lottery should not be promoted in derogation of nor as an alternative to employment, nor as a financial investment, nor a way to achieve financial security.

- Lottery advertisements should not be designed so as to imply urgency, should not make false promises, and should not present winning as the probable outcome.

- Advertising should not denigrate a person who does not buy a lottery ticket nor unduly praise a person who does buy a ticket.

- Advertising should emphasize the fun and entertainment aspect of playing lottery games and not imply a promise of winning.

- Advertising should not exhort the public to wager by directly or indirectly misrepresenting a person's chance of winning a prize.

- Advertising should not imply that lottery games are games of skill.

Minors:

- Persons depicted as lottery players in lottery advertising should not be, nor appear to be, under the legal purchase age.

- Age restriction should, at a minimum, be posted at the point of sale.

- Advertising should not appear in media directed primarily to those under the legal age.

- Lotteries should not be advertised at venues where the audience is reasonably and primarily expected to be below the legal purchase age.

- Advertising should not contain symbols nor language that are primarily intended to appeal to minors or those under the legal purchase age.

- The use of animation should be monitored to ensure that characters are not associated with animated characters on children's programs.

- Celebrity or other testimonials should not be used that would primarily appeal to persons under the legal purchase age.

Game information:

- Odds of winning must be readily available to the public and be clearly stated.

- Advertising should state alternative case and annuity values where reasonable and appropriate.

Beneficiaries:

- Lotteries should provide information regarding the use of lottery proceeds.

- Advertising should clearly denote where lottery proceeds go, avoiding statements that could be confusing or misinterpreted.

Source: *National Gambling Impact Study Commission Report*, National Gambling Study Commission, Washington, DC, 1999

data concerning lottery operations in the United States. The data should include information on volume of purchase; demographics of lottery players and demographic patterns of play; nature, content, accuracy, and type of advertising spending aimed at problem and pathological gamblers; spending on regulation; and other relevant matters.

- States with lotteries should reduce their sales dependence in low-income neighborhoods and on heavy players by various means, including limiting advertising and number of sales outlets in low-income areas.

- States with lotteries should create a private-citizen oversight board that would make data-based policy decisions on types of games to offer and marketing strategies to follow, etc.

- States should curtail the growth of new lottery games, reduce lottery advertising, and limit locations for lottery machines.

The Commission recognizes that lotteries and convenience gambling may play a major role in the development of youth gamblers. It recommends that all relevant governmental gambling regulatory agencies enact and enforce harsh penalties for abuse in this area involving underage gamblers. Penalties and enforcement efforts regarding underage gambling should be greatly increased.

CHAPTER IX

BINGO AND OTHER CHARITABLE GAMES

HOW MUCH MONEY IS BET ON CHARITY GAMING?*

Charity gaming activities are conducted by and for charitable non-profit organizations and include bingo, charity game tickets, pulltabs, jar tickets, breakopens, instant bingo, Lucky 7's, pickle cards, raffles, casino nights, and various other games of chance.

Charity gaming is permitted in all states except Arkansas, Hawaii, Tennessee, and Utah. According to NAFTM, charity gambling is intended

> to fund activities in local communities … to fund activities that no longer enjoy the benefit of state or federal support … to add value to the lives of members of the local community by providing services and programs which might otherwise be neglected for lack of funds.

Since 1986, the National Association of Fundraising Ticket Manufacturers (NAFTM, Minneapolis, Minnesota) has annually surveyed states permitting charitable activities to determine how much money is raised at charity gaming throughout the United States. The 1998 survey included data from the 22 states and seven Canadian provinces that provided information for the report. The NAFTM survey does not include statistics for gaming conducted on Native American reservations. (For information on gambling on Native American reservations, see Chapters III and VII.)

According to NAFTM, charitable gambling constitutes 4.7 percent of the total amount wagered for legalized gambling in the United States. (See Figure 9.1.) In 1991, charity gaming made up 3.7 percent of the total amount bet. The NAFTM estimates that $6.7 billion was wagered in 1998 in the 22 states that reported receipts from charity gaming. Minnesota ($1.4 billion) was, by far, the lead-

---

* The National Association of Fundraising Ticket Manufacturers (NAFTM) estimate of the total amount of money wagered is based on the information provided by only the states that responded to its survey. Within those states, the type and amount of information gathered may vary. As a result, NAFTM advises that figures in its report are low estimates and that "it is important to realize that actual charity gaming amounts are considerably higher than the figures reported." The NAFTM refers to the total amount wagered as annual gross receipts as noted, for example, in Table 9.1. The amount earned by the charitable game is referred to as "net proceeds to charity" as noted in Table 9.2 (which does not cover three states — Indiana, New York, and Wisconsin — that are included in Table 9.1).

International Gaming and Wagering Business (IGWB; August 1999) estimated gross wagering for total charitable gaming, in 1998, at $10.1 billion. Approximately two-fifths ($4 million) came from bingo. Since Eugene Christiansen and Will Cummings, in their annual report in *International Gaming and Wagering Business*, estimate the total handle for the whole country, their estimate will be higher than the NAFTM estimates, which cover only responding states.

TABLE 9.1
WAGER PER CAPITA

State	Gross Receipts	Population[1]	Wager per Capita	Games Included
Colorado	$217,071,991	3,747,000	$58	Bingo, Pulltabs, Raffles
Connecticut	$55,871,657	3,275,000	$17	Bingo, Pulltabs, Raffles, Casino Nights, Other
Idaho	$8,487,765	1,163,000	$7	Bingo, Raffles
Indiana	$521,970,657	5,803,000	$90	Bingo, Pulltabs, Raffles, Casino Nights
Iowa	$47,275,395	2,842,000	$17	Bingo, Raffles, Casino Nights
Kentucky	$539,571,980	3,860,000	$140	Bingo, Pulltabs, Raffles, Casino Nights, Other
Louisiana	$220,300,000	4,342,000	$51	Bingo, Pulltabs, Raffles, Casino Nights
Massachusetts	$190,062,009	6,074,000	$31	Bingo, Pulltabs, Raffles, Casino Nights, Other
Michigan[2]	$333,627,272	9,549,000	$35	Bingo, Pulltabs, Raffles, Casino Nights, Other
Minnesota	$1,432,630,000	4,610,000	$311	Bingo, Pulltabs, Raffles, Other
Mississippi	$138,234,948	2,697,000	$51	Bingo, Pulltabs, Video Bingo, Video Pulltabs
Missouri	$169,807,300	5,324,000	$32	Bingo, Pulltabs, Raffles
Nebraska	$271,356,261	1,637,000	$166	Bingo, Pulltabs, Raffles, Keno
New Mexico	$46,943,263	1,685,000	$28	Bingo, Pulltabs, Raffles, Other
New York	$445,756,342	18,136,000	$25	Bingo, Pulltabs, Raffles, Casino Nights
North Carolina	$33,420,768	7,195,000	$5	Bingo
North Dakota	$263,836,527	641,000	$412	Bingo, Pulltabs, Raffles, Other
Oregon	$77,887,374	3,141,000	$25	Bingo, Raffles, Casino Nights, Other
Texas	$604,587,795	18,724,000	$32	Bingo, Pulltabs
Virginia	$271,290,343	6,618,000	$41	Bingo, Pulltabs, Raffles, Casino Nights, Other
Washington[3]	$777,213,360	5,431,000	$143	Bingo, Pulltabs, Raffles, Casino Nights, Other
Wisconsin	$73,137,829	5,123,000	$14	Bingo, Raffles

Province[4]	Gross Receipts	Population	Wager per Capita	Games Included
Alberta	$913,265,000	2,656,000	$344	Bingo, Pulltabs, Raffles, Charity Casinos
Manitoba	$106,200,000	1,105,000	$96	Bingo, Pulltabs, Raffles, Charity Casinos
New Brunswick	$63,152,862	738,000	$86	Bingo, Pulltabs, Raffles, Charity Casinos
Newfoundland	$66,737,000	570,000	$117	Bingo, Pulltabs, Raffles, Charity Casinos
Ontario	$2,305,000,000	10,768,000	$214	Bingo, Pulltabs, Raffles, Other
Prince Edward Island	$14,848,011	131,000	$113	Bingo
Saskatchewan	$192,260,000	978,000	$197	Bingo, Pulltabs, Raffles

[1] Source: Encarta 2000 New World Almanac 1998, Helicon Publishing, Ltd. [2] Only 54% of all Raffles are reported. Raffles with prizes of less than $500 per drawing are not required to report to the state. [3] Includes some commercial activity. [4] Canadian Dollars.

Source: *Charity Gaming in North America, 1998 Annual Report*, National Association of Fundraising Ticket Manufacturers, St. Paul, MN, n.d.

ing charity game state, followed by Washington State ($777.2 million), Texas ($604.6 million), and Kentucky ($539.6 million). Canadians wagered approximately $3.7 billion, most of it in Ontario ($2.3 billion) and Alberta ($913.3 million). (See Table 9.1.)

How Much Went to Charity?

NAFTM reported that in the 19 states that reported net proceeds, $548.2 million was raised for charitable organizations in 1998 — 9.6 percent of the total raised. Charities received the most money from charitable gambling in Minnesota ($77 million), Washington ($74.5 million), and Michigan ($62.9 million). In Canada, about $516.8 million was raised for charity — 14.9 percent of the total raised. Most of the money went to charities in Ontario ($346 million) and Alberta ($128.6 million). (See Table 9.2 and Figure 9.2.)

How Much Went to Tax Revenue?

According to the NAFTM, charitable gaming in the states that provided data, through taxes and license fees, contributed $164.7 million in 1998 to

TABLE 9.2

DISTRIBUTION OF DOLLARS

State	Gross Receipts	Prizes Paid	% of Gross Receipts to Prizes	Net Proceeds to Charity	% of Gross Receipts to Charity	License Fees & Taxes	% of Gross Receipts to LF&T	Expenses[1]	% of Gross Receipts to Expenses	Games Included
Colorado	$217,071,991	$168,244,724	77.51%	$28,603,391	13.18%	$946,977	0.44%	$19,276,899	8.88%	Bingo, Pulltabs, Raffles
Connecticut	$55,871,657	$28,021,440	50.15%	$18,816,718	33.68%	$1,349,320	2.42%	$7,684,179	13.75%	Bingo, Pulltabs, Raffles, Casino Nights, Other
Idaho	$8,487,765	$5,771,679	68.00%	$1,697,552	20.00%	$19,000	0.22%	$999,534	11.78%	Bingo, Raffles
Iowa	$47,275,395	$30,715,325	64.97%	$10,579,837	22.38%	$2,367,059	5.01%	$3,613,174	7.64%	Bingo, Raffles, Casino Nights
Kentucky	$539,571,980	$467,251,320	86.60%	$36,805,817	6.82%	$2,505,587	0.46%	$33,009,256	6.12%	Bingo, Pulltabs, Raffles, Casino Nights, Other
Louisiana	$220,300,000	$165,600,000	75.17%	$27,700,000	12.57%	$1,008,000	0.46%	$25,992,000	11.80%	Bingo, Pulltabs, Raffles, Casino Nights
Massachusetts	$190,062,009	$137,153,283	72.16%	$29,151,596	15.34%	$12,209,277	6.42%	$11,547,853	6.08%	Bingo, Pulltabs, Raffles, Casino Nights, Other
Michigan[2]	$333,627,272	$230,192,411	69.00%	$62,870,238	18.84%	$14,952,538	4.48%	$25,612,085	7.68%	Bingo, Pulltabs, Raffles, Casino Nights, Other
Minnesota	$1,432,630,000	$1,167,195,000	81.47%	$76,975,000	5.37%	$64,516,398	4.50%	$123,943,602	8.65%	Bingo, Pulltabs, Raffles, Other
Mississippi	$138,234,948	$100,167,584	72.46%	$19,852,042	14.36%	$238,352	0.17%	$17,976,970	13.00%	Bingo, Pulltabs, Video Bingo, Video Pulltabs
Missouri	$169,807,300	$130,461,292	76.83%	$20,476,057	12.06%	$4,087,237	2.41%	$14,782,714	8.71%	Bingo, Pulltabs, Raffles
Nebraska	$271,356,261	$203,651,398	75.05%	$27,397,037	10.10%	$6,294,344	2.32%	$34,013,482	12.53%	Bingo, Pulltabs, Raffles, Keno
New Mexico	$46,943,263	$35,651,752	75.95%	$5,564,353	11.85%	$198,855	0.42%	$5,528,303	11.78%	Bingo, Pulltabs, Raffles, Other
North Carolina	$33,420,768	$25,193,274	75.38%	$3,979,811	11.91%	$57,600	0.17%	$4,190,083	12.54%	Bingo
North Dakota	$263,836,527	$207,195,224	78.53%	$16,053,941	6.08%	$10,914,664	4.14%	$29,672,698	11.25%	Bingo, Pulltabs, Raffles, Other
Oregon	$77,887,374	$57,629,133	73.99%	$9,583,652	12.30%	$695,414	0.89%	$9,979,175	12.81%	Bingo, Raffles, Casino Nights, Other
Texas	$604,587,795	$431,961,474	71.45%	$42,737,244	7.07%	$30,135,136	4.98%	$99,753,941	16.50%	Bingo, Pulltabs
Virginia	$271,290,343	$206,762,956	76.21%	$34,853,100	12.85%	$3,543,817	1.31%	$26,130,470	9.63%	Bingo, Pulltabs, Raffles, Casino Nights, Other
Washington[3]	$777,213,360	$506,682,327	65.19%	$74,501,281	9.59%	$8,653,497	1.11%	$187,376,255	24.11%	Bingo, Pulltabs, Raffles, Casino Nights, Other
Totals	$5,699,476,008	$4,305,501,596	75.54%	$548,198,667	9.62%	$164,693,071	2.89%	$681,082,674	11.95%	

Province[4]	Gross Receipts	Prizes Paid	% of Gross Receipts to Prizes	Net Proceeds to Charity	% of Gross Receipts to Charity	License Fees & Taxes	% of Gross Receipts to LF&T	Expenses	% of Gross Receipts to Expenses	Games Included
Alberta	$913,265,000	$674,334,000	73.84%	$128,641,000	14.09%	$4,216,000	0.46%	$106,074,000	11.61%	Bingo, Pulltabs, Raffles, Charity Casinos
Manitoba	$106,200,000	$76,100,000	71.66%	$16,300,000	15.35%	$632,172	0.60%	$13,167,828	12.40%	Bingo, Pulltabs, Raffles, Charity Casinos
New Brunswick	$63,152,862	$43,805,658	69.36%	$12,889,303	20.41%	$22,185	0.04%	$6,435,716	10.19%	Bingo, Pulltabs, Raffles, Charity Casinos
Newfoundland	$66,737,000	$46,425,000	69.56%	$10,160,000	15.22%	$523,000	0.78%	$9,629,000	14.43%	Bingo, Pulltabs, Raffles, Charity Casinos
Ontario	$2,305,000,000	$1,639,000,000	71.11%	$346,000,000	15.01%	$14,497,507	0.63%	$305,502,493	13.25%	Bingo, Pulltabs, Raffles, Charity Casinos
Prince Edward Island	$14,848,011	$10,374,472	69.87%	$2,769,765	18.65%	$207,494	1.40%	$1,496,280	10.08%	Bingo
Totals	$3,469,202,873	$2,490,039,130	71.78%	$516,760,068	14.90%	$20,098,358	0.58%	$442,305,317	12.75%	

[1] Expenses figures were calculated for this report using the formula Gross Receipts-(Prizes Paid+Net Proceeds to Charity+License Fees and Taxes). [2] Only 54% of all Raffles are reported.
Raffles with prizes of less than $500 per drawing are not required to report to the state. [3] Includes some commercial activity. License Fees and Taxes figure does not include income
from ID stamps. [4] Canadian Dollars.

Source: *Charity Gaming in North America, 1998 Annual Report*, National Association of Fundraising Ticket Manufacturers, St. Paul, MN, n.d.

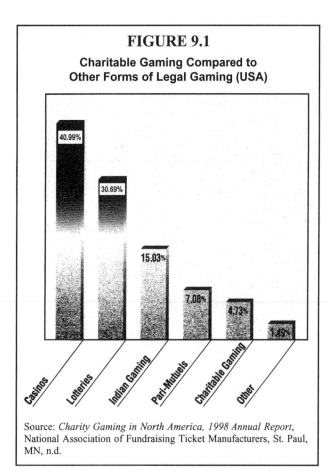

FIGURE 9.1

Charitable Gaming Compared to Other Forms of Legal Gaming (USA)

- Casinos: 40.99%
- Lotteries: 30.69%
- Indian Gaming: 15.03%
- Pari-Mutuels: 7.08%
- Charitable Gaming: 4.73%
- Other: 1.49%

Source: *Charity Gaming in North America, 1998 Annual Report*, National Association of Fundraising Ticket Manufacturers, St. Paul, MN, n.d.

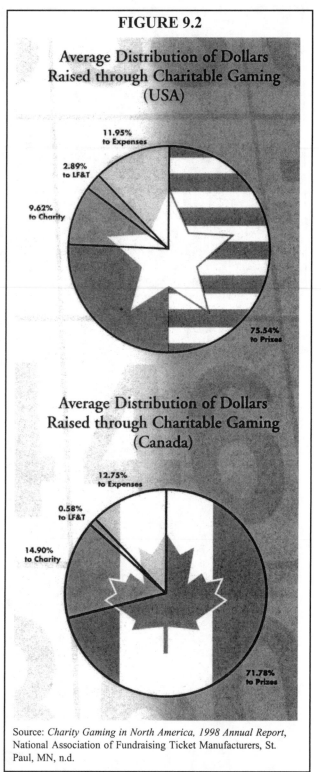

FIGURE 9.2

Average Distribution of Dollars Raised through Charitable Gaming (USA)

- 11.95% to Expenses
- 2.89% to LF&T
- 9.62% to Charity
- 75.54% to Prizes

Average Distribution of Dollars Raised through Charitable Gaming (Canada)

- 12.75% to Expenses
- 0.58% to LF&T
- 14.90% to Charity
- 71.78% to Prizes

Source: *Charity Gaming in North America, 1998 Annual Report*, National Association of Fundraising Ticket Manufacturers, St. Paul, MN, n.d.

the various states. State and local treasuries in Minnesota ($64.5 million), Texas ($30 million), and Michigan ($15 million) benefited the most. (See Table 9.2.) Table 9.3 shows how bingo, pulltabs, and raffles were taxed and how the revenue was used in the states that submitted information.

WHO PLAYS WHAT?

All the states that permit charitable gambling allow bingo. (Five states — Alabama, Georgia, Nevada, North Carolina, and South Carolina — permit bingo but not other charitable games. [See Chapter III, Table 3.1.]) The other most commonly permitted charitable games are raffles (32 states and Washington, DC); charity game tickets, such as pulltabs, breakopen, jar tickets or pickle tabs in which the player takes off the top of the tab to see if a winner is behind it (40 states and Washington, DC); and Las Vegas or casino nights (17 states). Table 9.4 shows what kinds of games are legal in the 22 states and seven Canadian provinces that provided data for the 1998 report.

BINGO — FROM UNKNOWN ORIGINS TO A UNIQUELY AMERICAN GAME

Historians are unsure of the origin of bingo. Experts attribute it to the English, the Dutch, or the Swedes. Others believe bingo developed ei-

120

ther from the sixteenth-century Italian game of lotto, or from the popular lottery game of keno, first played in New Orleans during the 1840s. In the 1920s, bingo was played at local movie theaters. Operated as a "raffle" to avoid state laws against certain forms of gambling, the movie theater games were the first to make bingo a form of public entertainment. The winner of the "raffle" drawing would shout "Bingo!" and claim the prize.

Modern-day bingo, also known as beano, is a simple game. It is based entirely on chance and played until a participant wins. Each player purchases a bingo card, which is made of cardboard or paper and contains five rows of five squares each. (At the end of the session, the cards are returned to the game manager to be used again.) One letter of the word BINGO appears above each of the vertical columns. All of the squares contain a number from 1 to 75, except the "free" center square.

In a typical game, an announcer calls a letter/number combination, such as "B-15." As a combination is called, players who have that combination on their card place "beans" or other markers on the correct square. When a player has covered five squares in a vertical, horizontal, or diagonal column, he or she shouts "Bingo." The announcer then checks the player's card against a master card, and if the cards match, the player receives a prize and a new game begins.

Bingo — The "Innocent" Gambling Game

Bingo is unique among the various forms of gambling. Many Americans learned to play the game as children and generally do not consider it to be gambling. Bingo sessions are a common form of fundraising by charitable organizations such as churches, synagogues, or service clubs, so many people consider the game socially and morally acceptable. It is also a relatively inexpensive way for people to do something together socially. Players can sit out a game or two and talk with their friends. All these factors give bingo a respectability that, until recently, was not enjoyed by most other forms

of gambling. Even commercial bingo (see below) is viewed favorably by many people.

Charitable Bingo Games Run by Commercial Bingo Operations

In most states, bingo games are legal only when they are operated as "charitable gaming activities," that is, at least part of the money bet must go to a charitable (or non-profit religious, educational, etc.) organization. Some charitable organizations run their own bingo games, but many turn to commercial operators to run the games for them. These commercial operators may set up permanent bingo parlors where players can find a game going at almost any time of the day or night.

For their services, commercial bingo operators charge a commission on the proceeds of every game. Their commission is deducted from the "donations" to the charitable organization, thereby reducing the charitable organization's revenue. But because professional operators have the time and money to invest in large-scale operations, charitable organizations generally realize more revenue than if they tried to operate the games themselves.

Almost Anyone Can Play

Only Arkansas, Hawaii, Tennessee, and Utah, which permit no charitable gambling of any type, do not allow bingo. The National Association of Fundraising Ticket Manufacturers (NAFTM) estimated the gross receipts for bingo in 1998 at about $2.49 billion from 21 states in the United States and $1.8 billion from 7 provinces in Canada (Table 9.5). *International Gaming and Wagering Business* (IGWB; August 1998) estimated charitable bingo wagering in the United States at $4 billion in 1998, considerably higher than the NAFTM estimate.

According to the NAFTM, Texas ($505.7 million), Indiana ($453.4 million), Washington ($174.2 million), and New York ($167.6 million) had the greatest handle in the United States, while Ontario ($1.2 billion) and Alberta ($333.8 million)

TABLE 9.3

Taxation Methods

State[1]	Bingo	Pulltabs	Raffles	How Revenue Is Used
Colorado	0.3% of Gross Receipts 1.1% of Net Sales paid by Manufacturers and Suppliers[2]	0.3% of Gross Receipts	0.3% of Gross Receipts	Regulation
Connecticut	0.5% of Adjusted Gross Receipts	10% of Gross Receipts	None	General Revenue Fund
Idaho	None	Not Applicable[3]	Not Available[4]	Not Available[4]
Indiana	Included in License Fee	10% of Sales paid by Suppliers	Included in License Fee	Charity Gaming Enforcement Fund
Iowa	5% of Gross Receipts	Not Applicable[3]	5% of Gross Receipts	General Revenue Fund
Kentucky	0.4% of Gross Receipts	0.4% of Gross Receipts	0.4% of Gross Receipts	Not Available[4]
Louisiana	5% of Bingo Supply Purchases	3% of Ideal Net Receipts	Not Available[4]	Charitable Gaming Regulation
Massachusetts	5% of Gross Receipts	Generated by Sale of Tickets to Licensees	5% of Gross Receipts	State Treasury and State Lottery Fund
Michigan	Included in License Fee	50% of Ideal Net Receipts less Supplier Commission	Included in License Fee	Charitable Gaming Regulation and General Fund
Minnesota	9% of Net Receipts	1.8% of Ideal Gross Receipts plus Additional Amount if Actual Gross Receipts exceed $500,000	9% of Net Receipts	General Revenue Fund
Mississippi	0.5% - 1% of Gross Receipts for each Bingo Session	5% of Net Receipts	Not Applicable[5]	Special Funds
Missouri	$0.002 per Bingo Face paid by Suppliers	2% of Sales paid by Suppliers	Not Available[4]	Not Available[4]
Nebraska	3% of Gross Receipts	10% of Net Receipts paid by Suppliers	2% of Gross Receipts	40% to Cash Fund 60% General Revenue Fund
New Mexico	$30 per event plus 3% of Net Receipts	$30 per event plus 3% of Net Receipts	$30 per event plus 3% of Net Receipts	General Revenue Fund
New York	0.5% of Gross Receipts 2% of Sales paid by Manufacturers and Suppliers	0.5% of Gross Receipts 2% of Sales paid by Manufacturers and Suppliers	0.5% of Gross Receipts	Not Available[4]
North Carolina	None	Not Applicable[5]	Not Available[4]	Not Available[4]
North Dakota	Excise and Gaming Taxes	Gaming Tax	Not Available[4]	General Revenue Fund
Oregon	0.95% of Gross Receipts	Not Applicable[3]	0.5% of Gross Receipts	Charitable Gaming Regulation
Texas	5% of Prizes paid by Winners	5% of Prizes paid by Winners	Not Applicable[5]	General Revenue Fund
Virginia	1.25% of Adjusted Gross Receipts	Not Available[4]	Not Available[4]	Charitable Gaming Regulation
Washington[6]	Up to 10% of Net Receipts	Up to 10% of Net Receipts Up to 5% of Gross Receipts paid by Commercial Operators	10% of Net Receipts minus Prizes	Gambling Enforcement by Local Governments
Wisconsin	2% of Gross Receipts	Not Applicable[3]	Not Available[4]	General Revenue Fund

[1] Taxes and Fees shown on this chart are paid by charities unless otherwise noted. [2] Throughout this chart "Supplier" is defined as the entity from which Charities purchase Bingo, Pulltab and/or Raffle supplies. [3] Pulltabs are sold as a lottery product only; they were not included in the data provided by the state. [4] Information was not included in the data provided by the state. [5] Game Type is not played in the state. [6] Local Government taxes.

Source: *Charity Gaming in North America, 1998 Annual Report*, National Association of Fundraising Ticket Manufacturers, St. Paul, MN, n.d.

had the largest handles in Canada (Table 9.5). *International Gaming and Wagering Business* estimated the amount of the handle retained was 24 percent, meaning that about 76 percent was paid out in prizes. The charities received about 6 percent of the total money bet, while the company administering the bingo game earned the rest.

Eugene Martin Christiansen, writing in *International Gaming and Wagering Business*, believes

TABLE 9.4
THE GAMES

State	Bingo	Pulltabs	Raffles	Casino Nights	Other
Colorado	✔	✔	✔		
Connecticut	✔	✔	✔	✔	✔
Idaho	✔		✔		
Indiana	✔	✔	✔	✔	✔
Iowa	✔		✔	✔	
Kentucky	✔	✔	✔		✔
Louisiana	✔	✔	✔	✔	✔
Massachusetts	✔	✔	✔	✔	
Michigan	✔	✔	✔	✔	✔
Minnesota	✔	✔	✔		✔
Mississippi	✔	✔			✔
Missouri	✔	✔			
Nebraska	✔	✔	✔		
New Mexico	✔	✔	✔		
New York	✔	✔	✔	✔	
North Carolina	✔				
North Dakota	✔	✔	✔		✔
Oregon	✔		✔	✔	
Texas	✔	✔	✔		
Virginia	✔	✔	✔	✔	✔
Washington	✔	✔	✔	✔	✔
Wisconsin	✔		✔		

Province	Bingo	Pulltabs	Raffles	Casino Nights	Other
Alberta	✔	✔	✔	✔	
Manitoba	✔	✔	✔	✔	
New Brunswick	✔	✔	✔	✔	
Newfoundland	✔	✔	✔	✔	
Ontario	✔	✔	✔	✔	
Prince Edward Island	✔				
Saskatchewan	✔	✔	✔		

Source: *Charity Gaming in North America, 1998 Annual Report*, National Association of Fundraising Ticket Manufacturers, St. Paul, MN, n.d.

that bingo is a mature sector of the gambling industry. This means that the public's demand for bingo has been met, and, as a result, revenues from bingo have leveled off and are unlikely to grow significantly in the future. (See Figure 9.3.) Christiansen also thinks the spread of casino gambling may likely hurt bingo's future as bingo players find another way to spend their money.

Bingo on Native American Reservations

These figures do not, however, include bingo on Native American reservations, which has grown dramatically and has been cutting into non-reservation bingo games. The handle on bingo played on Native American reservations rose from almost nothing 15 years ago to about $3.2 billion in 1998. Meanwhile, revenues earned from bingo reached

TABLE 9.5
BINGO, PULLTABS, AND RAFFLES

State	Bingo Gross Receipts	Bingo Net Proceeds	Pulltabs Gross Receipts	Pulltabs Net Proceeds	Raffles Gross Receipts	Raffles Net Proceeds
Colorado	$66,102,087	$8,975,917	$142,881,862	$14,870,262	$8,088,042	$4,757,212
Connecticut	$31,530,981	$6,527,835	$8,358,927	$2,159,751	$14,897,255	$9,417,666
Idaho[1]	$8,487,765	$1,697,552				
Indiana	$453,392,684	$46,761,957	$43,568,610	$7,039,907	$11,891,808	$5,589,461
Iowa[2]	$38,716,854	$8,675,466			$8,558,541	$1,904,371
Kentucky[3]	$113,775,378	$36,805,817	$410,695,395		$5,125,218	
Louisiana[3]	$124,600,000	$27,700,000	$78,400,000		$10,100,000	
Massachusetts	$116,433,303	$3,962,915	$53,594,506	$16,078,351	$18,863,060	$8,677,008
Michigan[4]	$161,691,215	$20,970,756	$114,515,285	$14,630,518	$50,866,256	$24,817,826
Minnesota	$77,090,000	$4,142,034	$1,333,165,000	$71,630,760	$3,792,000	$203,744
Mississippi[5]	$104,171,675	$19,852,042	$9,142,283			
Nebraska	$19,630,057	$675,274	$96,153,628	$11,403,820	$3,263,822	$1,762,464
New Mexico	$31,224,068	$2,683,658	$15,290,195	$2,607,980	$259,977	$103,691
New York	$167,555,946	$61,472,474	$269,779,846	$52,356,793	$5,185,472	$2,499,304
North Carolina	$33,420,768	$3,979,811				
North Dakota[3]	$48,650,772	$16,053,941	$176,480,491		$1,975,800	
Oregon[6]	$73,746,224	$7,242,063			$4,141,150	$2,341,589
Texas[7]	$505,690,713	$42,737,244	$98,897,082			
Virginia	$114,862,326	$20,565,559	$67,287,764	$10,469,685	$5,419,387	$3,385,856
Washington[8]	$174,227,734	$14,531,554	$539,870,359	$45,737,035	$5,991,954	$3,045,754
Wisconsin[6]	$26,375,018	$6,857,505			$46,762,811	$26,413,141

Province[9]	Bingo Gross Receipts	Bingo Net Proceeds	Pulltabs Gross Receipts	Pulltabs Net Proceeds	Raffles Gross Receipts	Raffles Net Proceeds
Alberta	$333,753,000	$57,339,000	$47,708,000	$8,838,000	$55,088,000	$18,731,000
Manitoba	$80,000,000	$9,400,000	$15,000,000	$2,500,000	$11,000,000	$4,300,000
New Brunswick	$54,266,629	$9,396,001	$1,160,298	$172,979	$7,590,468	$3,245,220
Newfoundland	$34,394,000	$2,216,000	$19,599,000	$3,683,000	$12,173,000	$3,947,000
Ontario	$1,200,000,000	$180,000,000	$945,000,000	$125,000,000	$160,000,000	$35,000,000
Prince Edward Island	$14,848,011	$2,769,765				
Saskatchewan	$119,940,000	$23,867,000	$45,605,000	$8,936,000	$26,715,000	$9,330,000

[1] **Bingo** figures include Raffles activity. Pulltabs are sold as a lottery product only; they were not included in the data provided by the state. [2] Pulltabs are sold as a lottery product only; they were not included in the data provided by the state. **Raffles** figures include Casino Nights activity. [3] **Bingo Net Proceeds** figure includes Bingo, Pulltabs, Raffles and Other. [4] Only 54% of all Raffles are reported. Raffles with prizes of less than $500 per drawing are not required to report to the state. [5] **Bingo Net Proceeds** figure includes Bingo, Pulltabs and Other. [6] Pulltabs are sold as a lottery product only; they were not included in the data provided by the state. [7] **Bingo Net Proceeds** figure includes Bingo and Pulltabs. [8] **Pulltabs** figures include some commercial activity. [9] Canadian Dollars.

Source: *Charity Gaming in North America, 1998 Annual Report*, National Association of Fundraising Ticket Manufacturers, St. Paul, MN, n.d.

$954.2 million in 1998. (These are figures for Class II gambling on Indian Reservations, almost all of which is bingo.)

Bingo revenues on Native American reservations have leveled off. Just as non-reservation bingo has been affected by the expansion of casino gambling, so has Native American bingo. In fact, with 160 tribes in 24 states having signed compacts to open casinos, the leveling off of revenues from bingo, rather than a sharp decline, would seem to attest that bingo has a firm base of support. Of course, whether the customer chooses to visit the bingo hall or the casino, in many cases, the money will go into the same tribal coffers.

CHARITY GAME TICKETS

Charity game tickets are also known as pulltabs, jar tickets, breakopens, instant bingo, and pickle cards. According to the NAFTM, in 1998, far more money was wagered on charitable game tickets in the United States than on bingo ($3.5 billion — with just 16 states reporting — compared to $2.49 billion), while about $1.1 billion was bet on charity games in Canada, with six provinces reporting. Minnesota ($1.3 billion) had, by far, the greatest amount of money wagered on charity games, followed by Washington ($540 million) and Kentucky ($411 million). In Canada, Ontario ($945 million) had the largest handle by far, followed by Alberta ($47.7 million). (See Table 9.5.)

RAFFLES

Many states that permit raffles do not require organizations that operate them to report them to the state. As a result, the NAFTM notes that the gross proceeds figure is only a fraction of the actual amount bet. Seventeen states reported raffle wagering of about $205 million, while six Canadian provinces reported $272.6 million. (See Table 9.5.)

CHARITABLE GAMBLING STILL GROWING, BUT SLOWLY

Eugene Christiansen, in *International Gaming and Wagering Business,* estimated that about $6.2 billion was wagered on non-bingo charitable games in 1998, producing about $1.6 billion in revenues for a retained amount of 26 percent, or a payout of around 74 percent. Bingo has been leveling off since the mid-1990s (Figure 9.3), and, in 1996, consumer spending on charitable games rose only 1 percent. Realizing that the high consumer price of pulltabs and other non-bingo games put charitable games at a disadvantage when competing with lower-priced slot machines and lottery gambling,

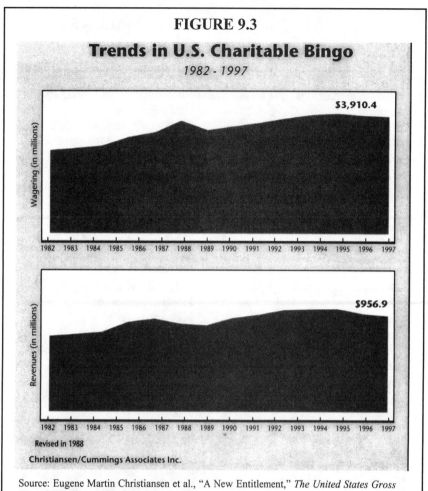

FIGURE 9.3

Trends in U.S. Charitable Bingo
1982 - 1997

Source: Eugene Martin Christiansen et al., "A New Entitlement," *The United States Gross Annual Wager — 1997.* Copyright © 1998, *International Gaming and Wagering Business* magazine. Reproduced with permission.

some states began to approve higher payouts. In addition, pulltab manufacturers began to improve graphics and themes, and added new game variations. These improvements resulted in a 6 percent increase in gross revenues for charitable games in 1997.

Charitable gambling has several advantages over commercial gambling. The players often feel they are doing something good for their community, especially for their more immediate community, such as the church, synagogue, fraternal organizations, or veterans group. Charitable gambling also offers an opportunity for a social gathering. The gambling is only one part of having a good time with friends and acquaintances.

On the other hand, charitable gambling cannot offer the professional embellishments, such as

TABLE 9.6
LICENSING METHODS

State[1]	Bingo	Pulltabs	Raffles	Bingo
Colorado	C	C	C	$62.50 Annual Fee
Connecticut	C	C	S	$75 (Class A), $5 (Class B) and $50 (Class C) Annual Fee based on License Class
Idaho	C		C	$100-$300 Annual Fee based on Gross Receipts
Indiana	C	C	S	$25-$25,000 Annual Fee based on Gross Receipts
Iowa	S			$15-$150 Fee based on License Period from 14 Days to 2 Years
Kentucky	C	C	C	$100-$300 Annual Fee based on Gross Receipts
Louisiana	C	C	C	$50 Annual Fee - $25 per License Modification
Massachusetts	C	C	S	$50 Annual Fee
Michigan	C	C	S	$55 or $150 Annual Fee for Weekly Bingos - $10 or $50 for Special Bingos
Minnesota	C	C	C	$150 to $400 per site Biennial Fee
Mississippi	C	C		$50 Annual Fee
Missouri	S	S		$50 Fee for a Regular License - $25 Fee for a Special License
Nebraska	S	S	S	$35-$120 Annual Fee
New Mexico	C	C	C	$100 Annual Fee
New York	S	S	S	$18.75 Fee per Occasion
North Carolina	C		C	$100 Annual Fee per Organization
North Dakota	C	C	C	$150 Annual Fee
Oregon	S		S	$20-$100 Annual Fee based on License Class (4 classes)
Texas	C	C		$100-$2,500 Annual Fee based on Gross Receipts
Virginia	C	C	C	$200 Annual Fee
Washington	S	S	S	$52-$12,492 Annual Fee based on License Class
Wisconsin	S		S	$10 Fee per Occasion - $5 Fee to Register Financial Officer

Province[1]	Bingo	Pulltabs	Raffles	Bingo
Alberta	S	S	S	$30 or $3,000 per Event based on Prizes (less than or greater than $15,000)
Manitoba	S		S	1.5% of Gross Receipts
Newfoundland	C	C	C	1% of Prizes
Ontario[7]	C	C	C	Up to 3% of Prizes
Prince Edward Island	S		S	2% of Prizes
Saskatchewan	S	S	S	$5 or $50 Annual Fee based on Prizes (less than or greater than $1,000)

(continued)

bright lights and fancy interiors. Winnings are usually limited so that charitable gaming cannot always offer the excitement and payoff some gamblers require. Nonetheless, charitable gambling has been able to maintain its niche in the gambling industry.

REGULATION AND ENFORCEMENT

Despite the popularity of bingo and other forms of charity gambling as fund-raisers and their reputation as harmless pastimes, they are as susceptible to abuses as any other forms of gambling. While Americans might conceive of charitable gambling as just the bingo game at the corner church, the Las Vegas New Year's party at the local synagogue, or the slot machines at the American Legion Hall down the street, charitable gambling is big business. Eugene Christiansen and Will Cummings, of Christiansen/Cummings Associates, Inc., estimate the gross receipts from charity gambling at about $2.5 billion.

While charity gambling revenues in 1998 were estimated at $2.5 billion, on-track revenues from horse racing were about $3.3 billion. Although the revenues are nearly comparable, the administration of horse racing and charitable gambling are

TABLE 9.6 (Continued)

Pulltabs	Raffles
See Bingo	See Bingo
See Bingo	$10-$100
Not Applicable[3]	See Bingo
See Bingo	$25-$25,000 Annual Fee based on Gross Receipts
Not Applicable[3]	Not Available[4]
See Bingo	See Bingo
See Bingo	See Bingo
See Bingo	$10-$50 Municipal Permit Fee
See Bingo	$15-$50 per Event
See Bingo	See Bingo
See Bingo	Not Applicable[5]
$10 per Event	Not Available[4]
$120-$220 Annual Fee	$35-$45 Annual Fee
See Bingo	See Bingo
$25 Annual Fee	$25 Annual Fee if Net Proceeds exceed $30,000
Not Applicable[5]	See Bingo
See Bingo	See Bingo
Not Applicable[3]	$20 or $50 Fee based on License Class
See Bingo	Not Applicable[5]
See Bingo	See Bingo
$527 or $9,880 Annual Fee based on License Class	$52 - $1,326 Annual Fee based on License Class
Not Applicable[3]	$25 Annual Fee

Pulltabs	Raffles
1.5% of Gross Receipts	1.5% of Gross Receipts if Prizes exceed $10,000
Not Available[6]	1.5% of Gross Receipts
See Bingo	See Bingo
See Bingo	See Bingo
Not Applicable[8]	2% of Prizes Awarded
$20 Annual Fee	$5 or $20 per Event based on Prizes (less than or greater than $5)

[1] Charity licensing only. Licensing methods for other entities (ie, manufacturers, distributors, etc.) are not included in this chart.
[2] C indicates a combined license is issued for the designated activities. S indicates a separate license is issued for the activity.
[3] Pulltabs are sold as a lottery product only; they were not included in the data provided by the state. [4] Information was not included in the data provided by the state. [5] Game type is not played in the state. [6] Information was not included in the data provided by the province. [7] Licenses are issued by either the province or the municipality. [8] Game Type is not played in the province.

Source: *Charity Gaming in North America, 1998 Annual Report*, National Association of Fundraising Ticket Manufacturers, St. Paul, MN, n.d.

not. Horse racing is run by professionals with many years of experience. If the management of a horse racing track is sloppy or inattentive, the track will lose money and the manager, his or her job. On the other hand, volunteers, who have often never managed any type of gambling operation, run charitable gambling. Since the administrative positions are usually voluntary, they turn over frequently so the volunteers develop little experience. If they do not do a good job, they probably will not be asked to do it again the next year.

Because they have little experience, charitable groups frequently hire outside administrators to manage the program. Often, a considerable amount of money is involved, and there is little oversight by the charitable organization. Dishonest agents may take advantage of the situation. Racketeers are suspected of controlling some commercial bingo operations; however, when commercial bingo games are held under the sponsorship of a charitable organization, questions are seldom asked.

Skimming — the practice of under-reporting income from games and pocketing the difference — is thought to be the biggest problem facing officials who enforce bingo regulations. As with other forms of gambling, it is required that the revenues from bingo operations be reported to the government. The government considers skimmed money as not just stolen money, but also as untaxed money. Therefore, both charitable groups and the government, through the loss of tax revenue, lose money when it is skimmed by dishonest bingo operators.

All states require bingo licenses (Table 9.6), but few have license control boards. Law enforcement officials generally ignore illegal or dishonest bingo or charitable games because their efforts to regulate them are resisted by the general public.

Few municipal or state budgets have funds for bingo investigation. In addition, many police officers believe bingo is a "victimless" crime, too insignificant to merit substantial enforcement time and effort. As a result, bingo and other forms of charitable gambling continue to have the potential for large revenues with little regulation by government or law enforcement agencies.

Several states have brought charitable gambling under state regulation, and many others are planning to. While government regulation is usually considered an interference, it also can provide legitimacy to charitable groups and provide them with guidelines that will help make their charitable gambling operations less susceptible to dishonest administrators.

CHAPTER X

ILLEGAL GAMBLING IN AMERICA

Illegal gambling, like legal gambling, is deeply rooted in American society. Despite innumerable federal and state laws and competition from state-supported legal gambling, illegal wagering remains a part of American life. In 1999, the Gallup Organization, in *Social Audits: Gambling in America 1999: A Comparison of Adults and Teenagers*, asked respondents if they had participated in any form of illegal gambling during the past year — 24 percent of adults and 18 percent of teenagers had. (See Chapter 11 for more on public opinion about gambling.)

TYPES OF ILLEGAL GAMBLING

The four principal forms of illegal gambling are

- The numbers.

- Horse books (betting on horses).

- Sports books (betting on sporting events).

- Sports cards.

The Numbers Game

The forerunner of modern numbers gambling was a game called "policy." Policy was often a sideline game of the lotteries. Originally, lotteries were used to raise money for civic or charitable causes, while policy was played to earn money for the lottery company, since policy can be played more quickly than a lottery. It is commonly believed that the game of policy gave rise to gambling syndicates, which raised the large sums of money required to operate a policy shop.

Policy gambling radically changed when "numbers" was introduced as a separate and rival game. (See below for how the games are played.) During the 1920s, Black Americans migrated from the rural South into northern cities where more opportunities existed. Policy and numbers appealed to members of poor Black communities and political organizations. During the 1930s, ex-bootleggers fought for control of Black policy and numbers operations.

Using their political connections and money gained from bootlegging, White mobsters forced Black policy and numbers operators to join with them or risk being put out of business — or worse. This conflict usually ended in a partnership, with the original Black owners staying on as managers and operators and the White mobsters providing such services as "protection," financial backing, regulation of competition, and legal representation in court when required.

How the Numbers Game Is Played

As mentioned above, policy was the forerunner of modern numbers gambling. Policy is a simple game in which the bettor selects one to four numbers from 1 to 78, hoping that one of those will be among the 12 that are drawn. Policy feeds on a large volume of small bets and is especially popular among the poor.

To be successful, numbers games require the participation of many people. The bettor places his or her bet for any desired amount on a number from 000 to 999 and receives a receipt indicating the chosen number and the amount wagered. One-digit numbers have an 8-to-1 payoff ($8 is won for every $1 wagered), two-digit numbers have a 60- or 70-to-1 payoff, and three-digit numbers pay 550- or 600-to-1.

The wager money is left with a "collector" (who often operates a numbers game as a sideline to a restaurant, candy store, drugstore, gas station, or other business that involves a lot of public contact). A "pickup man" collects the wagers from the collector and delivers them to the "bank," which is a central headquarters or processing center where the winning numbers are determined and payoffs are made, usually based on the results at a local racetrack or a stock market closing.

Usually, the collector does not know what bank the pickup man works for, so if a collector is arrested, the entire operation will not be jeopardized. Gross profit for the bank may be as high as 40 percent of the total amount wagered, but the administrative costs are also high. The net profit for numbers games is usually about 1 percent and rarely exceeds 10 percent.

One of the Most Popular Forms of Illegal Gambling

Although illegal, most numbers operations take place openly while law enforcement officers may be paid to look the other way. In fact, numbers is often cited as a primary source of police corruption. When the occasional police raid does occur, numbers operators and their customers view them as a minor nuisance.

The game still thrives in New York City, especially in economically depressed neighborhoods, and is probably the most lucrative form of illegal gambling in the city. Some politicians and observers believe that the numbers racket is so deeply entrenched in the culture of poor neighborhoods

that it has become part of the local economy. Recent immigrants and many poor people may not even know that the game is illegal and that it often supports organized crime. Various types of lottery games are easily available in states where they are legal, giving bettors an option to play lottery games that they never had before.

Horse Books — How a "Bookie" Operates

The bookmaker or "bookie" was first identified with the gambling business during the 1870s, when racetracks licensed them to accept bets at the tracks. For that privilege, bookies paid the racetrack operators a daily fee, usually around $100 (a very large sum in those days). Once established, bookies branched out into (illegal) off-track betting parlors in the cities to provide services to bettors who could not attend races.

When placing a bet with a bookie, the bettor makes his or her choice from a scratch sheet that contains information on post (starting) times, post positions, a horse's lineage and past performance, expected odds, and handicappers' picks. The bookie pays off the same amount as the track, keeping the 15 percent normally charged by the track for himself. After expenses, the bookie normally makes a 10-to-11 percent net profit.

To have enough financial support to cover bets, bookies generally form syndicates. The syndicate gives each bookie the latest information about jockey changes, betting odds, and racetrack conditions.

Sports Books — The Most Popular Form of Illegal Gambling

While many forms of gambling in the United States have been legalized, gambling on sporting events continues to be illegal in all but four states (Delaware [not operative], Montana, Nevada, North Dakota, and Oregon) and is legal statewide only in Nevada. Some sources estimate that professional football alone attracts $50 billion in wagers per season or possibly as much as $10 million per football weekend in major cities. This figure does not include wagers on college football games. According to Eugene M. Christensen of *International Gaming and Wagering Business*, sports betting is the fastest growing type of illegal gambling. This is especially true since gamblers can now bet legally in many states on the lotteries (which are similar to the illegal numbers games), but still cannot legally bet on sporting events.

The "Point Spread"

A sports bookie is literally playing both ends against the middle (trying to balance the bets), hoping to come out on top. The line, or "point spread," is manipulated to try to keep the betting on both teams even. A bookie must be careful not to change the spread too much or he might end up paying off both sides. Lines vary among bookmakers, and some bettors shop around for the spread that is most acceptable.

During the football season, the "early line" is posted every Tuesday in the legal sports books in Nevada. For example, in a game in which the Washington Redskins are playing the Dallas Cowboys, the line might start at Dallas +6. This means that, for the Cowboy supporter, Dallas must win by 7 points for the bettor to win because 6 points will be subtracted from the Cowboys' final score. A good bookie does not care who wins. He or she moves the point spread up or down in order to keep the betting even. If the line goes from Dallas +6 to Dallas +8, it is because that is what is needed to get more people to bet on Washington instead of Dallas.

Both the legal line in Las Vegas and the illegal line created by the bookies fluctuate during the week, usually because of the bettor's interpretation of everything from changes in the weather to the condition of the players' health. Competent bookies, however, will move the line only in response to how much money is being bet on each team, not conjecture about players and the weather. Normally, by the end of the week as the game approaches, the legal and illegal point spread will usually be very close, if not the same.

The point spread is not the only thing the gambler may bet on. In the over/under (O/U) bets, the gambler wagers on how many points will be scored by both teams. On big games, such as the National Football Conference or American Football Conference championship games or the Super Bowl, odds and lines are posted so that gamblers can bet on any number of aspects of the game. Some of these may include total touchdown passes, the first player to score, total number of running or passing touchdowns, the total number of fumbles lost by both teams, which team will score the most points in the first quarter or first half, or whatever the gambler can convince a bookie to accept.

Today, most bookmaking operations are partnerships that employ several workers to record bets and compute the day's business. The bookmakers decide how to shift the point spread, when to lay off bets (get help from other bookies in covering bets), what limits to set for bets, and how much credit to extend to customers. Just as in most other types of businesses, the computer has helped the illegal gambler organize his business and make it more efficient.

As with numbers games, illegal sports betting sometimes requires that law enforcement officials be unobservant. In order to avoid confrontations with the law, bookies use various methods to conceal their operations, such as frequently moving, using answering services, and changing telephone numbers.

Sports Cards

Sports cards are very popular for the $1 to $10 sports bettor. Sports cards list a particular week's sporting events, along with the point spreads. The cards are distributed no later than Tuesday for games that will take place the coming weekend. The bettor selects the team(s) he or she thinks will win, tears off the card stub, and submits it to the bookie before the game takes place.

SPORTS WAGERING

According to the National Gambling Impact Study Commission (NGISC) Report released in June 1999, estimates of illegal sports betting in the United States range from $80 billion to $380 billion annually, making sports betting the most common and most popular form of gambling in America. Sports betting is illegal in most states and, therefore, does not contribute to any local economies (in a way that can be measured) or create many new legal jobs like casinos or other destination resorts do. Sports betting can ruin families and careers, can threaten the honesty and uprightness of sports, and can put adolescent gamblers at risk for future problems.

Professional and College Sports Gambling

College officials nationwide are expressing alarm at the phenomenal increase in betting on college sports. Many people fear betting poses a threat to the integrity of sports. "Point shaving" scandals (paying a player to deliberately score fewer points than he or she might have during a particular game) still occasionally surface. Basketball is considered the easiest game to "fix" because it is so easy to purposely miss shots without appearing to be doing so. A player on a team that is winning might easily rationalize missing a basket here and there in order to stay within the point spread — his team will win anyway and so, he or she thinks, neither team nor fans get hurt. A missed shot, however, can be very important to someone betting on a specific point spread.

The issue of point spread sometimes comes up at the end of a football game when a team does something that appears to make little sense. For instance, the losing team goes for a field goal when the game is far out of reach and the almost-certain three points mean little, or a team that is leading by a wide margin goes for an extra touchdown.

Illegal Gambling on Campus

Illegal sports wagering continues to grow and is believed to exist in one form or an-

other on virtually every college campus in America. — Bill Saum, NCAA anti-gambling representative

The problem of illegal gambling on college campuses has troubled schools for 50 years. Between 1947 and 1950, 32 players at seven schools were implicated in a plot to fix games. In the past decade alone, there have been sports scandals at more than 10 schools, including Arizona State University, where one basketball player and four other men, some of them former students, pleaded guilty to federal charges that they had helped shave points in four games in 1994. The former Arizona State students were tried and found guilty. Their sentences ranged from 46 months in prison to combinations of jail time, home detention, fines, and community service.

In 1996, 13 football players at Boston College were suspended for gambling on games; two players bet against their own team. In 1995, five athletes, including the quarterback of the football team at the University of Maryland, were suspended for gambling on sports. At Northwestern, in 1994, a football starter and a basketball starter were suspended for betting on college games. In 1992, five basketball players at Bryant College were suspended. They had amassed a $54,000 gambling debt. A former player and a student were arrested and charged with bookmaking.

A nationwide survey conducted in 1996 by the University of Cincinnati (Ohio) involving Division I (large schools) basketball and football players found that one-fourth of the players had gambled on other college sports, and nearly 4 percent said that they had gambled on a game in which they had participated. Three athletes admitted that a gambler had paid them for not playing well in a game. An athlete gambling on his or her own team is a serious issue, because the athlete may have the opportunity to help himself with his bet.

In early 1998, a 20-year-old student at Columbia University in New York City and a 27-year-old Columbia alumnus and law student at New York University were arrested for accepting bets on sporting events from other students. The wagers, usually between $40 and $200, were telephoned to a gambling ring based in Queens, New York, operated by people with links to organized crime.

School officials were concerned that Columbia's athletes had bet on their own games and even tried to affect the results. Following the arrests, school administrators and the National Collegiate Athletic Association (NCAA) began an investigation and urged any athlete who had bet illegally on professional or college games to come forward. A number of current and former Columbia athletes interviewed after the arrests said that they knew athletes who had made illegal bets. They also claimed that it was easy to find illegal gambling on and around the campus. The NCAA believes that there are student bookies on every campus in America.

In December 1998, four former Northwestern University football players were indicted for perjuring themselves (lying) before a federal grand jury when they denied betting on Northwestern games in 1994. The former athletes were accused of trying to lose by more than the predicted point spread. One player was accused of fumbling the ball on the goal line to protect a bet.

Northwestern hired a former assistant U.S. Attorney to investigate the allegations as soon as it heard about the gambling, and the school turned over the findings to the federal authorities and the NCAA. Prior to the scandal, the university had distributed NCAA anti-gambling literature to athletes several times each year. Beginning in 1998, in addition to receiving the literature, members of every school-sponsored team are required to watch a video about the dangers of sports gambling. Moreover, once a year, the coaches and players must attend a speech given by either a reformed gambler or a former FBI agent who has investigated sports gambling.

LIVING WITH GAMBLING

Gambling represents a quandary for the National Football League. While it is absolutely nec-

essary that fans believe in the integrity of the game, a good proportion of those watching (an estimated 20 to 30 percent) are watching because they have money bet on the game. In fact, these gamblers may be more committed viewers than those who do not have bets on the game. A game in which the Oakland Raiders are beating the Philadelphia Eagles by a score of 31-15 may be considered a lost cause to an Eagles fan, who may change the channel. On the other hand, a bettor who has the Raiders +10 is only a touchdown away from winning. He or she is more likely to stay tuned and watch more of the commercials that pay for the overhead of the NFL.

Radio, television, and newspapers, the major media that promote football and other sports, also contribute to the huge amount of betting on sporting events. Most local newspapers make the point spreads readily available to the general public, and it is not unusual for sportswriters and sportscasters to predict the outcome of a game and include the "point spread" in their predictions. After all, anyone can predict that 12-0 St. Louis will trounce 0-12 Dallas. The "real" question for the prognosticator is, can they beat the "point spread." The "point spread" is very much a part of the hype that increases the interest in upcoming games and helps ensure that many millions of fans will watch the games and the commercials that support the league.

Many bettors consider the advice of these professional sportswriters and sportscasters before they call their bookies to make bets. Since sports betting is legal in only a few states, the media is quite aware that some people will be using these point spreads and the advice given by sports commentators to make illegal bets.

While the NFL reports who is injured and not likely to play for the information of fans, it is also reported for gamblers. The information that an important a player like Emmitt Smith of the Cowboys or Kurt Warner of the Rams had been injured would certainly help determine whether to bet on the Cowboys or Rams. The NFL is concerned that, if such information were not reported and a gambler found out about it, this knowledge would give the gambler an "edge" — an advantage.

Many gamblers would do a lot to get such an edge, including offering players money to report who is unable to play. Once the player had been compromised by giving such information, the gamblers could put greater pressure on the athlete to do other things, including throwing a game. Consequently, the NFL feels it is better to voluntarily give out information that gamblers want to know rather than create a situation that could threaten the integrity of the game.

Trying to Fix the Problem

Many professional and amateur sports organizations have recognized the importance of attempting to stop illegal sports betting and have established rules for punishing those who illegally bet on sports. The National Football League, Major League Baseball, and the National Basketball Association have all stated that any athlete or coach who bets on his or her own sport may be dismissed. The case of Major League Baseball's refusal to permit Pete Rose's entrance into the Baseball Hall of Fame indicates how seriously this policy is taken. Each league offers referral services for treatment of problem or pathological gambling, as well as for other addictions. The National Collegiate Athletic Association (NCAA) has adopted legislation forbidding university athletics department members, athletics conference office staff, and student athletes from betting on intercollegiate or professional sporting events. Violators may be expelled, dismissed, and/or fined. In addition, the NCAA has a full-time staff member who deals with gambling issues.

HOW POPULAR IS
ILLEGAL GAMBLING?

It is virtually impossible to accurately estimate how much money is bet illegally in the United States. So much has happened in gambling over the past decade and a half that it is hard to determine exactly how illegal betting has been affected by the development of legal gambling. The easy availability of legal lotteries has undoubtedly hurt the numbers game. In addition, the growth of the drug trade in poorer urban areas has attracted some people to drug dealing who, in an earlier time, might have been running numbers operations.

Although off-track betting is more available than ever, many bettors still prefer an illegal bookie. Sometimes it is more convenient to deal with a bookie who is located nearby. More importantly, if the bettors win big, and most hope that they will, the Internal Revenue Service (IRS) will not become involved. When bettors win big at the racetrack, the IRS either takes a percentage immediately, or the track reports the winnings so that the bettors will have to pay taxes. When bettors wager with an illegal bookie, they never have to worry that the IRS will be informed.

With the increased acceptance of state-sanctioned legal gambling, it is not surprising that Americans are less concerned about gambling. High school students bet on weekly basketball and football games. For many people, it is a tradition to have some money bet on the Super Bowl or the World Series. With all that parents worry about with their children, discovering that a son or daughter bet on the World Series does not compare with their concern that they might be using drugs, drinking alcohol, or engaging in sex. Finally, a generation ago, crime and the criminal underworld were often associated with gambling. Today, they are overwhelmingly associated with drugs.

With the continued growth of amateur and professional sports and the improbability that legal sports gambling will extend beyond the states in which it is currently legal in some form, illegal sports betting will likely continue to grow and be the most important part of illegal gambling. (See Chapter II — Professional and Amateur Sports Protection Act of 1992.) Many Americans consider betting on major sporting events as American as apple pie, and there will likely always be an illegal bookie available to take a bet.

INTERNET GAMBLING

Internet gambling was introduced on the World Wide Web in 1995. By May 1998, there were about 90 on-line casinos, 39 lotteries, eight bingo games, and 53 sports books. By 1999 — one year later — there were 250 on-line casinos, 64 lotteries, 20 bingo games, and 139 sports books available to the public over the Internet. According to Sebastian Sinclair, a gambling industry analyst for Christiansen/Cummings Associates, total gambling revenues for 1998 totaled $651 million, more than double the 1997 figure of $300 million. Estimates have put Internet gambling revenue for 1999 at $1.2 billion, and Sinclair forecasts revenues will reach $2.3 billion by 2001.

It is difficult to track the amount of money that is bet on the Internet, since there is no global sanctioning body to keep track of the sites or to regulate them. However, industry experts estimate that there are 800 to 1,000 online gambling businesses operating out of nearly 50 countries worldwide. The Wire Communications Act of 1961 (PL 87-216) makes it illegal to place bets over telephone lines, but when the law was passed, there was no Internet and thus, the law does not address e-gambling wins and losses. Many legislators oppose Internet gambling, but stopping cyber casinos is difficult since they do not operate in the United States.

In its 1999 comprehensive study on gambling, the National Gambling Impact Study Commission (NGISC) claimed that even if Congress were to pass Internet gambling legislation, the hardware and software required by Internet service providers to block access to such a large number of sites would be too expensive and difficult to put into practice. (See Chapter III for more on Internet gambling.)

ILLEGAL OFFSHORE GAMBLING

Wagering on sports is illegal everywhere in the United States, except for Delaware (currently not operative), Montana, Nevada, North Dakota, and Oregon. In recent years, a number of American bookmakers have relocated to West Indies countries, such as Antigua, where sports gambling is legal. Local governments license these operations, which use advanced technology to communicate, set odds on games, and record wagers. To receive a license, applicants must pay the government $75,000 for telephone gambling operations and $100,000 for on-line enterprises. The industry has created hundreds of jobs for local residents and built an offshore sports book business that analysts say is taking in 1 to 5 percent of the estimated $80 to $380 billion that is bet illegally on sports each year in the United States.

Approximately 60 offshore sports books operate throughout the Caribbean and Central America. Of those, 25 are based in Antigua, where local officials created a free trade zone in 1994. This permits bookies to operate without paying corporate taxes.

Many of the sports books also operate on-line casinos, which allow customers to bet on interactive games, like slot machines, blackjack, and poker. The sudden popularity of these offshore gambling operations has called attention to the Wire Communications Act of 1961, a federal law that prohibits using telephone lines for gambling. Gambling opponents are calling for new laws banning Internet casinos and offshore sports books from doing business in the United States. Foes of offshore gambling claim it will be too difficult to regulate the fairness of interactive casino games, which will pose a great threat to consumers.

The Money

Customers of offshore betting on the World Wide Web set up an account by transferring money through wire cashier's check or credit card debit. The customer receives a toll-free number to call, a personal identification number, and an on-line password.

Until recently, offshore companies have used Western Union as one of their preferred means of receiving wagers and sending winnings. However,

Florida's attorney general and Western Union have agreed that Western Union will no longer wire money for the offshore companies. The offshore bookies will now have to depend on bank wires, cashier's checks, and overnight mail.

Government Action

Several states have attempted to halt offshore gambling, claiming that while it may be legal to gamble in the country where the bookies are located, it is not legal in the states where the bets are being placed. (See Chapter III.) However, according to the Justice Department, since the offense has not taken place on U.S. soil, the government has no jurisdiction in these offshore locations.

The bookmakers have started their own lobbying effort in Washington. They are currently searching for a sponsor of legislation that would legalize and regulate their industry. The bookies claim that they would be willing to pay taxes and "do everything by the book" if the government would allow them to. They point out that the government will not receive any tax revenue as long as bookmaking operations are kept offshore. (Offshore bookmakers are not under any obligation to report winners' earnings to the Internal Revenue Service.) Currently, prospects for legalization are not bright. However, in hard economic times (that may develop sometime in the future), some legislators may decide the taxes from such gambling could benefit the nation.

GAMBLING ARRESTS

In 1982, police arrested 41,200 people for illegal gambling. In 1987, they arrested 23,000. In 1990, police arrested only 19,300; in 1992, 17,100; and in 1994, 18,500. This huge drop in the number of people arrested for gambling occurred during a time when the overall number of arrests was increasing. The 15,900 people arrested for gambling in 1997 made up .01 percent of all those arrested.

More than 11 times as many people were arrested for curfew violations (182,700), and nearly 7.5 times as many were arrested for forgery and counterfeiting (120,100). With the increase in violent crime and drug-related crimes and the growth and general acceptance of legal gambling, illegal gambling has become a low priority for both the nation's citizens and their police.

CHAPTER XI

PUBLIC OPINIONS ABOUT GAMBLING

Between April 30 and May 23, 1999, the Gallup Organization, in *Social Audits: Gambling in America 1999: A Comparison of Adults and Teenagers,* surveyed 1,523 American adults over the age of 18 and 501 teenagers. The poll found that 63 percent of adults and 52 percent of 13- to 17-year-olds approved of legalized gambling; 32 percent of adults and 47 percent of teenagers opposed it.

When Gallup asked those adults who approved of legalized gambling why they approved, 30 percent responded that wagering is an individual freedom, and that if people choose to bet, it is their choice. About the same proportion (29 percent) saw gambling as fun and entertainment. Another 18 percent of adults considered gambling to be a good source of state revenue. Teens who approved of legalized gambling generally agreed, with 30 percent approving of wagering because they considered it to be fun and 20 percent believing betting to be a right for those interested in taking part. About 1 of 5 (18 percent) of 13- to 17-year-olds also saw gambling as a way to make or win money. (See Table 11.1.)

Of the adults who disapproved of gambling, one-fourth (25 percent) responded that wagering can ruin lives and devastate finances, while 20 percent considered betting to be addictive. Another 16 percent of adults associated gambling with crime and violence, and saw it as corruptive. The disapproving teenagers agreed, with 29 percent seeing the potential for gambling to ruin lives and finances. Another 14 percent of 13- to 17-year-olds considered wagering to be a waste of time and money, 12 percent believed it was wrong, and 10 percent thought it was addictive. (See Table 11.1.)

The survey asked respondents whether or not they agreed that legalized gambling provides necessary monies to states to pay for government programs and control taxes. More than half of adults and teenagers (58 and 60 percent, respectively) agreed, and 39 percent of both groups disagreed. Respondents were asked whether or not they approved or disapproved of their state offering different forms of gambling for cash prizes as a way in which to help their state raise money. In 1999, 74 percent of adults and 86 percent of teenagers approved of playing bingo for cash prizes. About two-thirds (63 percent) of adults and 61 percent of teens approved of casino gambling as a way to help the state raise money. Three-fourths (75 percent) of adults and 82 percent of teens approved of lotteries as a means to raise money for the state. Off-track wagering on horse races, professional sports events, and video poker all received less support. (See Table 11.2.)

GAMBLING BEHAVIOR

About 7 of 10 adults and 26 percent of teens have participated in some form of legal gambling during their lives. In 1999, 11 percent of adults had played bingo for money, up from 9 percent in 1992 and 1996, but down from 16 percent in 1963. In 1999, 31 percent of adults and only 2 percent of teens gambled at a casino, while 9 percent of adults and 5 percent of teenagers had bet on a horse or dog race. (See Table 11.3.)

TABLE 11.1

What are the one or two most important reasons why you (approve or disapprove)
of legal gambling? (Based on those who approve or disapprove)

APPROVE OF GAMBLING	ADULTS (n=964) %	APPROVE OF GAMBLING	TEENS (n=251) %	DISAPPROVE OF GAMBLING	ADULTS (n=485) %	DISAPPROVE OF GAMBLING	TEENS (n=241) %
Choice/Right/Freedom	30	It's fun/enjoy/like it/entertainment	30	Ruins lives/people lose everything/get into debt /misuse finances	25	Ruins lives/people lose everything/get into debt /misuse finances	29
Source of state revenue/decrease taxes/provide funding	18	Choice/right/freedom	20	Addictive	20	Waste of time and/or money	14
It's fun/enjoy/like it/entertainment	29	Way to make money/win money	18	Crime/violence/corruptive	16	It's wrong/bad	12
See nothing wrong with it/harmless	8	See nothing wrong with it/harmless	14	Religious convictions	14	Addictive	10
People will gamble anyway	7	Source of state revenue/decrease taxes/provide funding	6	Causes problems for family	9	Religious convictions	9
Way to make money/win money	6	It's legal	5	People in lower income or on welfare gamble	8	Don't like it	8
Better to be legalized/controlled	5	Better to be legalized/controlled	2	Waste of time and/or money	7	Lose money	6
Creates jobs/brings business	4	People need to be responsible	2	Don't like it	7	Crime/violence/corruptive	5
It's legal	2	Ruins lives/people lose everything/get into debt/misuse finances	2	It's wrong/bad	6	Causes problems for family	5
I gamble	2	People will gamble anyway	1	Lose money	4	Better ways to spend money	3
Revenue benefits Native Americans	1	Creates jobs/brings business	1	Better ways to spend money	3	Adults only/not for children	2
Adults only/not for children	1	Revenue benefits Native Americans	1	Moral issues	3	Wasn't raised to gamble	2
People need to be responsible	1	Adults only/not for children	1	Government misuses gambling revenue	2	It's fun/enjoy it/entertainment	1
Crime/violence/corruptive	1	Lose money	1	Adults only/not for children	1	People need to be responsible	1
Work in gambling industry	1	Causes problems for family	1	Wasn't raised to gamble	1	Other	11
Better ways to spend money	1	Other	7	Way to make money/win money	1	None	3
Other	8	None	4	Source of state revenue/decrease taxes/provide funding	1	DK/Refused	9
None	2	DK/Refused	10	Other	13		
DK/Refused	2			None	1		
				DK/Refused	2		

Source: *Social Audit: Gambling in America 1999*, The Gallup Organization, Princeton, NJ, 2000

Lotteries are the most popular form of gambling in the United States. In 1999, more than half (57 percent) of adults purchased a state lottery ticket, as did 15 percent of 13- to 17-year-olds. (See Table 11.3.) Since 1989, buying a lottery ticket, at least occasionally, has become part of most Americans' lives.

When it came to wagering on sports, a larger percentage of teenagers than adults had participated. In 1999, 27 percent of teenagers reported that they had bet on a professional sports event in the past year, compared to 13 percent of adults. Betting on college sports attracted 18 percent of teenagers and 9 percent of adults. Not surprisingly, the office pool garnered more wagers from adults (25 percent) than from teens (15 percent), simply because there are more adults working in offices. (See Table 11.3.)

Internet wagering apparently plays a tiny role in today's gambling business. About 75 percent of adults disapprove of this form of gambling. Most people believe that it is too easy for teenagers and gambling addicts to bet online, and fear that Internet access will increase gambling among those groups. Very few respondents to the survey reported using the Internet to wager for money — no adults in 1999, 1 percent of adults in 1996, and 2 percent of teens in 1999. (See Table 11.3.) Nonetheless, it should not be forgotten that, in 1995, the Internet was referred to as the "Information

TABLE 11.2

As you may know, some states legalize betting so that the state can raise revenues. Please tell me whether you approve or disapprove of each of the following types of betting as a way to help YOUR STATE raise revenue. First, do you approve or disapprove of (read and rotate A-F)? Do you approve or disapprove of it being legal?

A. Bingo for cash prizes

		Approve %	Disapprove %	No Opinion %	Sample size
ADULTS (18+)	99 Apr 30-May 23	74	24	2	1,523
	96 Jun 27-30	77	20	3	1,004
	92 Nov 20-22	72	25	3	1,007
	89 Apr 4-9	75	23	2	1,208
TEENS (13-17)	99 Apr 30-May 23	86	14	-	501

B. Casino gambling

		Approve %	Disapprove %	No Opinion %	Sample size
ADULTS (18+)	99 Apr 30-May 23	63	36	1	1,523
TEENS (13-17)	99 Apr 30-May 23	61	39	-	501

C. Lotteries for cash prizes

		Approve %	Disapprove %	No Opinion %	Sample size
ADULTS (18+)	99 Apr 30-May 23	75	24	1	1,523
	96 Jun 27-30	77	22	1	1,004
	92 Nov 20-22	75	24	1	1,007
	89 Apr 4-9	78	21	1	1,208
TEENS (13-17)	99 Apr 30-May 23	82	18	-	501

D. Off-track betting on horse races

		Approve %	Disapprove %	No Opinion %	Sample size
ADULTS (18+)	99 Apr 30-May 23	53	44	3	1,523
	96 Jun 27-30	55	41	4	1,004
	92 Nov 20-22	49	47	4	1,007
	89 Apr 4-9	54	42	4	1,208
TEENS (13-17)	99 Apr 30-May 23	55	43	2	501

E. Betting on professional sports, such as baseball, basketball, or football

		Approve %	Disapprove %	No Opinion %	Sample size
ADULTS (18+)	99 Apr 30-May 23	41	57	2	1,523
	96 Jun 27-30	40	58	2	1,004
	92 Nov 20-22	33	65	2	1,007
	89 Apr 4-9	42	55	3	1,208
TEENS (13-17)	99 Apr 30-May 23	60	40	-	501

F. Video poker machines at local establishments

		Approve %	Disapprove %	No Opinion %	Sample size
ADULTS (18+)	99 Apr 30-May 23	42	55	3	1,523
	96 Jun 27-30	37	59	4	1,004
	92 Nov 20-22*	38	52	10	1,007
TEENS (13-17)	99 Apr 30-May 23	53	46	1	501

*Video Poker

Source: *Social Audit: Gambling in America 1999*, The Gallup Organization, Princeton, NJ, 2000

Superhighway" with barely a mention of "E-commerce." It would be very surprising if gambling as a form of "E-commerce" did not become more available.

About one-fifth of teens (23 percent) and adults (20 percent) had played a video poker machine in 1999. Adults (10 percent) took part in riverboat gambling more often than teens (1 percent). (See Table 11.3.)

TABLE 11.3

Please tell me whether or not you have done any of the
following things in the past 12 months. First, how about (read A-J)?

A. Played bingo for money

		Yes	No	Sample Size
ADULTS (18+)	99 Apr 30-May 23	11	89	1,523
	96 Jun 27-30	9	91	1,004
	92 Nov 20-22	9	91	1,007
	89 Apr 4-9	13	87	1,208
	63 Jan 11-16**	16	84	1,525
	50 May 4-9*	21	89	1,343
TEENS (13-17)	99 Apr 30-May 23	13	87	501

*Play bingo
**During the past 12 months, did you, yourself, happen to do any of these?

B. Gambled at a casino

		Yes	No	Sample Size
ADULTS (18+)	99 Apr 30-May 23	31	69	1,523
TEENS (13-17)	99 Apr 30-May 23	2	98	501

C. Bet on a horse race or dog race

		Yes	No	Sample Size
ADULTS (18+)	99 Apr 30-May 23	9	91	1,523
	96 Jun 27-30*	6	94	1,004
	92 Nov 20-22*	12	88	1,007
	90 Feb 15-18*	9	91	1,235
	89 Apr 4-9*	14	86	1,208
	50 May 4-9*	8	92	1,343
TEENS (13-17)	99 Apr 30-May 23	5	95	501

*Bet on a horse race
**During the past year, have you.....

D. Bought a state lottery ticket

		Yes	No	Sample Size
ADULTS (18+)	99 Apr 30-May 23	57	43	1,523
	96 Jun 27-30	57	43	1,004
	92 Nov 20-22	56	44	1,007
	89 Apr 4-9	54	46	1,208
TEENS (13-17)	99 Apr 30-May 23	15	85	501

E. Bet on a PROFESSIONAL sports event such as baseball, basketball, football, or boxing

		Yes	No	Sample Size
ADULTS (18+)	99 Apr 30-May 23	13	87	1,523
	96 Jun 27-30	10	90	1,004
	92 Nov 20-22	12	88	1,007
	90 Feb 15-18	21	79	1,235
	89 Apr 4-9	22	78	1,208
TEENS (13-17)	99 Apr 30-May 23	27	73	501

F. Bet on a COLLEGE sports event such as basketball or football

		Yes	No	Sample Size
ADULTS (18+)	99 Apr 30-May 23	9	91	1,523
	96 Jun 27-30	7	93	1,004
	92 Nov 20-22	6	94	1,007
	90 Feb 15-18	11	89	1,235
	89 Apr 4-9	14	86	1,208
TEENS (13-17)	99 Apr 30-May 23	18	82	501

G. Participated in an office pool on the World Series, Super Bowl or other game

		Yes	No	Sample Size
ADULTS (18+)	99 Apr 30-May 23	25	75	1,523
	96 Jun 27-30	23	77	1,004
	92 Nov 20-22	22	78	1,007
TEENS (13-17)	99 Apr 30-May 23	15	85	501

(continued)

140

TABLE 11.3 (Continued)

H. Gambled for money on the Internet

		Yes	No	Sample Size
ADULTS (18+)	99 Apr 30-May 23	*	100	1,523
	96 Jun 27-30	1	99	1,004
TEENS (13-17)	99 Apr 30-May 23	2	98	501

I. Played a video poker machine

		Yes	No	Sample Size
ADULTS (18+)	99 Apr 30-May 23	20	80	1,523
	96 Jun 27-30	17	83	1,004
	92 Nov 20-22*	11	89	1,007
TEENS (13-17)	99 Apr 30-May 23	23	77	501

*Played video poker

J. Participated in riverboat gambling

		Yes	No	Sample Size
ADULTS (18+)	99 Apr 30-May 23	10	90	1,523
TEENS (13-17)	99 Apr 30-May 23	1	99	501

Source: *Social Audit: Gambling in America 1999*, The Gallup Organization, Princeton, NJ, 2000

TABLE 11.4

Not everyone is clear about what forms of gambling are legal or illegal. Have you ever participated in any form of LEGAL gambling?

		Yes	No	DK/Refused	Sample Size
ADULTS (18+)	99 Apr 30-May 23	69	30	1	1,523
TEENS (13-17)	99 Apr 30-May 23	26	71	3	501

As far as you know, have you ever done any gambling that was NOT COMPLETELY LEGAL?

		Yes	No	DK/Refused	Sample Size
ADULTS (18+)	99 Apr 30-May 23	24	75	1	1,523
	93 Sep 13-15*	20	79	1	802
TEENS (13-17)	99 Apr 30-May 23	18	81	1	501

*CNBC/Gallup Poll

Source: *Social Audit: Gambling in America 1999*, The Gallup Organization, Princeton, NJ, 2000

TABLE 11.5

Please tell me whether or not you have done any of the following things in the past 12 months. First, how about...(read A-J)?

% "yes, have done" this

	Total	Under $25K	$25-44.9K	$45-74.9K	$75K+
Bought a state lottery ticket	57%	53%	61%	65%	56%
Gambled at a casino	31	23	34	37	37
Participated in an office pool	25	13	27	35	36
Played a video poker machine	20	17	20	23	22
Bet on a professional sports event	13	9	15	15	16
Played bingo for money	11	10	12	10	8
Participated in riverboat gambling	10	6	12	12	13
Bet on a horse race or dog race	9	5	12	9	14
Bet on a college sports event	9	5	11	11	12
Gambled for money on the Internet	*	*	*	*	1

Source: *Social Audit: Gambling in America 1999*, The Gallup Organization, Princeton, NJ, 2000

TABLE 11.6

How much money do you usually spend each month on lottery tickets?
(Base: those who have ever gambled and those who have bought a state lottery ticket in the past 12 months)

		Less than $1	$1-$4	$5-$9	$10-$19	20-$29	$30-More	No Opinion	Sample size
ADULTS (18+)	99 Apr 30-May 23	15	24	25	18	11	6	1	756
	96 Jun 27-30	11	26	23	22	10	7	1	581
	92 Nov 20-22	14	28	17	19	11	9	2	567
	89 Apr 4-9	11	22	24	18	11	12	2	n/a
TEENS (13-17)	99 Apr 30-May 23	12	25	30	19	7	7	-	42

TABLE 11.7

Besides lottery tickets, how much money have you bet or wagered in the past 12 months? (Base: those who have ever gambled)

		Less than $1	$1-$4	$5-$9	$10-$19	20-$29	$30-More	No Opinion	Sample size
ADULTS (18+)	99 Apr 30-May 23	37	2	3	6	8	43	1	1,130
TEENS (13-17)	99 Apr 30-May 23	29	5	9	15	13	29	-	188

Source of both tables: *Social Audit: Gambling in America 1999*, The Gallup Organization, Princeton, NJ, 2000

The survey asked respondents if they had participated in any form of legal gambling during the past year — 69 percent of adults and 26 percent of teens had. The survey also asked if they had done any illegal gambling during the past year — 24 percent of adults and 18 percent of teenagers had. (See Table 11.4.)

More High-Income Earners Gamble

In 1999, according to the Gallup Organization, upper-income earners ($75,000) spent approximately three times as much on lotteries each month as did those with low earnings (under $25,000), and upper-income Americans spent nearly 10 times as much annually as did those in the $25,000 income bracket. Bingo was one exception, with more people earning less annually playing more than those earning more. While 37 percent of those earning more than $75,000 gambled at a casino, only 23 percent of those earning under $25,000 did, and persons earning $75,000 or more (36 percent) were more likely than persons earning under $25,000 (13 percent) to participate in an office pool. More

142

TABLE 11.8

Do you recall at what age you first lost money or made money as a result of a bet, a card game, or any other form of gambling? Please tell me what that age was. (Base: those who have ever gambled)

		Age First Lost/Made Money Betting								
		10 or less	11-15	16-20	21-25	26-30	31-35	36-40	41-45	Sample Size
ADULTS (18+)	99 Apr 30-May 23	7	14	30	19	5	4	3	2	1,130
	93 Sep 13-15*	6	13	22	4	1	1	1	1	802
TEENS (13-17)	99 Apr 30-May 23	29	58	2	-	-	-	-	-	188

		Age First Lost/Made Money Betting							
		46-50 %	51-55 %	56-60 %	61-65 %	66 or over %	Have never gambled (vol.) %	DK/RF %	Sample Size
ADULTS (18+)	99 Apr 30-May 23	1	1	*	*	1	-	13	1,130
	93 Sep 13-15*	1	1	*	*		22	15	802
TEENS (13-17)	99 Apr 30-May 23	-	-	-	-	-	-	11	188

*CNBC/Gallup Poll

TABLE 11.9

Considering all the money you spent on bets, wagers, or lottery tickets over the past 12 months, as well as your winnings, would you say you are ahead or behind? (Base: those who have ever gambled)

		Ahead %	Behind %	Broke Even (vol.) %	DK/Refused %	Sample Size %
ADULTS (18+)	99 Apr 30-May 23	26	49	15	10	1,130
	89 Apr 4-9	24	58	15	3	n/a
TEENS (13-17)	99 Apr 30-May 23	61	24	10	5	188

Source of both tables: *Social Audit: Gambling in America 1999*, The Gallup Organization, Princeton, NJ, 2000

TABLE 11.10

Do you sometimes gamble more than you think you should? (Base: those who have ever gambled)

		Yes	No	DK/Refused	Sample Size
ADULTS (18+)	99 Apr 30-May 23	11	88	1	1,130
	96 Jun 27-30	7	93	*	1,004
	92 Nov 20-22	9	91	-	1,007
	89 Apr 4-9	10	90	-	1,208
TEENS (13-17)	99 Apr 30-May 23	20	78	2	188

TABLE 11.11

Has gambling ever been a source of problems within your family?

		Yes	No	DK/Refuse	Sample Size
ADULTS (18+)	99 Apr 30-May 23	9	91	*	1,523
	96 Jun 27-30	5	95	*	1,004
	92 Nov 20-22	5	94	1	1,007
	89 Apr 4-9	4	96	*	1,208
TEENS (13-17)	99 Apr 30-May 23	10	89	1	501

TABLE 11.12

Do you know anyone outside your family for whom gambling has been a source of problems?

		Yes	No	DK/Refused	Sample Size
ADULTS (18+)	99 Apr 30-May 23	41	59	*	1,523
TEENS (13-17)	99 Apr 30-May 23	28	72	-	501

Source of above tables: *Social Audit: Gambling in America 1999*, The Gallup Organization, Princeton, NJ, 2000

people in every earnings category bought lottery tickets, with those making between $45,000 to $74,900 (65 percent) buying most often. (See Table 11.5.)

Monthly Spending

For most Americans, betting on the lottery seems to be an entertaining distraction involving little expense. In 1999, two-thirds (64 percent) of adults who played the lottery spent under $10 each month, up somewhat from 60 percent in 1996, 59 percent in 1992, and 57 percent in 1989. In 1999, 67 percent of teenage lottery players spent less than $10 each month. (See Table 11.6.)

The survey also asked those who gambled on other games in the past year how much they spent.

144

TABLE 11.13

Do you approve or disapprove of legalized gambling or betting using the Internet?

		Yes %	No %	DK/Refused %	Sample size %
ADULTS (18+)	99 Apr 30-May 23	20	75	5	1,523
TEENS (13-17)	99 Apr 30-May 23	33	66	1	501

As far as you know, is it easy for teenagers to use the Internet to gamble?

		Yes %	No %	DK/Refused %	Sample size %
ADULTS (18+)	99 Apr 30-May 23	76	9	15	1,523
TEENS (13-17)	99 Apr 30-May 23	70	21	9	501

Source: *Social Audit: Gambling in America 1999*, The Gallup Organization, Princeton, NJ, 2000

While 42 percent of adults and 43 percent of teens spent less than $10, 43 percent of adults and 29 percent of teens had spent more than $30. (See Table 11.7.)

Age When Respondent First Won or Lost Money Gambling

Gambling is certainly a part of growing up in America. Half (51 percent) of the respondents had gambled before they reached 21. One fifth (21 percent) had gambled before they were even 16, and 7 percent had bet on something before they left elementary school. (See Table 11.8.)

Respondents were asked whether, over the past 12 months, they had come out ahead, behind, or even financially. In 1999, 49 percent of adults admitted having lost more than they won, down from the 58 percent who reported losing more than they won in 1989. In 1999 and in 1989 about one-fourth claimed to have come out ahead, and in both years, 15 percent reported that they had broken even. In 1999, 61 percent of teens responding to the survey claimed they were ahead, 24 percent were behind, and 10 percent had broken even. (See Table 11.9.)

Is Gambling a Problem?

When asked if they thought they sometimes wager more than they should, 11 percent of adults and 20 percent of teens replied that they did. (See Table 11.10.) Adults and teenagers were both asked if gambling had ever been a problem within the family. In 1999, 9 percent of adults and 10 percent of teens reported that it had been. (See Table 11.11.) When respondents were asked if they knew anyone outside of their families for whom gambling had been a source of problems, 41 percent of adults and 28 percent of teenagers responded they did. (See Table 11.12.)

GAMBLING ON THE INTERNET

According to the *Gambling in America 1999* poll, there is not very much support for legalized online wagering. Most adults (75 percent) and teens (66 percent) disapproved of Internet betting, and large proportions of adults (76 percent) and teens (70 percent) were concerned that it was too easy for youngsters to use the Internet to gamble. (See Table 11.13.)

TABLE 11.14

For each of the following activities, please tell me whether you think of them as "gambling". How about (read and rotate A-E)?

A. Church-sponsored bingo

		Yes %	No %	DK/Refused %	Sample size %
ADULTS (18+)	99 Apr 30-May 23	59	40	1	1,523
TEENS (13-17)	99 Apr 30-May 23	25	75	*	501

B. Participation in office pools at work

		Yes %	No %	DK/Refused %	Sample size %
ADULTS (18+)	99 Apr 30-May 23	65	33	2	1,523
TEENS (13-17)	99 Apr 30-May 23	40	58	2	501

C. Investing in the stock market

		Yes %	No %	DK/Refused %	Sample size %
ADULTS (18+)	99 Apr 30-May 23	52	46	2	1,523
TEENS (13-17)	99 Apr 30-May 23	31	67	2	501

D. Buying state-sponsored lottery tickets

		Yes %	No %	DK/Refused %	Sample size %
ADULTS (18+)	99 Apr 30-May 23	78	22	*	1,523
TEENS (13-17)	99 Apr 30-May 23	65	35	*	501

E. Playing poker with friends for money other than in a casino

		Yes %	No %	DK/Refused %	Sample size %
ADULTS (18+)	99 Apr 30-May 23	67	33	*	1,523
TEENS (13-17)	99 Apr 30-May 23	62	38	*	501

Source: *Social Audit: Gambling in America 1999*, The Gallup Organization, Princeton, NJ, 2000

IS IT GAMBLING?

The Gallup poll asked respondents if they considered various activities to be gambling. More than half (59 percent) of adults considered church-sponsored bingo to be gambling, while 40 percent did not. Among teenagers, only 25 percent thought church-sponsored bingo was gambling, while 75 percent did not. (See Table 11.14.)

About two-thirds (65 percent) of adults thought that participating in office pools at work constituted gambling, while one-third (33 percent) did not. Two of five (40 percent) of teenagers thought participating in an office pool was betting, but most (58 percent) did not. (See Table 11.14.)

Half of adults (52 percent) and one-third (31 percent) of teens thought investing in the stock market was gambling. On the other hand, more than one-fifth (22 percent) of adults and one-third (35 percent) of teens did not think buying a lottery ticket was gambling. Similarly, one-third of adults (33 percent) and almost two of five (38 percent) teens did not consider playing poker for money gambling. (See Table 11.14.)

146

CHAPTER XII

THE INTRODUCTION OF GAMBLING IS A GOOD IDEA

PREPARED STATEMENT OF J. TERRENCE LANNI, CHAIRMAN OF THE BOARD AND CHIEF EXECUTIVE OFFICER OF MGM GRAND, INC., AND MEMBER OF THE NATIONAL GAMBLING IMPACT STUDY COMMISSION, JUNE 1999

With a budget of $5 million, the Commission conducted extensive research, traveled to numerous gaming destinations throughout the U.S., and heard from scores of local officials and residents in jurisdictions where casinos are located in an effort to comprehensively study the social and economic impacts of gaming....

... [M]ost of the Commission's recommendations were either suggested or supported by the commercial casino industry, or are already being implemented by that industry today.

... [C]ommercial casinos are credited by the Commission as being a well-regulated, responsible segment of the industry.... [T]his confirms what we in the industry already know — the public has great confidence in the integrity of this form of entertainment....

... Although the gaming industry is often mistakenly viewed as a monolith, this Commission draws clear distinctions among its various segments. One of those important distinctions was the Commission's conclusion that, especially in historically impoverished, underdeveloped communities, casinos have had a net positive economic impact. This conclusion was reinforced firsthand by the hundreds of individuals who testified before the commission about the good jobs casinos provide.

The casino industry recognizes that, although the percentage is small, pathological gambling affects a significant number of individuals. Many of the Commission recommendations in this area were based on steps we in the commercial casino industry have already undertaken. For example, commercial casinos created the first and only foundation to date dedicated to funding research in the area of pathological gambling — the National Center for Responsible Gaming....

TESTIMONY OF JEREMY D. MARGOLIS, FORMER ASSISTANT UNITED STATES ATTORNEY AND DIRECTOR OF THE ILLINOIS STATE POLICE, BEFORE THE HOUSE COMMITTEE ON THE JUDICIARY, SEPTEMBER 29, 1995

People often ask whether the presence of gaming in their community would cause an increase in street crime. The facts are these: Las Vegas, Nevada, the city that is synonymous with casinos, is among the safest cities in America. Illinois, the county's leading riverboat casino state, has experienced no increase in crime in some riverboat towns and measurable reductions in crime in others.

... Las Vegas' crime rate is significantly lower than many other tourist and convention-oriented cities, such as Miami, New Orleans, Los Angeles, Atlanta, San Diego, and San Francisco. It has a lower crime rate than college towns like Ann Arbor, Michigan, and heartland towns like Lincoln, Nebraska, and Lawrence, Kansas.

Significantly, it has a far, far lower crime rate than Orlando, Florida, the home of Mickey Mouse.

... A number of points must be made. First, comparing the demographics of problem-ridden pre-casino Atlantic City to the stable, family-oriented, economically sound, and socially responsible communities now considering casinos is like comparing night and day. Sadly, Atlantic City's problems of unemployment, drug use, extreme violence, and substandard public housing long predate the advent of casinos on the Boardwalk.

... The most exhaustive research on post-casino crime in Atlantic City was conducted by the noted criminologist and sociologist Jay Albanese ("The Effect of Casino Gambling on Crime," *Federal Probation*, 39-44, 1985).... He found that the individual risk of victimization in Atlantic City was actually less than it had been before the advent of casinos, and that the crime rate for people actually present was less than it had been before visitors tripled the city's average daily population.

The Illinois experience has surpassed all expectations, and crime has, simply put, not been an issue at all.... There is no better or more accurate way to say it; crime has not been a problem.... [C]rime in the six-block area around the downtown Joliet boat decreased approximately 12 percent.

Most other Illinois riverboat towns have also reported decreases in crime.

... Probably no issue arouses more passion or poses more of a community concern than does the question of the potential involvement of organized crime in legalized gaming. Based upon a combination of history and Hollywood imagery, some people allege that organized crime will be able to infiltrate and exert control. Recent experience in Las Vegas and the total experience of Atlantic City and Illinois riverboats refute this belief.

For many years, organized crime has not been a factor in Las Vegas. Aggressive and thorough regulators, and a very vigilant FBI (whose retired agents continue that work throughout the gaming industry), and highly efficient, tightly controlled, publicly owned companies have seen to that. In Atlantic City, organized crime never touched the casino industry.

As legalized gaming spread throughout the United States, we are seeing that those states with strong regulation and enforcement are not experiencing an influx of organized crime activity....

TESTIMONY OF FRANK J. FAHRENKOPF, JR., PRESIDENT AND CHIEF EXECUTIVE OFFICER OF THE AMERICAN GAMING ASSOCIATION, BEFORE THE HOUSE COMMITTEE ON THE JUDICIARY, SEPTEMBER 29, 1995

Forty-eight of the 50 states plus the District of Columbia and Puerto Rico have some form of legalized gaming. They have not taken that responsibility lightly.... The people and elected officials of each state know what is best for their own state.

I am not here today claiming that the gaming-entertainment industry does not have problems. We do, but the problems we have are no different than those of any large visitor-dependent entertainment industry.

... The American Gaming Association has met with prominent leaders in the field who tell us that the vast majority of Americans are social gamblers who can participate in a gaming activity without harmful effects. Some gamblers cannot, however, and are referred to as problem or compulsive gamblers. Prevalence studies conducted in fourteen states show that the percent of those with a problem ranges from 1.7 percent in Iowa to 6.3 percent in Connecticut. Our view is that one problem gambler is one too many, and as good citizens it is our responsibility to address the problem through public education, corporate training and basic research.

A number of our members have been working with state and national organizations for many years to develop proactive corporate policies, public service announcements, employee assistance programs, funding of hotlines, speaker's bureaus, and training of employees. The American Gaming Association will continue this effort. We have created an industry-wide task force to develop a long-range strategy to reduce gambling addiction, raise public awareness, and provide models for early intervention and treatment. Working in partnership with public and private organizations, we will promote industry-wide training programs and public outreach techniques.

... It is time the organized crime issue was put to rest. There is no showing anywhere, be it FBI reports or other law enforcement reports, of organized crime activity in today's gaming-entertainment industry.

... [G]aming entertainment today is owned by the same people who own other major industries — stockholders. More than 75 publicly traded companies, all under the stringent scrutiny of the SEC [Securities and Exchange Commission, the federal regulatory agency which monitors publicly traded companies], own gaming interests.

... In addition to the quality of ownership, no other industry has stricter regulation within the states.

... In fact, Jim Moody, supervisory special agent, FBI Organized Crime Program, in Congressional testimony in 1992 said, "As legalized gaming spreads throughout the United States, we are seeing that those states with strong regulations and enforcement are not experiencing an influx of organized crime activity."

Critics and naysayers notwithstanding, there is absolutely no credible evidence that shows the introduction of legal gaming, because of the nature of the business, increases crime. An increase in the number of tourists in any community will bring more crime regardless of the venue. A perfect example of this is what has happened in Orlando, Florida. No one would argue that Mickey and Minnie Mouse cause more crime, yet according to the FBI, Orlando has a higher crime rate than Las Vegas. And when you consider the visitor-adjusted population, Orlando's crime problem exceeds both Las Vegas and Atlantic City.

For example, in Illinois, State Police records indicate that overall patterns of service calls and crime incidents remained stable or even declined after the riverboats began service in the state.

... [D]on't take my word for it. Ask the more than one million men and women whose jobs directly or indirectly support the industry about the economic benefits. Or ask the state and local governments that receive billions of dollars of tax revenues. There is no question that, just as with any expanding industry, some areas of the country will do better than others, but in the overwhelming number of cases, gaming entertainment has been a boon to the communities where it is established.

Another culprit that opponents trot out is known as the "substitution theory." Somehow opponents argue every dollar spent on gaming, apparently unlike any other new industry, results in the loss of revenue somewhere else. That same logic for some reason isn't applied to money spent purchasing entertainment from theme parks, or movies, or baseball games. The "substitution theory" is highly controversial, to say the least.

The bottom line is there is a net increase in jobs and tax revenues, two positive economic indicators, when gaming entertainment is introduced into a community. In other words, the economic pie gets bigger. We will take the facts over the theory any time.

TESTIMONY OF REPRESENTATIVE FRANK A. LOBIONDO (R-NJ) BEFORE THE HOUSE COMMITTEE ON THE JUDICIARY, SEPTEMBER 29, 1995

While I respect my colleagues as thoughtful people, I fear that they are motivated by stereotypes and misinformation of the gaming industry....

I asked to come before you today in order to tell the other side of the story....

I represent a district that includes Atlantic City, New Jersey. It was the collective decision of the people of the entire state of New Jersey to require a heavily regulated, strictly controlled casino industry to operate in one city of the state in return for making a financial commitment to the people of the state.

Atlantic City is a perfect example of how a state, with the approval of its citizenry, is the best entity to determine what, if any, type of gaming should be permitted and what conditions should be applied to that permission.

First, the law approving casinos in Atlantic City was approved by a statewide, binding referendum. Second, the law established two state government oversight agencies....

Third, Atlantic City casinos must contribute to the betterment of the state. In an age when cities and states provide tax breaks to attract new industries, Atlantic City casinos are not only subject to all state and local taxes, but must pay substantial additional taxes and fees....

Finally, New Jersey casinos directly generate 45,000 jobs, and, in fact, Atlantic City casinos provide roughly one-third of all jobs in Atlantic County. When related jobs are taken into account, another 35,000 New Jersey residents owe their employment to the gaming industry.

Gaming's opponents will tell you that Atlantic City's casinos have increased the crime rate. This is simply untrue. The visitor-adjusted crime rate, according to the WEFA group, a private consulting firm in Pennsylvania, are comparable to, and in some cases lower than, cities such as Atlanta, Nashville, and Orlando. Our crime rate nationally is far too high for my taste, but there is no indication that Atlantic City casinos have contributed to that crime rate.

Gaming's opponents will also tell you that Atlantic City's casinos have lead to economic decline in other parts of the city. The fact is that Atlantic City's economy was on the decline long before the first casino opened in 1978. If anything, Atlantic City's casinos have brought a welcome economic stability to the city.

The point to all of this is that for Atlantic City and for the State of New Jersey, casino gaming was the right answer to some serious problems. That does not mean that it is the right answer for Virginia, or Illinois, or Indiana. What is right in those states is for the residents of those states to decide. It is not for Washington to say.

TESTIMONY OF WEBSTER FRANKLIN, EXECUTIVE DIRECTOR, CHAMBER OF COMMERCE, TUNICA COUNTY, MISSISSIPPI, BEFORE THE HOUSE COMMITTEE ON SMALL BUSINESS, SEPTEMBER 21, 1994

Historically, Tunica County has been known as "the poorest county in the Nation."

... Our community's jobs have all been based on agriculture prior to the legislation permitting dockside gaming. Large farms, which grow cotton, soybeans, and rice farms, provided jobs for our citizens. But due to the mechanization and new technology that has come into the farming industry, hundreds of our workers have been displaced.

Unemployment as recently as January of 1992 was as high as 26.2 percent, one of the highest in the State of Mississippi. Per capita income was $11,865, one of the lowest in the State. Fifty-three percent of all Tunica County residents received food stamps. We were known for our substandard housing, poor health care delivery, and sanitation problems caused by inadequate or antiquated sewage systems.

... [S]tudies all recommended basically the same thing: Government assistance. Due to this national attention, we received much-needed government money and assistance. But that did not solve our problem — which was jobs for our citizens. It was not until the gaming industry came into our county that those jobs surfaced.

... Since the arrival of gaming, our once defunct planning commission, now very active, has issued over $1 billion worth of building permits.

In 1993, we had 12 major casino constructions — in the construction phase. This allowed, for the first time, our citizens to go to work in the construction industry at salaries of $10 and upwards an hour. Every able-bodied person in the country was afforded, for the first time, the opportunity to acquire as many overtime hours as they could withstand; therefore, they had a skill that they could take to other jobs once these facilities had been constructed.

... Nine casinos currently operate in our county, employing approximately 9,000 people. There have been more jobs in our county in 20 months than there were people.... Our unemployment rate ... was 26.2 percent.... It has gone as low as 4.9 percent. Child support collections have increased.... [T]he number of welfare recipients has decreased 42 percent. Food stamp recipients have decreased 13 percent ... and that trend continues....

Business in Tunica County is, in fact, booming.... We have new housing, RV parks, restaurants, and motels.... In fiscal year 1994, our county recorded the highest percent increase of retail sales of all of Mississippi's 82 counties, a 299 percent increase....

... This new revenue source has allowed the county to continue the much-needed infrastructure improvements.

... Revenue from gaming has allowed our county to provide an additional $1.4 million of funding for this school year. This funding will go to new classes, much-needed equipment, and increase in teacher salaries.

... Our board of supervisors also recently voted to reduce its tax on property by 32 percent.

... [G]aming has had an extremely positive impact on our local economy.

PREPARED STATEMENT OF S. TIMOTHY WAPATA, EXECUTIVE DIRECTOR OF THE NATIONAL INDIAN GAMING ASSOCIATION BEFORE THE HOUSE COMMITTEE ON SMALL BUSINESS, NOVEMBER 28, 1994

Indian Gaming enterprises have, by necessity, relied on and become partners with local small businesses in order to survive. Tribal Gaming enterprises are large purchasers of local business services. It has been determined that, for survival, Indian Gaming, by and large, requires partnerships with local construction and building supply firms, local restaurants, local hotels, local lounges, local cleaning firms, local clothing/uniform manufacturers, local law enforcement/security, local limousine, taxi, bus, and air transportation, local grocers and food distributors, local public utility companies, positive relationships with the local population. There is no "Wal-Mart Syndrome" [big conglomerate business taking the place of and pushing out small business] in effect in Indian Gaming because of the reliance on the local business community to operate most Indian Gaming enterprises and because Indian Gaming creates a new type of business in a community where no business of this type existed before.

Finally, when a Tribal Gaming enterprise opens, many new small businesses are also created in order to provide necessary service to the new business. These can include restaurants, hotels, convenience stores, gas stations, banks, other entertainment ventures such as boating or skiing, childcare ventures, gaming employment training and management programs, etc. Indian Gaming enterprises are the genesis for an entire support network of business ventures. Literally hundreds of new businesses nationwide have been created as a result of Indian Gaming.

Certain trends have developed in local economies with the proliferation of Indian Gaming enterprises. These trends are as follows:

Indian Gaming Enterprises

- Stimulate and create new businesses, both Indian and non-Indian.

- Increase local economic activity, particularly increasing spending and employment.

- Reduce local public assistance rates and expenditures.

- Increase tourism and stimulate visitor spending.

- Increase federal, state, and local tax revenues.

- Result in decreased crime rates and increased local law enforcement and security expenditures.

- Result in lowered unemployment rates on the reservation and in local non-Indian communities.

- Increase Indian governmental services, economic development, and self-sufficiency.

- Nationwide, have created in excess of 100,000 direct jobs and an additional 110,000 indirect jobs, a total in excess of 210,000 jobs created as a result of the industry. These are generally jobs and work created in depressed areas where no previous employment opportunity was available.

... If Indian Gaming seems an economic and social panacea, it is because the industry has been designed to be so.

... Indian Gaming has provided positive benefits to Indian Tribes and to the local, regional and state areas in which the gaming is situated. This is particularly evident in counties which the U.S. Census has identified as the poorest in the U.S. All are Indian reservations. Unemployment is as high as 80 percent, a rate similar to Third World Countries. For these areas, Indian Gaming is the only economic development tool which has worked in 200 years.

Finally, it must be remembered that Gaming is an entertainment industry. People do this to have fun. The average loss at an Indian Gaming enterprise is less than $20. Tribes fully support, and have even created, programs to assist those who have a problem with gambling. But, the ultimate message is that people are having a good time. Their good time shouldn't be legislated out of existence.

CHAPTER XIII

THE INTRODUCTION OF GAMBLING IS NOT A GOOD IDEA

PREPARED STATEMENT OF JAMES C. DOBSON, PH.D., PRESIDENT AND FOUNDER OF FOCUS ON THE FAMILY (A NONPROFIT ORGANIZATION THAT PRODUCES HIS INTERNATIONALLY SYNDICATED RADIO PROGRAMS) AND COMMISSIONER OF THE NATIONAL GAMBLING IMPACT STUDY COMMISSION (NGISC), JUNE 1999

The central mission of the NGISC was to study the various implications of gambling and to assess the scope of problem and pathological gambling and its effects on individuals and families. The Commission's findings, from any reasonable perspective, depict a depth of pain and devastation in this country that compels a change in the way betting activity is regarded.

Clearly, gambling is a destroyer that ruins lives and wrecks families. A mountain of evidence presented to our Commission demonstrates a direct link between problem and pathological gambling and divorce, child abuse, domestic violence, bankruptcy, crime, and suicide. More than 15.4 million adults and adolescents meet the technical criteria of those disorders. That is an enormous number — greater than the largest city in this country....

One of the most scandalous features of the gambling industry, engaged in by many of our state governments, is the vigorous promotion of gambling among the poor, less-educated, and senior populations. Gambling is touted as the "ticket out of poverty," offering a last chance to riches. As such, it overtly preys on the desperation of the poor by peddling false hope.

The gambling industry pours vast sums into the campaign coffers of gambling-friendly politicians. It is time for the public to scrutinize those who are regularly jetted off to Las Vegas and other gambling centers to pick up these enormous contributions. We must ask, what service is being provided in return for this generosity? Republicans have been given $6.1 million and Democrats $7.6 million in recent years. During the last election in California, nearly $100 million was spent by casino interests to influence the outcome of various races and measures.

In summary, the illusion of pain-free riches promoted by the gambling industry has been exposed. The very appeal of gambling belies the claims of the gambling industry, which is sown in greed and the exploitation of human weakness. It robs from the poor and exploits the most vulnerable. It undermines the ethic of work, sacrifice, and personal responsibility that exemplify the best qualities of American society. And if you scratch beneath the veneer of gambling-induced prosperity, the pain, despair, and hopelessness of problem and pathological gamblers is recognized as a stark tragedy.

PREPARED TESTIMONY OF TOM GREY, EXECUTIVE DIRECTOR, NATIONAL COALITION AGAINST LEGALIZED GAMBLING, BEFORE THE HOUSE COMMITTEE ON THE JUDICIARY, SEPTEMBER 29, 1995

A battle is raging across our country. Ambitious gambling promoters have been invited into our communities by some state and local officials under the guise of prosperity, economic development, jobs, and a painless new source of government revenue.

The recent, rapid spread of gambling was never the result of a popular movement. Rather, it was driven by self-interested gambling pitchmen with money, high-priced lobbyists, and pie-in-the-sky promises. Cash-starved municipalities and legislatures, eager for a way to increase revenue while avoiding voter backlash, were vulnerable to the prospect of something-for-nothing.

The tide turned [against gambling] not simply because all of the major conservative Christian groups oppose the expansion of gambling, although they do. It is not simply because mainline churches — liberal, conservative, and moderate — are almost universally opposed to more gambling, although they are. Resistance to government-sponsored gambling is growing because voters from every walk of life recognize that legalized gambling is, based on the facts, poor public policy.

... To many Americans, government's promotion of gambling is a cop-out and a double-cross. We see public officials sacrificing our communities to a predatory enterprise — for money. Citizens see government living off gambling profits, taken from the poorest and weakest of our citizens, instead of facing up to rational choices regarding budgets and taxes.

... One could say that gambling has become the new national pastime.

... The pro-gambling initiatives must be stopped before our nation's economy, and its social fabric, are irreparably harmed.

... The expansion of legalized gambling is a major threat to business in the United States. The gambling enterprise cannibalizes existing businesses, stealing their customers and revenues. At the same time, gambling establishments bring new social costs that are inevitably paid by business.

... Pathological gamblers tend to engage in forgery, theft, embezzlement, and property crimes to pay off gambling debts. They are responsible for an estimated $1.3 billion worth of insurance-related fraud per year.

... According to a study by the Better Government Association of Chicago, "Law enforcement officials agree that the mob usually infiltrates ancillary (auxiliary) services to the casinos. New Jersey law enforcement officials believe that organized crime has infiltrated legitimate businesses, such as those which provide the casinos with ancillary services including limousines, linen, meat, and vending machines."

... Increased crime costs state and local governments not only the salaries of more police officers, but prosecutors, judges, court personnel, court facilities, and prisons.

... Legalized gambling triggers the mental disorder of pathological (or "compulsive") gambling. Pathological gambling destroys the lives of thousands of Americans and devastates their families, friends, and employers. The most common argument in favor of gambling expansion is that it will yield government revenues, which can be used for programs to "help" people. But helping some people by exploiting and destroying others is bad social policy, and simply unethical.

It is important to understand that gambling addiction is just as real, and its consequences just as tragic, as alcohol or drug addiction.

... Individuals who become gambling addicts accumulate debts averaging $35,000 to $92,000 before they seek treatment, are arrested, or commit suicide. Family savings are lost, marriages end, children go unsupported. A majority of pathological gamblers turn to some form of crime to support their addiction.

... Any expansion of legalized gambling is likely to trigger thousands of new victims of gambling disorders.

PREPARED STATEMENT OF PROFESSOR JOHN WARREN KINDT, UNIVERSITY OF ILLINOIS AT CHAMPAIGN-URBANA, BEFORE THE HOUSE COMMITTEE ON SMALL BUSINESS, SEPTEMBER 21, 1994

In recent economic history, legalized gambling activities have been directly and indirectly subsidized by the taxpayers. The field research throughout the nation indicates that for every dollar the legalized gambling interests indicate is being contributed in taxes, it usually costs the taxpayers at least three dollars — and higher numbers have been calculated. These costs to taxpayers are reflected in (1) infrastructure costs, (2) relatively high regulatory costs, (3) expenses to the criminal justice system, and (4) large social-welfare costs.

... In the context of social-welfare issues, it is well-established that legalized gambling activities act as a regressive tax on the poor. Specifically, the legalization of various forms of gambling activities makes "poor people poorer" and can dramatically intensify many pre-existing social-welfare problems. Demographic analyses reveal that certain disadvantaged socio-economic groups tend to gamble proportionately greater amounts of their overall income....

From the business perspective, businesses are not naive. With the exception of the cluster services associated with gambling, new businesses tend not to locate in areas allowing legalized gambling because of one or more of the aforementioned costs. In areas saturated with legalized gambling activities, pre-existing businesses face added pressures that push them toward illiquidity and even bankruptcy.

... More subtly, traditional businesses in communities which initiate legalized gambling activities can anticipate increased personnel costs due to increased job absenteeism and declining productivity. The best blue-collar and white-collar workers, the Type-A personalities, are the most likely to become pathological gamblers.

... Legalizing various gambling activities increases the number of problems related to pathological gambling in the context of the workforce, and these costs are reflected in increased personnel costs — such as "rehabilitation costs," which can easily range from $3,000 to $20,000 (or more) per pathological gambler.

Gambling activities and the gambling philosophy are directly opposed to sound business principles and economic development. Legalized gambling activities also negatively affect education — both philosophically and fiscally. In states with legalized gambling activities which were initiated allegedly to bolster tax revenues to "education," the funding in "real dollars" has almost uniformly decreased.

Those states which embrace legalized gambling activities can expect enormous socio-economic costs and declines in the quality of life. Unlike traditional business activities, legalized gambling activities cater to a market consisting of addicted and potentially-addicted consumers, and most pre-existing traditional businesses will find it quite difficult to compete for "consumer dollars" which are being transformed into "gambling dollars."

... Each newly-created pathological gambler has been calculated to cost society between $13,200 to $52,000 per year.

... Sociologists almost uniformly report that increased gambling activities which are promoted as sociologically "acceptable" and which are made "accessible" to larger numbers of people will increase the numbers of pathological gamblers.

PREPARED STATEMENT OF DR. VALERIE C. LORENZ, EXECUTIVE DIRECTOR, COMPULSIVE GAMBLING CENTER, INC., BALTIMORE, MARYLAND, BEFORE THE HOUSE COMMITTEE ON SMALL BUSINESS, SEPTEMBER 21, 1994

Let me make something very clear: ALL types of gambling can become addictive, regardless of whether one gambles on or with machines, races, tickets, or games. Fortunately, only certain people will become gambling addicts. However, the number of compulsive gamblers has been increasing at an alarming rate in the past twenty years — ever since the spread of casinos and state lotteries, which has turned this country into a nation of gamblers.

... Until the mid-1970s, the typical compulsive gambler was a white, middle-aged, middle-class male. A dozen years ago, a female compulsive gambler was a rarity. Lottery addicts were just beginning to surface. Teenage compulsive gamblers and senior citizens addicted to gambling were nonexistent.

The profile of today's compulsive gambler is truly democratic, all ages, races, religious persuasions, socio-economic levels, and education. Sixteen or sixty, the desperation and devastation is the same.

... Why? Because our governments are saying "Gambling is OK" and because gambling is now so readily available, with so very little regulation.

The formula is quite simple: availability leads to more gamblers, which leads to more compulsive gamblers. Casino gambling ... is particularly onerous because of the allure of escaping into fantasy, the fast action, and emphasis on quick money, all of which are basic factors in gambling addiction.

Gambling addiction increases socio-economic costs far greater than any amount of revenue generated for the government by the gambling industry.... Maryland's 50,000 compulsive gamblers cost the state $1.5 million per year in lost work productivity and monies that are abused (stolen, embezzled, state taxes not paid, etc.).

Other costs resulting from compulsive gambling are broken homes, physical and mental health problems, increase in social and welfare services, indebtedness, bankruptcies, and crime. Each and every one of these are far-reaching, affecting neighbors, employers, entire communities, and genera-

tions to come. These direct and indirect costs are staggering.

Taking just the issue of crime alone, virtually all compulsive gamblers, sooner or later, resort to illegal activities to support their gambling addiction. After all, money is the substance of their addiction, and when legal access to money is no longer available, these addicts will commit crimes. The crimes are typically of a non-violent financial nature, such as fraud or embezzlement or failure to pay taxes.

While in jail, the gambling addict is neither gainfully employed nor paying federal or state taxes. The family may be surviving on drastically reduced income or be on welfare. Well-paying jobs for felons are hard to come by, which means the gambling addict will most likely be earning less in future years, after he or she is released from prison.

... Ironically, while there are many education, prevention, and treatment programs for the substance abuser, supported by state and federal monies, what is there for the individual who becomes addicted to the government licensed or sponsored activity, gambling? Pathetically little in a few states, nothing in most.

... The casinos historically have failed to take any measure of responsibility for compulsive gambling, and only recently have a few Indian Reservations addressed this potential problem among their own people or among their customers. In short, the greed of the gambling industry is matched only by its lack of concern for its customers or the community in which it operates. That is not good business.

... First of all, it must face the fact that the problem exists, instead of continuing to ignore it or minimize it. Secondly, it must stop believing the deceptions perpetrated by the gambling industry, that legalization of casinos or race tracks or lotteries [is] the answer to governments' fiscal woes, the answer to unemployment, or the way to stop tax increases.

... The number of compulsive gamblers in this country today runs into the millions. Who will provide the treatment, and who will pay for it? Not the gambling addicts — they have neither the money nor the health insurance....

This country can ill afford to ignore the problems caused by the proliferation of gambling and the resultant increase in compulsive gambling. We do not need the economic ruin, broken homes, and crime brought on by this industry, which encourages instant gratification, something for nothing, while making a mockery of family, work, and community.

TESTIMONY OF ROBERT GOODMAN, DIRECTOR, THE U.S. GAMBLING STUDY, LEMELSON PROFESSOR OF ENVIRONMENTAL DESIGN, HAMPSHIRE COLLEGE, AND PROFESSOR OF REGIONAL PLANNING, UNIVERSITY OF MASSACHUSETTS, BEFORE THE HOUSE COMMITTEE ON SMALL BUSINESS, SEPTEMBER 21, 1994

In the process of studying and debating the economic consequences, I have come to understand why gambling industry executives and politicians were disturbed by criticism of this industry. Clearly, from the industry perspective, having a government monopoly — essentially, in many cases, government-sanctioned monopoly — gives them an immensely profitable position, and criticism can be seen as threatening to those profits.

But I think from the political perspective, criticism is also always threatening, but I think for more complex reasons, and these stem from, really, the limited opportunities for economic development in many parts of this country, and the introduction of gambling is really a symptom of that problem rather than a long-term solution to it.

Having to deal with downsizing by major private firms, having to bear the brunt of reduced federal aid and other problems that you are familiar with in the cities, any new enterprise which promises large numbers of jobs and revenue can give the appearance of salvation and economic revival. With constituents hurting, with more productive solutions very hard to come by, even desperate solutions can seem better than no solution....

That model of gambling as economic development does no longer exist in this country. Unfortunately, many communities are looking toward that model that no longer exists as a source of creating jobs and revenue.

... [W]hat you are finding in this convenience gambling economy is ... essentially that money, discretionary dollars that are being spent on other forms of entertainment and consumer expenditures, are now being shifted into casinos. That is not economic development in any real sense of the word. It is basically shifting dollars, and this is creating an onerous financial burden on future generations by simultaneously undermining what remains of America's productive economy.

... These governments are developing new partnerships with businesses in some of the most unproductive sectors of the economy, helping to expand an industry whose success increasingly depends on cannibalizing dollars from other businesses and whose expansion will create serious future problems for other businesses and governments to deal with in the future.

... [I]t seems to me the Federal Government has done little to protect American businesses, especially small businesses, against the predatory industry or process. I should call it, not simply an industry but a predatory process at home; those State and local government partnerships with the gambling industry whose monopolistic powers will have a devastating effect on large portions of the existing economy.

In the process of doing this kind of quick relief, quick-fix economic development, we are creating some enormous problems. Potential investment capital is being reduced. Existing businesses are losing consumer revenues, being pushed closer to decline and failure.

Using our own research findings, we have conservatively estimated that each problem gambler costs government and the private economy $13,200 a year. [In Iowa that would mean $73 million and in California $780 million.]

What do those costs have to deal with? This includes such costs to the private economy as money which problem gamblers borrow and don't pay back, work time lost to private industry by problem gamblers who are ineffective on the job, salaries lost by problem gamblers laid off as a result of their problems, private insurance losses as a result of fraud by problem gamblers, losses that result from embezzlement, check fraud.

In addition, there are the public costs of processing public gamblers through the criminal justice system, including the cost of keeping some of those people in jail for some period of time.

TESTIMONY OF EARL GRINOLS, PROFESSOR OF ECONOMICS, UNIVERSITY OF ILLINOIS, BEFORE THE HOUSE COMMITTEE ON SMALL BUSINESS, SEPTEMBER 21, 1994

The essence of the gambling debate from an economic perspective can be understood by asking the question: Does America need another form of entertainment so badly that it is willing to add another social problem to the list that it already deals with, such as crime, alcoholism, teen pregnancy, illegal drug use, and so on?

From the Federal Government's perspective, a good analogy might be the following: Imagine if a pharmaceutical company invents a new pharmaceutical. There are already other drugs available for the same purpose. The product works extremely well for 98.5 percent of the people who use it.

However, for 1.5 percent of the people who use it, the drug completely ruins their life. Would the FDA license this drug?

To see how gambling differs from other entertainment, we can ask, how would gambling have to be "sanitized" to make it like other forms of entertainment? I think at least three things are needed.

First, we would have to eliminate the 1.5 to 5 percent or so of the population who we know will become pathological or compulsive or addicted gamblers.

Second, we would have to eliminate those who gamble beyond the point of recreation or entertainment. Though gambling is a sterile transfer of money from one pocket to another, it does use time and resources. Gambling for nonrecreational or nonentertainment purposes reduces national income.

Third, we would have to eliminate the massive concentration into the hands of a small group in the gambling industry of money and influence, and especially its effect on the legislative process in statehouses and city councils across America.

... Were the Nation to introduce gambling everywhere, the damage would equal the costs of an additional 1990/91 recession every 8 to 15 years. Equivalently, this would be like the costs of an additional Hurricane Andrew, the most costly natural disaster in American history, or two Midwest floods every year in perpetuity.

... [Gambling draws] money away from other businesses, creating no economic development, but leaving social costs in its wake.

158

IMPORTANT NAMES AND ADDRESSES

American Gaming Association
555 13th St. NW, Suite 430 West
Washington, DC 20004-1109
(202) 637-6500
FAX (202) 637-6507
www.americangaming.org

American Greyhound
Track Operators Association
1065 NE 125 St., Suite 219
North Miami, FL 33161-5832
(305) 871-2370
FAX (305) 893-5633

American Quarter Horse Association
P. O. Box 200
Amarillo, TX 79168-0001
(806) 376-4811
FAX (806) 376-8304
www.aqha.com

Association of Racing Commissioners
International, Inc.
2 Paragon Centre, Suite 200
2343 Alexandria Drive
Lexington, KY 40504-3276
(606) 224-7070
FAX (606) 224-7071
www.arci.com

Colorado Division of Gaming
720 South Colorado Blvd.
Denver, CO 80222
(303) 205-1300
FAX (303) 757-8624
www.gaming.state.co.us

Compulsive Gambling Center, Inc.
924 East Baltimore St.
Baltimore, MD 21202-4739
HELPLINE (800) 332-0402

Council on Compulsive Gambling of
New Jersey, Inc.
1315 West State St.
Trenton, NJ 08618
(609) 599-3299
HELPLINE 1-800-GAMBLER
FAX (609) 599-9383
www.800gambler.org
ccgnj@800gambler.org

Gamblers Anonymous International
Service Office
P.O. Box 17173
Los Angeles, CA 90017
(213) 386-8789
FAX (213) 386-0030
www.gamblersanonymous.org
isomain@gamblersanonymous.org

*International Gaming and Wagering
Business*
888 Seventh Ave., 26th Floor
New York, NY 10106
(212) 636-2960
(800) 223-9638
FAX (212) 636-2961
www.gemcommunications.com

Harrah's Casino Hotels
1023 Cherry Road
Memphis, TN 38117
(901) 762-8600
FAX (901) 762-8637
www.harrahs.com

Illinois Gaming Board
101 West Jefferson St.
P.O. Box 19474
Springfield, IL 62794
(217) 524-0226
FAX (217) 524-0228
www.igb.state.il.us

Iowa Racing and Gaming Commission
Lucas State Office Building
Des Moines, IA 50319
(515) 281-7352
FAX (515) 242-6560
www.iowaccess.org/irgc/

Mississippi Gaming Commission
P.O. Box 23577
Jackson, MS 39206
(601) 351-2800
FAX (601) 351-2810
www.msgaming.com

Missouri Gaming Commission
1616 Industrial Drive
Jefferson City, MO 65109
(573) 526-4080
FAX (573) 526-4084
www.dps.state.mo.us/dps/mgc/
rbfin.htm

National Association of Fundraising
Ticket Manufacturers
1885 University Avenue West
St. Paul, MN 55104
(651) 603-8795
Fabian@scc.net

National Coalition Against Legalized
Gambling
110 Maryland Ave. NE
Washington, DC 20002
Phone and FAX (800) 664-2680
www.ncalg.org
ncalg@wavecom.net

National Council on Problem
Gambling, Inc.
P.O. Box 9419
Washington, DC 20016
(410) 730-8008
FAX (410) 730-0669
HELPLINE (800) 522-4700
www.ncpgambling.org
ncpg@erols.com

National Indian Gaming Association
224 2nd St. SE
Washington, DC 20003
(202) 546-7711
FAX (202) 546-1755
www.indiangaming.org

National Indian Gaming Commission
1850 M St. NW, Suite 250
Washington, DC 20036
(202) 632-7003
FAX (202) 632-7066

Nevada Gaming Control Board
P. O. Box 8003
Carson City, NV 89702-8003
(775) 687-6520
FAX (775) 687-5817
www.state.nv.us/gaming

New Jersey Casino Control
Commission
Tennessee Ave. and the Boardwalk
Atlantic City, NJ 08401
(609) 441-3200
FAX (609) 441-3840

North American Association of State
and Provincial Lotteries
2775 Bishop Rd., Suite B
Willoughby Hills, OH 44072
(216) 241-2310
FAX (216) 241-4350
www.naspl.org
nasplhq@aol.com

South Dakota Commission on Gaming
118 East Missouri
Pierre, SD 57501-5070
(605) 773-6050
FAX (605) 773-6053
www.state.sd.us

U.S. Trotting Association
750 Michigan Ave.
Columbus, OH 43215
(614) 224-2291
FAX (614) 224-4575
www.ustrotting.com

RESOURCES

The *National Gambling Impact Study Commission* (NGISC) was authorized by the National Gambling Impact Study Commission Act (PL 104-169) to conduct a "comprehensive legal and factual study of the social and economic implications of gambling in the United States." The study was released in June 1999. *Gambling in America* (Washington, DC, 1976), an earlier detailed government study, was published by the Survey Research Center of the University of Michigan. This extensive study covers gambling from the founding fathers down to its 1976 publication.

The U.S. Bureau of the Census reports the population growth of states in *National and State Population Estimates: 1990 to 1996* (Washington, DC, 1997) and the growth of cities and metropolitan areas in annual releases. The Indian Gaming Management Staff of the Bureau of Indian Affairs monitors the status of tribal-state compacts and periodically releases its statistics. The Federal Bureau of Investigation (FBI) maintains statistics on gambling arrests in its annual *Crime in the United States*. The General Accounting Office (GAO) investigates all areas of government activity. The GAO studied Indian gaming activities in *A Profile of the Indian Gaming Industry* (Washington, DC, 1997).

International Gaming and Wagering Business (IGWB), a monthly magazine devoted to the international gaming industry, contains invaluable information on every aspect of the industry. *IGWB* periodically publishes special reports on particular types of gambling activity, such as lotteries and casino gambling. Martin Christiansen and Will E. Cummings of Christiansen/Cummings Associates, Inc. (CCA) prepare an invaluable annual survey of gambling in America. Information Plus again extends its sincere appreciation to *International Gaming and Wagering Business* and CCA for permission to use selected material from their publication.

The Association of Racing Commissioners International, Inc. (Lexington, Kentucky), in its annual report, *Pari-Mutuel Racing*, summarizes statistics on horse racing, greyhound racing, and jai alai events. Information Plus would like to thank the Association for permission to use material from its publication.

The *Greyhound Network News* is a quarterly newsletter of general information and racing news from individual states. The publication focuses on the predicament of the American racing greyhound. The *Official Handbook of the American Quarter Horse Association* provides an overview of quarter horse racing in America.

The Nevada State Gaming Control Board, the New Jersey Casino Control Commission, the Colorado Division of Gaming, and the Illinois Gaming Board each publish a detailed yearly report on casino gambling in their states. The South Dakota Commission on Gaming, the Missouri Gaming Commission, the Mississippi Gaming Commission, and the Iowa Racing and Gaming Commission also produce annual statewide reports on casino gambling.

The National Association of Fundraising Ticket Manufacturers (NAFTM; St. Paul, Minnesota) annually surveys bingo, charity gaming, raffles, and other forms of gambling in *Report on Charity Gaming in North America*. Information Plus would like to thank the NAFTM for permission to use material from the publication.

As always, Information Plus expresses its sincere appreciation to the Gallup Organization (Princeton, New Jersey) for permission to use material from its surveys, in particular, *Social Audits: Gambling in America 1999: A Comparison of Adults and Teenagers* (1999).

The American Gaming Association (AGA), an industry trade group, published the first annual *State of the States: The AGA Survey of Casino Entertainment* in 1999. The survey is modeled after the longtime Harrah's surveys of U.S. casino gambling entertainment and gathers information from a number of sources, including Harrah's Entertainment, Inc., Christiansen Capital Advisors, Peter D. Hart Research Associates, Inc./The Luntz Research Companies, and The Evans Group, in addition to information from state gambling commissions. More than 80,000 people were polled, and the findings for the AGA survey are based on their responses.

The National Coalition Against Legal Gambling has prepared a useful packet of material opposing gambling. The American Gaming Association, which represents the gaming industry, has prepared information supporting gambling. The National Indian Gaming Commission, a government agency, and the National Indian Gaming Association, an association of the Indian gambling industry, supply information on Indian gambling. (See Important Names and Addresses.)

INDEX

INDEX (Continued)